DEMCO 38-297

A reference list of Harper Torchbooks, classified by subjects, is printed at the end of this volume.

ANCIENT HISTORY

by

MICHAEL GRANT

HARPER TORCHBOOKS ▼ The Academy Library

Harper & Row, Publishers

New York and Evanston

ANCIENT HISTORY

Printed in the United States of America.

This book was originally published in 1952 by
Methuen & Co. Ltd., London, and is here reprinted by arrangement.

First HARPER TORCHBOOK edition published 1965 by
Harper & Row, Publishers, Incorporated
49 East 33rd Street
New York, New York 10016

PREFACE

THE student who seeks to describe, in a limited space, any large tract of history is confronted with so many events and names that he has to think hard about the principles that will govern his selection. For, if he does not make a defensible decision regarding these principles and act consistently upon it, the reader will have more cause for complaint than if the narrative fails in any other respect: a haphazard choice of material is the equivalent of a falsified presentation. But the would-be historian can only avoid this charge when he has decided what is right and important, not only in the period which he is studying, but also in the modern world; for this, since he lives in it, cannot fail to colour his account.

So, in this book, I will not launch straight into narration, but will discuss also the matters of principle which seem to need clarification before the story can be completed, or even started. I want to anticipate the objection that, if one is going to judge ancient events (and it is impossible to discuss history without at least implying judgments), one ought to judge them by the ethical or other standards of their day rather than of 1951. In my opinion the question of anachronism hardly arises, partly because during most of the classical period (if not before) there already existed a minority of people with ideas about practical large-scale moral issues hardly inferior to the best which a minority can provide today. More illogical, to my mind, is the almost universal tendency to regard antiquity from the viewpoint of the nineteenth rather than the mid-twentieth century A.D.;

v

and the real anomaly—a serious danger in education —lies in the current habit of condoning in the ancient world (unlike many ancient thinkers themselves) pernicious conduct, such as aggression, which must not be condoned today.

I make this attempt with a keen sense of inadequacy. But that is an added reason why the machinery of my selective and narrative process should be laid bare to readers. They, too, will have to give thought before they can rebuild for themselves the mass of ancient history into any significant shape; and I hope that my own faulty reconstruction will incite them to improve on it. The same feeling of insufficiency has led me to include a good many quotations. These (like the numerous cross-references, which may be ignored if the reader prefers to do without them) may cause some annoyance. But so many good comments on this vast subject have already been made, and I did not want either to ignore all of them or to incorporate them as my own. I have acknowledged the names of many creditors, but space forbids the detailed citations of their works: I offer them all the deepest gratitude for their help.

MICHAEL GRANT
Edinburgh 1951

CONTENTS

vii

MAPS

Drawings by Richard Cribb

PART I
SELECTION IN ANCIENT HISTORY

CHAPTER I

SELECTION AND PLAN

THERE are two quite different sorts of history, with different purposes. There is the specialist history of those who attempt a detailed portrayal of a limited subject or group of subjects; and there is the general history of those who try to paint in broad lines. The present study is an extreme instance of the latter type of historical effort. It is an attempt to cram the essentials of a vast subject into 70,000 words.

If the attempt comes to grief, it at least deserves sympathetic condolences from several quarters. For example, the problem of compression which the present writer is thus setting himself is very similar indeed to the problem which the force of circumstances sets to many, indeed most, teachers of history in schools and universities. There, too, the number of words which they have the opportunity to utter is too limited for anything except the most rigorous compression to be possible; and that is particularly true today, when restrictions on time have increased further. But this whole question of historical compression is of special importance today for other reasons too. For there are also many people outside centres of learning, perhaps more than ever before, who want to know something about history and even

1

early history. It is desirable that attempts should be made to give them what they want.

When history is as general as it often has to be for such purposes, it is often called, much too portentously for this volume, 'universal history'. Experiments in 'universal history' go a long way back, but it is of the nineteenth and twentieth centuries that they have become a particular feature. The names of Hegel, Herder, Schiller, Kant, and Acton are prominent in this development. At the present time A. J. Toynbee is, in his highly individual and contestable manner, a master of it. Toynbee has emphasised that general history, if its generalisations are to have value, really must be 'universal'. We must not nowadays be too ready to leave out 'Orientals' and other incomprehensible people. It was said 'we cannot write a history of Western Europe and of China in the same work' (Headlam-Morley), and that the connection between European and Asiatic history is 'only occasional and incidental' (Freeman). But a perusal of our daily newspapers makes us very ready to discount this as regards the present; and for the dim past the spades of the archaeologists perform the same service. In a penetrating analysis of this subject Toynbee has pointed out that the difficulty was not felt by Voltaire or Gibbon, and that it largely arose in the nineteenth century from our desire to patronise the East—and from the annoyances that our closer political relations brought: hence 'the animus which we undisguisedly display towards the four non-Western civilisations that are alive today'—and this is not too strong a term for our complete neglect of the East—for example in our educational system, and especially in the teaching of history.

But even Gibbon could write firmly of 'the system of arts, and laws, and manners which so advantageously distinguish above the rest of mankind the Europeans and their colonies'. Likewise today, the West European is spoken of as naturally endowed with 'some unusual source of energy, some extraordinary purpose, some unprecedented strength' (P. McGuire). These are views which people may possess in their capacity as determined Europeans, but they belong to a range of ideas which should be alien to the historian.

There are, it is true, special reasons why Greece and Rome should be given prominence (pp. 107–9); but that again does not advocate complete silence concerning other parts of the world. Indeed, modern research generally is making it very difficult for the historian—and especially the 'universal' historian—to forget about those other regions. If they provide a 'standing challenge to the Western thesis that civilisation is one and indivisible' (Toynbee), then we must now succumb to the challenge and abandon the thesis, or transfer it to an altogether loftier and more general sphere.

For the time has gone by when we could dismiss the ancient Egyptians to archaeology, the Persians to 'barbarism', the Jews to divinity, the Indians to patronage, and the Chinese to an ignorance which popular attempts are only made to rectify during periods of political friendship. And now the number of known ancient civilisations has multiplied still further. One has only to think of the Minoans, Sumerians, Hittites, Mitannians, and people of Anyang and Mohenjodaro—names unknown when many of us were being taught history (see Ch. II).

However, this extension of the field must only be undertaken, even now, with some circumspection. Civilisations remote from us in time and in cultural affinities cannot be dealt with as extensively as others that are nearer. Only, their existence and salient features ought not to be forgotten altogether. The teacher will here complain that he only has time for the barest summary of the Greek and Roman civilisations, let alone the others. But if he has, say, twelve lectures to devote to ancient history, two or three (at least) ought to be devoted to the others, however brutal the compression thus involved. For otherwise the true position of Greece and Rome is incomprehensible.

It may sarcastically be suggested that, having extended the field thus far, we might as well apply to our studies the Buddhist view, as restated today by a scientist: 'we are not justified in making barriers between insect and human mentality' (R. W. G. Kingston). Whether we are or not, the barrier must here, for practical purposes, be made. Let us at least agree with Alexander Pope that

the proper study of mankind is man.

Our classical learning, for example, is 'based on the humanistic faith that man is worth studying for his own sake' (C. M. Bowra). 'Human beings are the element in our environment which is of most consequence to every child of man' (Temple). Without adding animals and insects, that is already quite a large enough field, even if the scope of the study were only a moment of time—much more so if it comprises centuries, as ancient history does (the delimitation of this vague term is discussed elsewhere, pp. 32, 127).

Indeed, at this point, a severer warning is needed. Anyone who reads general history, and still more anyone who tries to write it, will do well first to ponder some of the things that can be said about it. Let them consider, for instance, the trenchant comment of Butterfield. Universal history, he says, has created 'a new form of nonsense, a new realm of specious generalisations and vague plausibilities, built up out of confusions of thought that were not known before, characterised by the bold handling of concepts that do not represent anything capable of genuine concrete visualisation'. And this is how it seemed to C. W. C. Oman: 'the specialist may sometimes be narrow-minded, but he is not so repulsive to the true historian as another class of people, who "rush in where angels fear to tread", and try to generalise in history without having any sufficient detailed knowledge of it. We have all met the man who, after reading a dozen popular manuals, is prepared to lay down the whole scheme of the universe, ignoring all difficulties because he is not aware of their existence . . . "the second-rate at second hand" . . . the vulgarisateur will pretend to throw the entire mass into simple shape, by plastering over the whole of it with some worthless superficial mud-wash of his own invention, which hides all ragged corners and tiresome edges.'

These quotations show clearly the dangers that beset general history, and the reserves with which it must be written and read, and the necessarily sweeping character of the stereotypes that it must employ. But they do not lessen the extreme desirability of trying to overcome the dangers. As has been said, the teaching of history at most levels would come to an end if the attempt were not made. The strictures of Oman and Butterfield convey a more arduous lesson. They show that before general history is attempted by teacher or writer, the full implications of his task of compression—that is, selection—and the principles according to which it should be conducted, should be thought out. Lack of time or space is no valid objection to the carrying out of this procedure, since it should come before anything at all. Nevertheless, far too little thought, often no thought at all, has been given to the *method* of selection. Naturally there has been selection of a sort, since otherwise whole epochs could not be described (however badly) in a few hundred words. But it has been haphazard and arbitrary; whereas no selection at all can profitably be attempted unless first we sit down and decide the principles, the plan or plans, by which we shall operate it. 'Critical history must have a criterion' (Bradley). This decision will need to be preceded by an examination of first principles—of the writer's or teacher's fundamental views on a variety of subjects. For, unless the trouble is taken to operate according to some defensible and specified process of reasoning, we are contributing nothing to our audience. Indeed we are misleading them, since we are placing them at the mercy of the very same accidents as are guiding our own course. And a purely fortuitous distribution of emphasis is almost certain to be quite as misleading as a deliberately fallacious one. This is often the position today. Many teachers and writers are either nervous of choosing wrong or tendentious principles of selection, or they are regardless of the need to choose any at all; or at any rate they are too busy to spare the time for fundamental questions. In all such cases their selection of material is not thought out beforehand, and so is inevitably haphazard. But before any attempt is made to write or teach general history, these questions must be asked, and an attempt must be made to answer them: 'What is the yardstick according to which I shall decide whether to insert material or omit it? If I include or exclude this or that material, am I able to state clearly (at least to myself) why I am doing so?'

In practice, the yardstick often adopted, by unconscious as well as by conscious choice, is the *extent* of evidence available on one topic or another. That is to say, if a large amount of material has survived about a place or subject, that place or subject is given great prominence; and vice versa. It is by virtue of this passive method of selection that so many Histories of Greece rapidly become little more than Histories of Athens. Athens was of remarkable historical importance, but there were other very interesting Greek States as well—in Italy, Sicily and Asia Minor as well as Greece. None of these, however, provided nearly as much information about itself as Athens did; or at any rate, not nearly so much has survived (though Kathleen Freeman has taught us not to rely too much on this comfortable conclusion). The information about Athens is so exceedingly valuable that the historian would be ill-advised to ignore it; but he should try to use it to illuminate the more general aspects of his subject, since his study comprises the other Greek States as well. And, in any case, while using this information, he should not, consciously or otherwise, judge the relative *importance* of Athens in proportion to the *quantity* of this information. Toynbee has recently made this same point about the States formed out of the empire of Alexander: the fact that Ptolemaic Egypt has bequeathed to us valuable papyri does not mean that we must ignore the middle-eastern Seleucid State, which has not. We must try to use whatever information comes to hand, and the specialist researcher may well be excused for concentrating on regions and periods in which this is most fruitful; for 'pas de documents, pas d'histoire'. But the general historian must attempt to discount this factor, at least to some extent. We ought not to become the 'slaves of materials come into our hands by chance'; there is 'no rational correlation between importance and evidence' (E. Meyer).

This bewitchment by the quantity of surviving evidence is the legacy of another discredited historical technique which is sometimes described as the 'scissors and paste' method. This, as its nickname suggests, relied slavishly on the historical record, pasting history together from the surviving snippets, one piece uncritically fastened to the next, their choice dictated by the accident of survival. Here, naturally enough, the quantity of the extant material was the most important consideration. Unfortunately this 'scissors and paste' method is occasionally called the 'common-sense view'. But this is attaching much too humble a valuation to common sense. The 'scissors and paste' method was superseded as long ago as the seventeenth century; and so the 'universal' historian ought to have ceased distributing his emphasis merely according to the quantity of surviving material.

This custom, as has been said, provides one of the

reasons why the historical prominence of Athens, already great enough by other standards, is almost always exaggerated in what purport to be studies of the whole of Greece. But for this there is a second and even more dazzling, but equally irrelevant, reason. It is not only that the information that she has left us about herself is so great in quantity. There is the additional fact that this and her other surviving literature is, in many cases, of superlative quality, and represents a great stage in human achievement; and the same applies to the other Athenian arts. These are facts which must very much interest students of literature and the arts. But the historian has to think very carefully indeed before building his history round these facts—for that is what he is doing if (as usually happens) the importance that he assigns to Athenian history is consciously or unwittingly dictated by the fineness of Athenian literature and art. If the 'universal' historian does this, it means that he has, in effect, partly answered for himself the question: 'What is the yardstick according to which I shall decide whether to insert material, or omit it?'

He has answered that his yardstick, or at least one of his yardsticks, is literary and artistic. He is, unconsciously or consciously, making the assumption of Shakespeare that the true criterion of an age is its literary elegance (Sonnet XXXII). But it does not seem probable that this is a right assumption for the historian. It is true that, from the nineteenth century onwards, the revolt against narrow concepts of history caused its doors to be thrown open wide to include cultural as well as all other factors (e.g. by Schiller). But the *practical* difficulties of combining these with the others are insurmountable. Either the emphasis becomes so violently shifted to suit the cultural factors that the others are lost sight of (as has happened in the case of Athens); or, alternatively, the cultural development is often ignored during the greater part of a book but dragged in at the end, in a separate, lame, and brief chapter. Probably it is beyond the bounds of possibility to write a general history into which the cultural history is interwoven as an integral part. The historian is perhaps best advised to attend to his other preoccupations instead —to note the literary and artistic record when it illuminates them, to note it, that is, for its historical value (which is often great), but certainly not to build his history round it *because of* its literary and artistic excellence.

It is curious to observe that the latter undesirable practice occurs far more frequently in general ancient histories than in general modern histories. English history, for example, is usually recounted more or less independently of English poetry and English cathedrals and painters. This difference is probably due to a certain inferiority of status in the ancient historian. This is easily detectable in the evolution of our universities. For a very long time, and indeed in many cases even today, their teachers of ancient history have been restricted to the history of the ancient Greeks and Romans. This is because the *literatures* of those peoples have long formed an important part of the curriculum. That is to say, ancient history is auxiliary and ancillary to classical literature. That, too, is why ancient history concentrates so greatly on Athens—namely, because Athens is the centre of interest for the students of literature;

and it is to aid them that most courses and text-books
of ancient history have been designed.

It would seem more correct and beneficial that the
ancient historian should be free to adopt his own
more truly historical standpoint and disciplines. If
so, he will need to be emancipated from this subordi-
nation. This can be achieved, in schools and universities, if the teachers of ancient literature will
themselves sketch in the historical backgrounds of
the Greek and Latin works that they are expounding.
This does not seem too much to ask (even if it means
leaving out something else), and many of them do it
already; but the ineptitude of the historical notes in
many editions of classical authors shows that it is
not very near to complete realisation. Meanwhile,
the ancient historian would gradually be able to forget his subservience to literary brilliance, and to
consider the ancient world from a less highly specialised point of view. Incidentally, he would thereby
also be able to give sufficient prominence to non-
literary sources. This is very important. The scope
of this book does not permit a discussion of sources;
but it may be observed that every year the percentage
of historical knowledge derived from literature dimin-
ishes a little in proportion to that derived from
inscriptions, coins, seals, etc.

By the adequate utilisation of these and by other
means, the ancient historian may become able to
apply the independent standards of his own trade.
But it still remains to be asked what these standards
are. A great many attempts have been made to
answer this question. Some of these are called the
'philosophies of history'. In general, philosophies of
history follow one or the other of two main lines. If

they follow the one line ('mystic' school, e.g. Hegel), they enunciate general principles of life—without necessarily looking first at the past; and then they look at the past, and fit it into the preconceived picture. Followers of the other line ('naturalistic' school) look at the past first, and in doing so endeavour to discern in it the main lines of development, i.e. the principles which should guide the historian in the choice of material. It has rather cynically been remarked that the first of these two methods, which does not profess to deduce its principles from the facts, is perhaps the more honest of the two.

Followers of either method have, from a very early date, sought to detect an evolutionary rhythm in history, an essential nature, a dominant movement —on a cosmic scale—in some direction or another. This is a voluminous subject which could not be dealt with adequately in the present book, and perhaps should not and need not either. Humanity has been regarded by various groups of historical philosophers as moving in all of the different directions that could be thought of, namely:

(1) forwards—the doctrine of Progress, held, for example (according to their special criteria), by the Marxists;

(2) backwards—Retrogression, a common view in the ancient world;

(3) in circles—the theory of Cycles.

Sometimes a complex process is presumed. Thus Toynbee regards the larger movement as Progressive, but within this, and as its constituent parts, sees (perhaps a little inconsistently) not progress but a series of Cycles—all civilisations being thought of as having their own Cycles of rise and fall (the fall of one often leading to the rise of another) according to analogous rules or laws.

It is true enough that, looked at from certain points of view, a rise, zenith, and fall can be detected in all civilisations. But no one would assert that they are therefore identical; and indeed the definition of the term 'civilisation' presents difficulty (p. 31). It has been well remarked that 'every event is at once (*a*) unique, (*b*) like some other' (Delisle Burns). It is therefore probably more accurate not to speak of laws or rules. 'Life is not a game to be played under immutable rules. It is, among other things, a grand free-for-all fight over what the rules should be' (Lawrence Dennis). It is better to talk not of rules but of uniformities. It is sometimes possible to find uniformities in fairly clear-cut form. But often, also, the uniformities are not so clear as is supposed. The same applies to Progress and Retrogression. On whatever definition of the terms and of the fields in which they are held to operate, the protagonists of either have to admit that they are 'zigzag'.

Study of the history of the past 5000 years undoubtedly does not show Progress, Retrogression, or Cyclical movements proceeding in any clear, easily definable, or universal form. Even those who see one of these principles operating must admit that during this period 'the picture presented is frankly chaotic' (Childe). This need not worry those who have put forward their philosophy of history in philosophical rather than historical form, i.e. basing the past on it rather than it on the past. But it does involve a terribly large number of qualifications on the part of those who wish to erect into immutable principles such uniformities or tendencies as can be detected.

Bertrand Russell has recently summed up this difficulty: 'I have spoken of a twofold movement in past
history, but I do not consider that there is anything
either certain or inevitable about such laws of historical development as we can discover. New knowledge
may make the course of events completely different
from what it would otherwise have been; this was,
for instance, a result of the discovery of America.
New institutions also may have effects that could not
have been foreseen. . . .' Personality is another of
these potent accidents. What can only be described
as 'Providence', or chance, seems to play its part; so
we cannot use history to foretell the future. It is, of
course, possible that this chaotic appearance of the
past may in part be due to our undoubted ignorance
of a vast amount of it: the story we have may be too
short for any pattern that there may be to have
displayed itself (H. J. Randall). But on the whole
it is likely that the surprising turns which we see in
the course of events are as much a part of it as the
circles, or upward and downward or parallel lines. 'I
can only see one emergency following another as
wave follows wave', said H. A. L. Fisher; for him
this was the only uniformity (cf. p. 128).

So the historian cannot very profitably utilise any
'philosophy of history' as the basis of his selection
of material. This is another negative conclusion.
The conclusions from this survey have so far all been
negative. It set out to try to establish principles on
which the general historian, and his counterpart in
schools and universities, should select their material
from the large store available—and should distribute
their emphasis. Thus far five conclusions have been
suggested:

(1) that the selection should not be influenced by prejudice against the East;

(2) that it should not be haphazard;

(3) that it should not be too much affected by the *quantity* of material by which this or that field is represented today;

(4) that it should not be excessively influenced by the literary or artistic talents of communities, or of individuals among them;

(5) that it should not be based on an assumption of cosmic cycles, progressions, or retrogressions.

The task of establishing positive principles of selection still remains. Clearly, one wants to select what is important. It is therefore desirable to avoid the 'innumerable *culs-de-sac* in the history of the race' (J. Murphy); it is necessary to concentrate on the things and thoughts that have produced consequences; or, in material terms, tools and discoveries that are untransmitted are of no value or interest (Childe). 'The wider the circle is, over which the effects of a historical event extend, the more important it is' (E. Meyer). So much may be agreed. But there is a great difference of opinion as to what *is* important. And that is only to be expected; for there is no hard-and-fast infallible way of settling this point, nor could there be. For in a subject so complex and many-sided, 'the limits of what is to be considered of historical importance and found worthy of record are of a purely subjective nature' (E. Meyer). That is not, of course, in contradiction with our conclusion that the selection should not be haphazard. On the contrary, it casts an even heavier responsibility on the writer and teacher of history. For it allows him no ready-made pattern to work by. He is obliged to undertake his selection for himself, and his only way of doing that sincerely is to search his own mind to try to find the pattern for that selection. In fact, in a sense it is true to say that he must form 'a definite conception of the nature and significance of history as a whole' (Collingwood).

But it has been suggested that this definite conception is not provided ready-made by any 'philosophy of history'. What, then, provides it? It is provided by the recognition of the real purpose of studying history, namely, its educative value today, its usefulness to this as to any other generation. History would not have been studied as it has been if it had not been found to be useful. As long ago as the sixth century B.C. Confucius remarked that even 'in the old days men studied [the past] with a view to their self-improvement'. This utility can be of very varied kinds. One particular kind is strikingly illustrated by Bertrand Russell: 'education should be designed to counteract the natural credulity and the natural incredulity of the uneducated . . . few things are more useful in a citizen of a democracy than skill in detecting, by reading newspapers, what it was that took place'. The citizen who does this is exercising his historical faculty—and in a very important way, for the study of propaganda in either the modern or the ancient world is invaluable. But the utility of history takes innumerable other forms also. In general, 'the study of history is capable of stimulating, of widening, and of assisting thought in many ways' (J. W. Allen). In particular, the study of civilised peoples or societies has unique value for every seeker after knowledge (Toynbee). These assertions are by no means invalidated by paradoxical

assertions that all history is uninteresting because it
must be false (R. Walpole), or 'the only thing that
we learn from history is that no one ever learns
anything from history'. It is true that it is hard to
get at the truth about the past, and it is also true
that its lessons are all too rarely appreciated, but
that does not mean that they are not there; they
are.

In other words, history is studied because we hope
it will be useful to us today. 'The prize of all history
is the understanding of modern times' (Acton). The
aim of history, however ancient, is the explanation
of the present—our environment and ourselves.
Teachers of the classics, among others, 'should be
ready to trace with pupils of every type and interest
those strands in ancient history which gave the
ancient world its widest and strongest claim to notice
in the modern age' (H. M. Last). General history, in
particular, seeks to show how the present came to be
what it is. It has already been suggested that no
'philosophy of history' justifies the claim that history
can foretell the future. In the future, as in the past,
there will be an element of the unforeseen and un-
foreseeable. Nevertheless history will help to fortify
us against the future. For example, 'failure has . . .
the important negative value of a warning' (Pratt).
History will fortify us against the future by making
the present clearer to us.

For this is the function of history—the elucidation
of the present. That has often been said. Indeed, it
was already a commonplace in ancient times. But it
has been given far more lip-service than practical
attention. Its implications have much too rarely
been transferred to the practical plane. This is

regrettable, especially today when teachers and 'universal' writers have little time and space—for this gives added urgency to their task of enabling their students to concentrate on what is truly essential in history.

For the main and most neglected implication of this topical interpretation of history may be described in the following way. Since the aim of history, including ancient history, lies in the present, the general historian, and the teacher of history, must select their material in accordance with the chief needs and problems of the present—that is, *of their readers and hearers.* 'The selection of facts depends upon the historical interest taken by those living at the present time' (E. Meyer). But this principle of selection, though a logically necessary one, is rarely observed, as a glance at history text-books will readily show.

A word of warning is necessary here. First, our desire to make history of present-day, topical interest must not induce us to *distort* the past—to force it into a modern mould. Nothing could be less desirable than that. The Roman emperor Augustus was neither an anticipatory Hitler, nor, on the other hand, was he a combination of the Archbishop of Canterbury and a Guards Officer. If we allowed our delineation of him to take either of these forms, we should be inducing our interest in the twentieth century to overstep its bounds and warp our judgment about the past—just as we should if we allowed current East-West animosities to blind us to the part that the East has played in history (p. 2). But this does not indicate that the historian's interest in the present is unjustifiable or unnecessary. It merely shows that

even a great guiding principle like this must leave his
judgment unimpaired. And, in any case, the desire
to make Greeks, Romans, etc., seem 'like ourselves'
is only a feeble and superficial way of serving the
cause of topicality. They are quite as interesting to
the modern world when they are different; indeed
that is one of the most interesting things about
them.

So the avoidance of distortion does not mean the
avoidance of topicality. It remains the most urgent
task of the general historian, however ancient his
period, to ensure that his selection of material is
governed by the principal needs and problems of the
present day. Unfortunately, there is not the slightest
doubt what is the greatest problem in the world
today. It is the question whether, by some means or
other, human beings of this and other countries, as
peoples and as individuals, *can avoid destruction*. The
Utilitarian doctrine of the 'Greatest Happiness of the
Greatest Number' has boiled down to that. Everything of value, 'of no matter what kind, is precarious
and may at any moment be destroyed by war'
(Russell). This is far the greatest problem of the
present day, and no amount of emphasis on other
problems must allow its absolute pre-eminence and
primacy to be lost sight of. Similarly, therefore, this
is the problem which must never leave the mind of
the historian, ancient or modern; for his subject is
man, and his selection must be based on the problems
of the present day. This most urgent of all problems,
then, is the one which must prompt the choice of
historical material.

The answer to this problem rests with governments and with the politicians who comprise them,

who are thus invested with a degree of responsibility that has never been exceeded. In other words, the problem is a political problem. When this danger hangs over our heads, all cultural and social questions are subordinate to this political one. Most people, in a crisis, subordinate even class to nation (p. 146). Subordinate, too, are economic questions. For, in direct contradiction of the view of Marx (who reversed the process), *economic power is based on the power of the State* (Bertrand Russell, Spitz); that is to say, it is based on political power, and is one of its chief parts. Control of the latter will give control of the former (cf. p. 220).

This state of affairs automatically provides the 'universal' historian with his main principle of selection. That, we concluded, must be adopted in accordance with the most pressing problems of the day. Much the most pressing problem of the day is political. So the material which the general historian or teacher must select will be mainly political too. This decision must take precedence over all the arguments that have been launched against the political method. Of these some of the most persuasive are those of J. B. S. Haldane; but even he grudgingly admits a merit in the subject, and a most important one too. 'History,' he says, 'as generally taught in schools, is the story of the political squabbles of the last 2000 years, and is, on the whole, rather a futile story. It becomes valuable when it is studied in detail, because it illustrates the psychology of politicians and those of crowds.' His criticisms of political history do not so much invalidate the subject as point out the undoubtedly common faults of bad political history; the shortness of historical view, the desire to use it as a vehicle for one's own political opinions, the failure to remember that man's hands have been important as well as his mouth. These are criticisms which induce humility in the prospective political historian, but they do not prevail against his conclusion based on overriding grounds. Popper, too, in criticising political history, the history of power, as due to the enforcement of this subject by those who possess the power, and as due to the worship of power owing to fear ('a relic of the time of the cage'), is obliged to give as another reason the very relevant fact that *power affects us all.*

The general historian who decides that politics is his central theme can, at least, console himself by the thought that, if he does his job properly, such criticisms, and the process of time, have in one respect put him in a better position than the nineteenth-century protagonists of political history. That is to say, he will have learnt from the materialists (and archaeologists—not always the same thing) not to ignore the role of technology as a factor in his politics. He will also have learnt from G. M. Trevelyan of that wider conception 'social history' which comprises them both, and many other things too. And he will have learnt from Lord Acton that some of his political events are caused by ideas emanating from non-political sources (p. 205).

But, as has been suggested, his chief preoccupation must nevertheless be with politics. Indeed, where his canvas is so limited by circumstances that it will take up nearly all his space and time merely to avoid under-stressing politics, then he must deal with it and little else. The damage done by his omission of other topics will be less than the damage done by a false emphasis; and where he only has 70,000 words to write or speak, a false emphasis will be hard to avoid unless he concentrates to an overwhelming extent on this aspect which is of overwhelming modern importance.

It is possible to specify further. The great problem today is not only political, it is that of political unity. We are now, slowly, becoming accustomed in this country to the somewhat uncongenial idea that it cannot work out its salvation by itself. In a sense we led the way to it by creating the British Commonwealth of Nations. But it is now widely agreed that even this great step in political thought is not enough to secure our safety. In 1935 Lord Lothian observed: 'While public opinion today may be far from thinking in these terms, events are driving the issue to the front with tremendous speed.' 1950 and 1951 are, perhaps, accustoming public opinion to this instinctively unpalatable but unavoidable and indeed all-important truth. In a sense, it is always true: 'it would be generally conceded that an important part of what we mean by social progress is the extension of positive social relationships to ever larger units' (John Baillie). But it is today of an importance transcending other matters. 'Modern technique has not only facilitated the psychology of cohesion in large groups; it has also made large groups imperative both from an economic and from a military point of view. . . . Modern developments . . . make a few large organisations much more productive than a number of smaller ones' (Russell). The groups of which he writes are political; their creation is an intricate and difficult operation, which is the main task of world politics today.

That is to say, the greatest of our present-day problems is that of political unity. And it again follows from the conclusions that we have reached that this must be the subject on which the teacher of ancient history, and his literary counterpart the general historian, need to concentrate their attention—if necessary (since their time and space are so limited) to the exclusion of many other matters.

For centuries arguments have raged concerning the proper subject-matter of history. It is clearly a question on which an enormously wide range of opinions can be held, all of them legitimately. The historian is at liberty, if he wishes, to say with the Latin dramatist Terence 'Everything that concerns man concerns me too.' But in practice, of course, systematic selection is necessary here again. For example, it has been suggested earlier that cultural matters are best handled separately (p. 10). But even if this is agreed, the field remains enormous, too enormous. This began to be explicitly recognised during the nineteenth century. Since then, perhaps the greatest of many controversies has been concerned with the question whether political or economic history should take first place. First Von Ranke, Freeman, and Seeley asserted the absolute supremacy of politics. This view was flatly contradicted by Marx, who held that what determines the processes of social, political, and intellectual life in general is the mode of production in material life—the economic factor. The Marxist formulation was a necessary corrective to the snobberies and cruelties of nineteenth-century social and economic conditions; and much of it has now passed permanently into systems of thought that are

by no means 'Soviet'. But in 1951 it meets the case
less well than the opposing view—not because our
relations with Russia are strained today, but because
that strain (the gravest and potentially most far-
reaching factor in our lives) is primarily political and
not economic. Present conditions, and the desirability that our ancient history should serve them and
help us to understand them, must bring all who are
not specialists back at least within hailing distance
of the position of Seeley: 'history is past politics;
politics is present history'.

Now this conclusion on grounds of principle might
be very inconvenient, in practice, for the ancient historian if it so happened that the subjects of politics
and political unity were those in which ancient
history had sparse developments to show. Fortu-
nately, however, the very opposite is the case. Ancient
history is a great storehouse of political developments
of every kind. 'No one can understand the present,
unless he has a clear conception of the evolution *of
government* and civilisation in the ancient world'
(Rostovtzeff: the italics are mine). Moreover, as
Russell again has pointed out, the central problem
of the ancient world, as of the world today, was
mostly that of the control of political power. Then,
as now—but perhaps to an even more marked extent
—the question of economic superiority was subordinate to that of political control. Two of the most
famous pairs of enemies in antiquity are Alexander
the Great and Persia, Rome and Carthage. Alexander
and the Romans were incomparably inferior in economic resources to their opponents, but they won;
their military power was the decisive factor, and the
political control which it gave them was incomparably

more important than their economic inferiority.[1] Nor can these be described as the class-struggles which, according to Marx, play the predominant part in wars (cf. pp. 214ff.). They were struggles between one political power and another, like the fights between popes and emperors in the Middle Ages.

Moreover in political unity, as well as in the subject of political control in general, ancient history has information of supreme significance to impart. During the ancient world, indeed, political unity was invented, and nearly all its main stages and degrees were invented too. Stonehenge shows enforced co-operation on a large scale, which would not be possible in a condition of anarchy. The creation of the first towns is widely recognised as comprising one of the greatest revolutions in the world's history (p. 32). Others time the end of one vast epoch and the beginning of another with the creation—still in the ancient world—of the first supra-national community (O. Halecki). This emphasis on the magnitude of social and political organisations, an emphasis —in a sense—on mere *size*, is not arbitrary or illegitimate. Indeed the anthropologist, too, tentatively and conjecturally concludes, in regard to early society, that 'the complexity and coherence of the social order follow from the size of the group' (R. R. Marett). So the subjects of politics and political unity are conveniently accessible to the ancient historian, owing to their extreme prominence and importance in ancient history itself.

But that was not the primary reason why they were

[1] More frequently, of course, superior economic resources *contribute to* superior political power, i.e. they are both in the hands of the same contestant (cf. pp. 219f.).

indicated here as constituting the foremost subject of
the general historian. The reason for that was their
topicality—their relevance to the chief problems of
1951. This was because 'the prize of all history is the
understanding of modern times'—that is to say, because of the educative value of history; because of its
value as a source of lessons and warnings. For
history, as Confucius observed, was studied because
it is useful and instructive; and Plato too was insis-
tent on its value from this point of view. This is a
point which may justly be mentioned again now that
we have decided to give the central position to
political factors; for it is the *political* instructiveness
of history that has been most persistently and most
justly stressed.

Other types of advantage to be derived from history have also been emphasised from time to time.
For example, ages disposed to point a moral have
invariably found morals enough to point in history.
'Men have always been adjured to study history to
learn how sinners perish' (R. R. Betts). Now there
ought not to be any objection to pointing a moral
where, after consideration with full intellectual
honesty, it can be detected; indeed some—though
this is a disputed point—consider it the historian's
duty to do so. But the careers of sinners throughout
history unfortunately do not seem to justify the
student in drawing any very clear-cut or satisfactory
moral. It is true that much of the record is missing;
but from that extensive part of it which remains it
appears, to put it briefly, that sinners have often
done rather well. Sometimes they came to grief
(p. 140); the fall of Nineveh is a fine bull's eye for the
moralist. But it is not playing fair to dwell on this

while avoiding all mention of the numerous men who, though undoubtedly sinners by any definition of the word, prospered and continued to prosper. Ancient moralists seem to have appreciated this difficulty, for to some of these successful villains they imaginatively attributed gory or worm-eaten deceases. But that is of no use to the historian, who must refrain from regarding history on such evidence as is available to him, as conveying moral lessons; though that does not mean that he should condone the more obvious forms of evil when he sees them (p. 151).

But it remains nevertheless true that there are *political* lessons to be learnt from history, and learnt in abundance. When Bolingbroke remarks 'the study of history seems to me, of all other, the most proper to train up to private and public virtue', we may query the first part of this assertion, but its second part is unmistakably true and has been recognised as such by people and also governments of many epochs. This educational importance of political history was expressed strongly, but not too strongly, by Seeley: 'history is the school of statesmanship. Without at least a little knowledge of history, no man can take a rational interest in politics, and no man can form a rational judgment about them without a great deal. It is an important study to every citizen; it is the one important study to the legislator and ruler.'

Thus a political subject is instructive as well as topical; and this will particularly apply to the ancient world, which, as has been said, is very rich in political themes. It is true that, here too, warnings are necessary. They have been voiced vigorously by a recent reviewer (*The Times Literary Supplement*; reviewing L. Waddy, *Pax Romana and World Peace*). 'The circumstances of the modern problem are so different as to reduce the historian's proffered guidance to little more than platitudinising. The topicalities impart to his survey of a past age a certain piquancy and poignancy like that which a shop-window display may have for a hungry urchin.' This criticism is valuable in that it makes us take heed not to indulge in too sweeping or facile comparisons. But it does not by any means justify us in coming to the nihilistic conclusion that general political history, ancient or modern, is no use at all. It is exceedingly useful if we can only make the necessary effort to see where the utility lies.

It may be added, too, that we Western Europeans (unlike, for example, Indians, whose historical tradition is very slender) have always tended to receive a historical training which emphasises politics. 'The political plane . . . is the plane on which the Western Society chiefly lives' (Toynbee). At all events, in the West, rival schools of historiography have never wholly ousted that of political history. And it is, on the whole, still true today that, despite a tendency to synthesis, 'political history retains its central position' (J. R. M. Butler). For the reasons that have been given, this remains all the more desirable in 1951.

The next duty of the teacher, or aspirant to the writing of general history, is to attempt to put before his hearers or readers some brief description of the ancient world. But this cannot be dealt with as a whole. Into what units shall he divide it? The answer has to a large extent been provided by our previous discussion. He will have to concentrate on the units which have chiefly contributed to the history of politics, and in particular to the history of political unity. The bogy of selection here arises again. He clearly cannot cram into his limited time and space an account of the whole political careers of such units.

To a large extent, then, he must concentrate on their most vital periods—the periods of their greatest political significance and, very often, of their greatest political expansion. That is to say, without necessarily committing himself to any 'philosophy of history', he must to a considerable degree adopt 'the happy artifice of Condorcet' (Comte) 'whereby the story is made to pass from one culture to another, and from one part of the world to another, the culture and region selected to represent each period being the culture and region which were at that time most advanced' (John Baillie). This artifice has its dangers (p. 141); but if one did not make at least some use of its technique, it would be difficult to write or teach 'universal' history at all. A book or course in which the units selected were the *least* advanced (or even much less advanced than others) would possess only the interest of a *tour de force*, and would not satisfy the essential requirement of modern significance.

However, it will not be quite enough just to flit from one unit to the other after 'pin-pointing' each at the climactic moment of its career. This aeronautic method is concisely summarised by verses of Ralph Hodgson, which Baillie quotes:

> Last week in Babylon,
>   Last night in Rome.
> Morning, and in the crush
>   Under Paul's dome; . . .
> Off to some city
>   Now blind in the womb.
> Off to another
>   Ere that's in the tomb.

To some extent every 'universal' historian must here declare himself *touché*. But he can and must minimise the ill-effects of this method by saying a little, in each case, about the processes that had led to these climactic moments—he must show briefly how and why they came about. Here, too, he must try to benefit from the improvements in political historiography that have resulted from the research of the present century (p. 21); for these make it possible to call other historical disciplines into play to explain the political developments.

This cannot be done adequately if the brief account of the ancient world is merely to be divided among political units as such. To take a single example, a number of different political units arose in the same place at different moments in the ancient world; Babylon is an example of this phenomenon. If the climaxes of these units are merely dovetailed with the climaxes of others to form a chronological sequence, the reader or hearer will be able to obtain no idea of the special character of Babylonia and its peoples as promoters of civilisation. Thus a mere enumeration of political units will not provide an adequate basis of classification.

What, then, are we to enumerate? Are we to look, for our basis of classification, to some of the other terms that are used, accurately or loosely, to denote social entities—cultures, societies, civilisations, races, or linguistic units?

For various reasons none of these terms provides a suitably clear and unequivocal type of heading for the subdivisions that we want. For example, 'culture', 'society', and 'civilisation' are all very variously defined terms. The historical materialist will define

'culture' strictly in terms of technology and equipment. We, with our decision to concentrate on
politics, must—while not forgetting technology—cast
our net a little wider; cultures must be regarded as
social as well as material. But they become most
important of all to our selected subject of study when
they come to form part of a civilisation—'a group of
cultures having certain distinct features in common'
(Glyn Daniel). However, its distinction from 'culture'
may clearly become arbitrary; and one of the least
satisfactory features of Toynbee's great work is his
employment of 'civilisation' and 'society' without
precise definition (H. M. Last).

The terms may none the less be used. But where
so great a master of the art of 'universal history' has
incurred criticism it would be as well for others to be
cautious. So it is preferable that the student should
not use 'cultures' or 'civilisations' as the actual
headings of the units into which he is going to divide
the ancient world.

This avoidance will make him chary also of the
various *types* into which archaeologists divide cultures or civilisations. Indeed large epochs covered
by these classifications may in any case be eliminated
as irrelevant, because of the political consideration
which has been established as our guiding principle.
For many of the periods thus classified had run their
course long before politics or political unity can
properly be spoken of. Political organisations and
relations involve a certain prior degree of social
cohesion, and we may legitimately take the view that
this did not reach a sufficiently large extent or high
standard until the village was superseded by the
town. Primitive societies are not grist to history's

mill (J. Murphy). It is, indeed, possible to trace a measure of co-ordination in pre-urban days—for example, the mass-labour of Stonehenge—but on the whole it must be agreed with Childe that 'this urban revolution . . . ushers in civilisation'.

According to one way of subdividing history, *homo sapiens* has experienced four or five great revolutions—the Food-gathering, Food-producing, Urban, Industrial, and perhaps the Atomic. With the Industrial and Atomic Ages we do not have to deal here, other than to repeat that it is they, the world of today, that has dictated our political subject. That subject begins with the Urban Revolution or successive revolutions, consisting of the creation of towns at various centres, first of all at a date which is now believed to be near 3000 B.C. Man (or, perhaps more often, woman) had already long been a producer of food—perhaps for five millennia or more. 'Every single cultivated food plant of any importance has been discovered by some nameless barbarian society' (Childe). Before Man the Farmer thus came into existence, the world had only known Man the Hunter (Stuart Piggott)—the food gatherer, hunting and fishing. But we are not concerned with Man the Hunter, nor even with Man the Farmer until his villages grew to towns. It is at the Urban Revolution that our story begins.

At some centres this coincides with the first use of bronze, a great improvement on the copper that had earlier come into use in place of stone. Here were a further set of 'revolutions', and they too have been used (originally by Lord Avebury) in an attempt to divide great epochs from one another. These include the Palaeolithic or Early Stone Age, in which man

merely chipped his stone tools into shape; the Neolithic or Later Stone Age, in which he had learnt to
grind and polish them; and then the Copper, Bronze,
and Iron Ages.

The creation of the earliest towns known to us
seems, in some cases, to have coincided with the first
use of Bronze—that is to say, with the inauguration
of a 'Bronze Age'. But this type of classification
carries with it certain important reserves. Tools of
chipped stone, polished stone, copper, bronze, and
iron came into use in different areas at widely
different epochs (there are still Stone Age peoples in
the world today). Some regions missed out one or
another of these stages altogether. Some achieved
a high degree of civilisation without using metals at
all. Some contained, at one and the same moment,
people or peoples at different stages of this process.
Some reverted from one stage to an earlier one. So
it is not correct to talk of *the* Bronze Age, Iron Age,
etc., though it is legitimate to speak of a certain area
entering upon *its* Bronze Age, etc. In this sense it
can be said that the earliest Urban Revolutions
known to us, in *c.* 3000 B.C., in some cases coincided
with the earliest Bronze Ages known to us.

These Urban Revolutions, at the earliest of which
our story begins, occurred—according to Childe's
reconstruction—when 'society persuaded or com-
pelled the farmers to produce a surplus of foodstuffs
over and above their domestic requirements'. A new
population of specialists and officials arose. This
more systematic grouping of population, and the
saving of labour thus introduced, quickly inspired
other great discoveries in addition to the alloying of
bronze. One of these discoveries pointed towards a

degree of social cohesion even more extensive than that provided by the city. For, with a view to the more conduct of trade, men agreed together, at about this time, that certain symbols should be held to possess certain fixed meanings: writing was discovered (though for a long time it did not become alphabetic, p. 93).

Towns and writing were two institutions which looked ahead to even larger groupings. Political history had begun—and its record as well. From now on an increasing number of peoples experienced urban revolutions and thus began to form part of this picture. These are the peoples whom it is our duty to enumerate. But how are we to do so, since, as has been suggested, enumeration by 'cultures', 'societies', and 'civilisations' is apt to be confusing?

Most historical text-books tacitly assume that a proper basis for classification is afforded by race. But such classifications, unless put in the most general terms, are hopelessly misleading. 'Race', in its present sense, is quite a recent word, and a highly ambiguous one. On any definition, 'races' are quite different things from 'nations' or 'nationalities', and from national or other 'ways of life'—as well as from 'cultures' and 'societies'. These and 'races' mutually overlap to an endless extent.

Another serious difficulty is provided by the fact that nearly all the racial groups to which names have been affixed are elaborately mixed, and the mixture has been proceeding ever since the earliest times of which we have any knowledge. 'Every civilised group of which we have any record has been a hybrid one' (R. Linton). 'Despite the restrictive effect of social sanctions, wherever and whenever men have met they have mingled their ancestral strains' (Trevor). It would, therefore, be as true of ancient times—and of any region—as it is of today, to say that 'in every single nationality of Europe the various elements of the continental population are represented' (Boas). And the effort of distinguishing and identifying the different blends is not made any easier when the people concerned have long been dead.

So we must abandon any idea that words like 'Roman', 'Hittite', or 'English' have a clear racial significance. It is for the identification of such national designations with racial concepts that the severest strictures have been reserved. For 'rarely does racial homogeneity among a whole people reach such a high level that strict racial terms can be applied in the analysis of phenomena' (Pratt). 'The student of history will find it prudent to ignore the idea of race in its biological sense and all theories founded upon it' (H. J. Randall). Racialist use of the word 'blood' represents an old biological error (J. Huxley and Haddon). And 'race' itself 'is an empty phrase, an utter swindle' (F. Müller).

It remains, however, possible to attempt cautiously certain broad groupings of mankind according to combinations of physical characteristics. This, too, is by no means plain sailing, as even so sweeping a classification is a deeply disputed matter. Research has made it certain that no single physical criterion is sufficient—neither the shape of the head or nose, nor the colour or form of hair, nor the colour of the skin. However, it remains a practical convenience to speak of certain great groups which, though frequently merging in various mixtures, are nevertheless roughly distinguishable by their physical characteristics. Even with regard to these, however, the current terminology frequently changes. To use a very recent 'working hypothesis' which takes the chief physical criteria into account, the main groups existing today may be described as the Caucasiform, Mongoliform, Negriform, Khoisaniform (Bushmen and Hottentots) and Australiform (J. C. Trevor)— the suffix '-iform' stressing that it is *characteristics* rather than alleged origins by which the classification is guided. Possibly even these very general headings are 'nothing but an illuminating set of classificatory abstractions' (Toynbee).

Of these five groups only two are of interest to the student of ancient history. Negroes, Khoi-San and Australasians achieved no leading ancient civilisation or supremacy; nor have they achieved any modern ones, though the turn of at least the Negroes is likely to come relatively soon. The ancient civilisations were created by Caucasiform and Mongoliform peoples (in popular speech 'white' and 'yellow', though these are misleading in view of the marked variations in colouring). Naturally these general headings, despite racial mixtures, admit of further subdivision to a certain extent. For example, the leading branch of the Mongoliform group—with its broad faces, high cheek-bones, coarse straight hair, and round heads—was, and is, that of the Chinese. Other branches are believed by many to be represented by the American Indians ('Amerinds', or 'Red race'). The Caucasiform group can also be subdivided up to a point. Its main subdivisions may be described as the 'Mediterranean', 'Alpine', 'Nordic' (and 'Baltic'), 'Erythriote' (Ethiopian), and 'Chersiote' (parts of India).

These subdivisions of the Caucasiform group had, even in very ancient times, undergone lengthy and incessant processes of intermixture. But the subdivisions in question can nevertheless be regarded as representing certain different physical characteristics. The average 'Mediterranean' had an elongated (long to medium) head, a sallow complexion, very dark hair and eyes, straight nose, and wavy hair. The average 'Alpine' was broad-headed, thickset and of medium height. He generated one type more prevalent in Europe (of which part used to be called 'Dinaric'), and another type more prevalent in Asia ('Armenoid' or Anatolian). The latter had pronounced features—a very broad high head, broad face, and prominent aquiline nose with long wings. The 'Nordics' were generally fair with blue or grey eyes and florid or reddish-white skins, but their most fundamental characteristics were their long heads and faces, prominent narrow noses and well-developed chins. The Ethiopian 'Erythriote' type does not figure in our study. The 'Chersiote' does, in the form of many Dravidian-speaking early peoples of India; they were slender, with long high heads, bulbous foreheads, and usually narrow faces.

Some have likewise claimed to be able to identify innate different psychological characteristics in these groups—the emotional temperament of the Chinese (in spite of their 'inscrutability' in so many films); the impulsive, extrovert vivacity of the 'Mediterranean'; the steadiness of the 'Alpine'; and the introspection, individualism, and determination (sometimes bellicosity) of the 'Nordic'. But these sweeping statements come under almost as heavy fire as the old-fashioned assertions, which we have all heard, that the French have such-and-such a character, the Americans such-and-such a character, and so on. Such general statements ignore the differences imposed by class, wealth, and culture or the lack of it; and heredity, though not a myth, operates in too complex and devious a way to warrant facile generalisations.

Moreover, a vast proportion of the genes in individuals are common to every population, and there is no definite evidence that there exist innate temperamental, mental, cultural, or moral differences between human groups. A summary of the Report of the UNESCO committee on Race questions (1950) includes the following passages: 'Whatever group differences of the kind there might be are greatly overridden by the individual differences, and by the differences springing from environmental factors . . . as for personality and character, these may be considered raceless . . . wherever it has been possible to make allowances for differences in environmental opportunities . . . tests have shown essential similarity in mental characters among all human groups'; and the same is then said to apply to culture and morals. W. Fagg, Honorary Secretary of the Royal Anthropological Institute, writes expressing certain unspecified reservations concerning the report in general; but he too concludes: 'there is general agreement with its main thesis—that there is no scientific justification for racial discrimination'. The view that any one 'race' is endowed with superior talents to any other is absurd (p. 193).

We shall therefore be well advised, in using terms like Caucasiform and the names of its subdivisions, to think only in terms of physical characteristics.

With this and all other reservations made, it seems possible to assert that at a very early date, for reasons that are not understood, *homo sapiens* became differentiated into great groups with physical distinctions. Ten or twenty thousand years ago there were comparatively unmixed 'Mediterraneans' in southern Europe and western Asia. Probably the 'Alpines' came rather later from elsewhere. The chief period of infiltration by 'Nordics' seems to have been the second millennium B.C.

Linguistic studies neither assist very much in the determination of racial origins nor provide us with the basis for our enumeration of ancient peoples. Languages are no better than passports as guides to race. In fact, they are entirely fallible. Language and race cut right across each other, and so linguistic and racial classifications must be kept rigorously apart. Terms like 'Indo-European', 'Aryan', 'Semitic', or 'Dravidian' should not be thought of as describing groups or units of a racial character; although they occasionally happen to coincide with peoples of more or less homogeneous race, they are purely linguistic.

So we must try to attribute a language to our ancient peoples quite separately from the race or races which we may, or may not, be able to attribute to them. In the case of the ancient world this attribution of languages is not always easy, for there are a number of important ancient languages of which we do not know even the main characteristics. However, where the languages are well known, the problem of classification is not usually particularly acute. It is true that, here again, systems of classification vary, and that occasional 'hybrids' occur, but the main groups of languages are easily distinguishable. These are the Semitic (technically described as 'triliteral'), Hamitic (distantly related to it), Uralian and Altaic ('agglutinative'), Indo-European ('flexional'), Caucasian, Sino-Tibetan (now 'isolating'), Dravidian, and perhaps several American ('polysynthetic') families. These are comprehensive terms, each divisible into branches, and in some instances (notably that of the Indo-European tongues —contrary to De Gobineau) it is very doubtful whether any language that can be described as 'original' ever existed. But the families, despite bastards, are authentic and distinguishable. Many attempts have been made to determine the areas in which they originated. It is thought that the Semitic languages were first spoken in the Syro-Arabian desert; and, as regards the much disputed home of the Indo-European tongues, 'speculation tends now to prefer a site beside the Baltic' (W. J. Entwistle).[1]

Linguistic differences, it may be repeated, are essentially independent from differences of race. Language is a part of 'culture', by most definitions of the latter (p. 31). However, language, though it is a most important form of culture and one about which and from which we have a great deal to learn, is only one form; its classification overlaps constantly not only with 'race', but also with every other form of culture, such as the use of different metals, religions, agricultural systems, clothes, etc.—not to speak of political organisations (Fichte's view that

[1] Another strong school of thought locates their origin among the early agriculturists of the steppes of S. Russia, east of the Caspian. It is sometimes maintained that the earliest Indo-European speech was a blend of Uralian and Caucasian (?) elements.

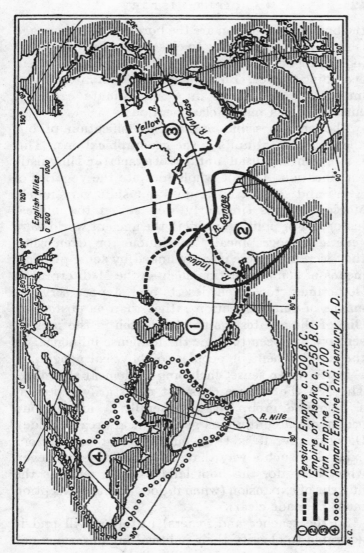

I. THE LARGEST ANCIENT EMPIRES

Persian Empire c. 500 B.C.
Empire of Asoka c. 250 B.C.
Han Empire A.D. c.100
Roman Empire 2nd. century A.D.

English Miles
0   200   1000

the borders of a nation are the borders of its language is naïve). So it is no use to classify the latter according to language, any more than it is to classify them according to race. Both questions are of interest and importance, but only in a subordinate capacity, cutting across major classifications.

The only possible primary classification of our ancient political units is the geographical one. This is free from the disadvantages of a racial and linguistic classification. On the whole (despite the vagaries of rivers and sea-coasts) it does not shift very much. Moreover, it is singularly well suited to political history. For political units in the ancient world were generally geographically continuous, or, even when they were not, were usually linked by some physical means of communication such as the Mediterranean (sometimes, too, even deserts and steppes serve as means of communication rather than as obstacles). One of the greatest gains of research in the present century has been to show the immense influence, on the development of peoples, of physical geography —in its wider sense, including geological structure. Thus, 'if the culture does not necessarily represent a linguistic group, it is generally a local group occupying a continuous geographical area' (Childe). Occasionally, it is true, cultures and civilisations expand in such a way that this is not true; but even when they do, the homeland usually remains the nucleus of expansion (when it does not, the exception must be made clear).

So the teacher and general historian will find it desirable to classify their political organisations not according to 'culture', 'civilisation', 'race', or language, but according to the geographical situations of their nuclei. There is obviously no natural order in which these can be arranged. It is convenient to group them in major geographical divisions. Perhaps it is salutary for the Westerner not to put Europe, or even the Near East, first (p. 2). Let us therefore employ the following five main headings:

(I) Pakistan and India
(II) China
(III) America
(IV) Mainland of Western Asia
(V) Mediterranean.

Within each of those subdivisions, the order in which geographical areas are placed will to some extent reflect the 'artifice of Condorcet' (p. 29); that is to say, the order will be roughly guided by the dates at which the areas gained political prominence or pre-eminence. Such pre-eminence was usually gained by military aggression, but it must be remembered that at least as many aggressors failed and so have not found their way into the main lines of history (p. 15).

The accounts under each heading will here be of the briefest possible character—mere skeletons or sketches of the form which it is suggested that treatment might take.

CHAPTER II

ANCIENT HISTORY

I. PAKISTAN AND INDIA (Map I)

1. *Indus Valley.* The Indian sub-continent is no more a single unit, and as hard to make into one, as Europe. Geographically it falls into four main areas, each provided with its own system of river communications and irrigation. These areas are: (i) the Valley of the Indus and its four main tributaries in the north-west (the main part of Pakistan); (ii) the Valley of the Ganges and its tributaries in the north-east; (iii) the Deccan plateau in the centre; and (iv) southern India. The first of these regions possesses natural protections—mountains to north and north-west, desert to east; it is also a well-watered area, and that was true in ancient times not only of the Punjab but of Sind, which is now a waterless desert. These regions produced what was, as far as we know, much the earliest high civilisation of India. For during the past twenty years two great cities, dating back to the middle of the fourth millennium B.C., have been discovered at Mohenjodaro in Sind, in the alluvial plain near the mouth of the river, and Harappa in the Punjab.[1] These cities possessed an advanced material culture, including the use of copper and some bronze, and of writing. It is striking to note that their culture (a somewhat

[1] Of the 14 known sites of ancient villages and small towns not far from Harappa, 12 are east of the Indus in the modern State of Bhawalpur.

drab one) is uniform; indeed it seems probable that already at this early date there was a uniform culture over the whole of this great area of Pakistan, and there may have been political unity also—though the two main centres were 350 miles apart.

Harappa products lack 'even the cheery *nouveau riche* vulgarity of Early Dynastic Sumer (p. 60), and display instead a dead level of bourgeois mediocrity in almost every branch of the visual arts and crafts' (Stuart Piggott). The combination of architectural size, centralisation, elaborate religion and technical backwardness, recalls the early cultures of Central America (*q.v.*). 'The picture is one of a rigid and highly evolved bureaucratic régime . . . little conducive to the political liberty of the individual' (R. E. M. Wheeler). There was, moreover, an unchanging quality reminiscent of ancient Egypt; this culture, which we first discover ready-made, hardly changed or developed in a thousand years.

We know neither who these people were, nor where they came from. Some plant geneticists tell us that S.E. Afghanistan was the home of a wheat that they cultivated. We do not know what language or languages they spoke, since we cannot read their writing. These are some of the most important questions in all history, and probably, if conditions permit, we shall know some of the answers within fifty years. Meanwhile it is important to note that, from *c*. 2300 B.C., they possessed close contact with the contemporary society of the Akkadians (see IV, 7, S. Iraq).

Nearly half of the skulls which this civilisation has revealed are of 'Mediterranean' type; the residue are mixed—Alpine, Mongoloid and even Australiform.

We do not yet know to what extent the people of these cities were linked racially or linguistically, or both, with the earliest Indian group of which we have clear knowledge—that great group which includes the people who spoke Dravidian and still do so in millions today: this group is sometimes classified as a separate subdivision of the Caucasiform 'race', the 'Chersiote' branch. These 'Chersiote' people may have inherited, or seized, part of the Indus civilisation. They may have come south and east to Pakistan and India from Baluchistan, driven on by some early element in the wanderings of the peoples. The Dravidian language is regarded as forming a 'family' distinct from any other—though it contains 'agglutination', and this has led to unsubstantiated conjectures that it is linked with the Altaic and Uralian groups (such as Turkish), which do the same.

The cities of Mohenjodaro and Harappa possessed fortified citadels, but in c. 1500 this whole civilisation was destroyed by war. The fertile Punjab has always attracted the tribes of Central Asia: now it succumbed to 'Nordic' incursions.

2. *Ganges Valley*. During the second, and early part of the first, millennium B.C., India and Pakistan were entered by successive waves of 'Nordic' immigrants and invaders, speaking Old Indian or Aryan, a language of the Indo-European family akin with Old Persian; Sanskrit is a literary form of this. The new occupants intermarried with the previous inhabitants, or sometimes relegated them to the lower regions of a rigid caste system. This mixed population did not achieve any important political units in the Indus Valley, of which, indeed, part passed to the Persians (sixth century B.C.) and then to Alexander

the Great. The first great Indian civilisation to arise
after the invasions was in the region lying eastwards,
'Hindustan', the alluvial plains of the Ganges and its
tributaries, bounded on the north by the Himalayas
and on the south by the Vindhya mountains.

The age of Buddha and Mahavira (sixth to fifth
centuries B.C.) witnessed no unification of this area,
which remained divided among a number of warring
states. But in the late fourth century B.C., for nearly
150 years, one of the kingdoms on the Ganges
succeeded in extending its rule from Afghanistan,
Kashmir, and Nepal over all northern India (except
Assam) and even the Deccan. This was the state of
Magadha with its capital at Pataliputra (Patna). Its
two emperors, grandfather and grandson, belonging
to the Maurya dynasty, are of uncertain origin. They
were sharply contrasted figures, except in their outstanding talent as organisers.[1] Chandragupta Maurya
(322–298 B.C.) was a brilliant militarist, who had met
Alexander the Great and married a daughter of
one of his successors, Seleucus, who yielded to him a
large part of Pakistan—already impregnated with
Hellenism.

Chandragupta's vast conquests passed to Asoka
(273–232 B.C.). Asoka, a Buddhist, renounced war,
and in an astoundingly far-reaching programme (still,
remarkably enough, almost wholly unknown in the
West) made the most serious attempt that has ever
been made to base the government of a great area on
strictly ethical standards. His envoys (or missionaries) visited the Seleucids in Syria and the Ptolemies

[1] Piggott suggests that here much was owed to the 'bureaucracy and mercantile organisation' of Mohenjodaro and
Harappa.

in Egypt, and also Burma and Ceylon. For the great inscriptions on which he summarised the principles of his rule he used not Old Indian (Sanskrit, etc.) but Middle Indian (Prākrit)—another literary language but one closer to the spoken tongue; but the Brāhmī script employed for these monuments appears to be of Semitic origin.

After the death of Asoka, the empire began to break up. The process was accelerated by invasions from Bactria, a Greek kingdom on the N.W. Frontier of Pakistan. Unity was not to come to the whole Ganges Valley again for five centuries (under the Guptas, A.D. 320–647).

3. *The N.W. Highlands.* The next unifying movement after that of the Mauryas came from an unexpected quarter. In the first century A.D. the measures of the Chinese government against the Huns (Hsiung-nu) caused the latter to move westwards, displacing another great group of tribes, the Yüeh-chih, in a westerly and southerly direction. One of these peoples, the Kushans, crossed the mountains into the Punjab in *c.* A.D. 48, and with their capital high up at Peshawar extended control not only over the northern and central parts of the Indus Valley, but also above a huge area in the upper reaches of the Ganges. They also controlled a large part of what is now W. Sinkiang, to the north of Kashmir, spanning the great East–West trade-route along which silk travelled from China (which succeeded in exacting tribute for a time, though not for long) to Rome. The creators of this remarkable State, with its even more variegated populations than usual, were apparently of very mixed race, possibly incorporating both 'Alpine' and 'Mongol' elements; but their rulers at

least seem to have spoken an Indo-European tongue (some form of Iranian). Their greatest ruler, Kanishka (A.D. 120–162), was a leading patron of Buddhism and friend of the Romans. He was 'a tall, bearded, burly man, with a big nose. He wore a long, quilted coat . . . and soft leather riding boots, and sat on a chair in European fashion' (H. G. Rawlinson). Soon after his death the kingdom disintegrated and the local wars usual in the area were resumed.

II. CHINA

4. N. China. The student might reasonably expect that the Mongols should be classified among the Mongoliform ethnic groups; but according to some authorities they are instead 'connected . . . with some branch of "Alpine" . . . man' (L. H. D. Buxton), and thus are in part Caucasiform. If this is so—though it is not certain—the northernmost area populated by the truly Mongoliform groups is N. China proper —the land watered by the Yellow River (Hwang Ho), up to the Great Wall, as opposed to S. China, the land of the Yangtse-kiang. Nowadays the northerners are considerably taller and less round-headed than the southerners, from whom they indeed differ markedly in many respects. Some of these differences may be due to comparatively recent racial mixtures, but the beginnings of such mixtures go back to a very remote date.

As far as we know, the greatest ancient civilisations and political unions of the Chinese sub-continent were achieved in the north. Neolithic sites are spread over N. and N.W. China, Mongolia, and Manchuria. But in N. China we come to something more. We also have a clear illustration of Toynbee's theory that

great steps forward are the 'response to a challenge'.
For the Yellow River is encumbered by thick under-
growth and a network of streams; but if these
difficulties could be controlled, the soil (loess) was
very fertile.

So it was in this area that the first great Chinese
civilisation arose. North of the river, in the modern
Honan (due west of the great peninsula opposite
Korea), there was discovered, in 1928, the great
capital city of Anyang. It shows a high civilisation
apparently developing gradually and directly from
the Neolithic culture. The people of Anyang used
bronze, and wrote. They did not perhaps ride, but
they used horses for chariots; and their formidable
monarch must have exercised feudal control over a
large area. The beginnings of Anyang must be dated
to c. 1400–1300 B.C. This provides valuable confirma-
tion of Chinese tradition, which records a great
feudal régime called 'Shang' at precisely this period
and in this area, controlling no less than eighteen
hundred city-states or fifty larger units. But the
tradition records that it began rather earlier than
anything yet found at Anyang (c. 1550 B.C.), and
shifted its capital several times; and archaeology will
probably show this tradition also to be right. More
mysterious is the equally circumstantial record of
a great unified State even earlier than 'Shang'—
allegedly already acquainted with bronze. This was
known as the 'Hsia', and its beginnings are claimed
to have been in c. 2200–2000 B.C. It is tentatively
located to the north of Anyang—in S.W. Shansi,
near the huge right-angled bend of the Yellow River.
No evidence of it has yet been found, but it is significant that the implements and writing found at

Anyang are already so developed 'as to presuppose the passage of a long, a very long past' (T. M. Tchang).

The heritage of 'Hsia', if it ever existed, passed to 'Shang'. 'Shang' were a warlike people, somewhat suggesting the Assyrians. Their characteristic weapons, the chariot and the composite bow, secured them the military ascendancy. But in the end, perhaps the frontier peoples were too much for them, for they fell in *c.* 1100–1000. Unity, however, was maintained, for they were replaced by another formidable dynasty, the 'Chou'. These were feudal chariot-fighters (still using bronze) who bear a singular resemblance to the 'Nordics' who poured into India and occupied Mycenae at the same period. This resemblance has tempted some scholars to ascribe the same origin to the 'Chou' rulers. It is true that they differed in certain respects from their 'Shang' predecessors—they seem to have had pastoral habits—but this may be due not to a fundamental racial difference but to their origin from a more westerly part of N. China (Shensi, where their capital was, and Kansu). However, they may have gained their Chinese character by cultural assimilation only, and it is not impossible that they and the Mycenaeans are, directly or indirectly, products of the same great series of movements.

The 'Chou' monarchy, the 'classical' period of China, broke up in the eighth century B.C., and there followed centuries of frequent war on which Confucius (551–479 B.C.) had no immediate effect; and attempts at federation proved immature. In the third century B.C., however, unity was re-established, and now it was unity over a far vaster area still, comprising almost all China. The unifiers were again a people based on Shensi, in the north-west. These were the 'Ch'in'; they were comparatively backward, and may like their predecessors have been Chinese by acquired culture rather than by race. Again like the 'Chou', they first founded their power on the vast food-producing plain to the south of their homeland (Szechuan). To the north, they shut themselves off from the mixed 'Hun' (Hsiung-nu) populations by the construction of the Great Wall. Their ruler Shih-huang-ti, from 220 B.C. the 'First Universal Emperor', proposed to dispense with the traditional feudal system. He insisted on a uniform standard of education and writing, and by military and totalitarian means established a rigidly centralised government.

This system proved impossible to maintain, and his dynasty fell with it, to give place to the 'Han' (202 B.C.–A.D. 220, with brief intermission). Their system, however, became provincial rather than feudal; this is the 'true Imperial' period. At two moments, c. 90 B.C. (Wu-Ti) and A.D. 90, the territory concentrated peacefully under one rule reached portentous dimensions. The early Han ruled, still from the Yellow River, as far as northern Korea to the east and the borders of Afghanistan to the west. The later Han added much of Indo-China and even obtained suzerainty over the Kushans (see 1, Indus Valley). Vast trading relations were established—for instance, with Rome, Arabia, and Japan—and for many there was unprecedented prosperity. But throughout the period there was trouble with the Huns. These were finally displaced westwards (to the ultimate regret of the Romans); but this necessitated the advance of the frontier far to the north of the Wall and caused a very heavy drain on resources. Towards the end of the second century A.D., the central control succumbed to class-warfare and palace revolutions. A lifetime of fighting followed, and China was not effectively reunited until the sixth century A.D.

III. AMERICA (Map II)

5. *Central America.* In this volcanic, mountainous, heavily forested isthmus there exist a startling series of stone remains to testify to the extent and significance of the early Maya civilisation. During the period of the Roman Empire this was rising to its climactic period (*c.* A.D. 400–900 (?)) on the borders of N. Guatemala and in N.W. Honduras. Colonies were planted in about the fifth century A.D., 100 to 200 miles farther north in Yucatan, to which, for some reason not yet known (war or fever (?)), the whole civilisation was transferred some hundreds of years later.

It is the earlier of these two areas of settlement, that of the Huaxtecan Mayas, that the student of the ancient world must bear in mind. Their chief crop was maize, and they must have exerted a great effort to subject these rich but tropical lands to its cultivation. They were ignorant of metals; 'the copper or bronze ages are not synonyms of an essentially higher civilisation in America' (Nordenskiöld). They were also ignorant of the arch, but nevertheless fabulously skilful in their use of stone for architecture, as for sculpture.

The Mayas are, as far as we know, the only American people to have written in symbols rather than pictures. A high proportion of their writings is concerned with their elaborate astronomy and calendar. But the chronology that can be deduced from these is still seriously disputed. Possibly objects can be dated back to 98 B.C. (H. J. Spinden); possibly the first stone carvings that we possess may belong to about the second century A.D. But these early objects show such an advanced art that they must have a long history behind them. Indeed, the Mayas themselves dated their calendars from the seventh century B.C., and their legends went back to the third or fourth millennium B.C.

Some part of this vanished past may perhaps some day be extracted from the numerous sites, often in difficult territory, which remain unexplored. Meanwhile it is possible to say that the various cities exhibit a considerable degree of uniformity; for example, their calendars possess fundamental resemblances from an early date. This justifies the supposition that they formed some sort of a confederation (G. H. S. Bushnell). At first the leading cities were Copan (Honduras), Uaxactun and Tikal (N. Guatemala), and Palenque (just inside Mexico). The Mayan language is still spoken by half a million people today. It is 'polysynthetic'—that is to say, a whole sentence may be included in a single polysyllabic word. This phenomenon is not precisely found in the Eastern hemisphere. But it is shared with other American tongues, despite their bewildering variety (the number of American linguistic *families* still existing is estimated at forty-five). So the 'Amerinds', or American Indians, must have been in America a long time; and it is in America that they appear to have developed their culture from a very early stage. But they seem to possess a common

racial origin; and 'it is highly improbable on zoo-
logical grounds that man originated on the American
continent' (G. C. Seligman). Some see remote Austra-
lasian cultural influences; but a strong body of
opinion regards the American Indians as 'Mongols'
who originally came from Asia at a wholly uncertain
date (c. 20,000–4000 B.C.)—perhaps a gradual infiltration began soon after the last Ice Age. Now, their
skulls are very varied; in the United States alone
there are eight main groups. The Mayans have
strongly round heads, and high cheek-bones.

6. *W. Bolivia and S.E. Peru.* The Mayas owed
their greatness to triumph over a tropical environment; but a contemporary American people overcame
the no less formidable challenge of a bleak plateau
(over 6000 ft.) and its grudging soil. This was the
people that came before the Incas, the pre-Incas, the
first great name (if we knew their name) among the
civilisations of the Andes. Again, theirs is a civilisation of stones; and the stones are of such vast
dimensions as to suggest comparison with the Egyptian pyramids. But, unlike the pyramids, the great
central city of the pre-Inca culture is 13,000 feet
above sea-level. This is Tiahuanaco, near Lake
Titicaca and Bolivia's frontier with Peru. The mono-
liths that made this city and a rectangular 'Stonehenge' that accompanied it are situated on a great
plain surrounded by unexplored mountains.

They lacked metal; yet their masonry is polygonal,
and even shaped into re-entrant angles. They also
lacked the potter's wheel; but their pottery is perhaps
the most remarkable of any made without it. The
art of these pre-Incas gives us many details of their
dress and physique, but that is all we know about

them. They were apparently very distant relatives, in race and culture, of the Mayas; but their art and architecture suggest that 'central American influence upon Peru lies very far back in time' (Nordenskiöld). Their main crop, too, was different: on the plateau, where maize could not ripen, they developed frost-resisting varieties of the potato.

The culture of Tiahuanaco appears in closely similar form on a great hill outside Cuzco, and in remoter imitations at centres on the Pacific. This measure of uniformity is significant, particularly in view of the almost rainless equatorial desert which separates the two regions; for it strongly suggests 'a great empire throughout the highlands, and even . . . conquest of part of the coast' (T. A. Joyce). Its origins are wholly uncertain. 'A puzzling feature of Peruvian architecture is that many high cultures first appear fully-fledged' (G. H. S. Bushnell). Some of these were far to the north; in these northern high-lands the earliest known culture is that of Chavin.

The ancient inhabitants of Tiahuanaco are sup-posed to have spoken an earlier version of a still surviving language, Colla by name. By now this language has taken about one-third of its vocabulary from another tongue, the Quechua (from which the Spaniards also borrowed words for objects unfamiliar to them). But we do not know when to date this, or indeed any of the other leading events in the history of the pre-Inca civilisation, any more than we know the story of the Mayas. So no further discussion of these peoples will be attempted in the present volume; it is enough to remember their existence and to hope that one day we shall obtain more insight into their political development.

II. ANCIENT AMERICAN CIVILISATIONS

IV. MAINLAND OF W. ASIA (Map III)

7. *S. Iraq.* Mesopotamia, the valleys of the Tigris and Euphrates, forms with Palestine and Syria a plateau of limestone that is sometimes called the 'Fertile Crescent'—though Mesopotamia used to be much more fertile than it is now. In antiquity this great crescent, based at one end on the Persian Gulf and at the other on Sinai, was fertile enough for its lands to be coveted by countless people of the mountains to the east and north of it, and of the desert between its horns; and that is its history.

The Tigris and Euphrates, when they have come down from the northern mountains, first pass through rolling pastureland. That is northern Iraq. Then, north of Baghdad, southern Iraq and the last stretch of the Fertile Crescent begin. Thenceforward there is only flat, alluvial mud. This is the 'Plain of Shinar' of the Bible. It did not exist until about 4000 B.C.; then the rivers deposited it, and the coastline of the Persian Gulf moved south—though still some fifty miles short of where it is now.

This region provided its inhabitants with fish, game, and date-palms. It needs careful irrigation, for the flooding of the rivers is unpredictable; but then, 'by contrast to the arid desert on either side, this jungle must have seemed a paradise' (Childe)—for the average yield on a crop of barley could be eighty-six times the sowing. Now the area is an utterly desolate sandy waste. But in ancient times, as an alluvial plain, it produced an extraordinary series of ancient civilisations. Most important are the Sumerians, the Akkadians, the Babylonians, and the Chaldaeans (neo-Babylonians).

Before 3000 B.C., in the southernmost part of this
alluvial area—between Babylon and the coast as it
then was—there already existed the very highly
developed civilisation of the Sumerians. These people
lived in well-built and elaborately administered cities,
using bronze, and writing on cylinder-seals in the
'cuneiform' (wedge-shaped) script which is, with the
possible exception of the Egyptian hieroglyphics
and Elamite ideographs, the earliest writing that has
been found anywhere.[1] This remarkable people was
almost totally unknown thirty years ago. Its race
and origin are highly problematical, and among the
most significant historical enigmas of our time. The
wheat that they cultivated may well have originated
from S.E. Afghanistan; and their culture was undoubtedly connected with that of the Indus Valley,
where similar wheat was grown. This has encouraged
some to seek linguistic and racial connections also.
But this does not help very much owing to our
extreme uncertainty regarding the language and race
of the Indus Valley people. Possibly they spoke some
variety of Dravidian (p. 46); and the Sumerian language, it is true, shared certain agglutinative features
with the Dravidian; but it also had a tendency to
monosyllables and composition by fixed groups, such
as we find in Chinese. It was rich both in consonants
and vowels.

The skulls discovered fall into two classes, 'Alpine'
(Armenoid) and 'Mediterranean'. This reminds us
that already now, at the dawn of city-life, the
population of S. Iraq was of exceedingly mixed race.

[1] This was a product of trade. 'Writing was not a deliberate
invention, but the incidental by-product of a strong sense of
private property' (Speiser). I borrow this quotation from
Stuart Piggott.

Very early sites have revealed at least three distinct sorts of people (one at least from Asia Minor); and the Sumerians were probably composed of more than one of these. They dressed largely in sheepskins and woven wool, and their women wore 'curiously folded, fringed skirts' (Seton Lloyd).

When we first meet them, these people are governed by kings ruling over independent city-states. The latter were often at war with each other, usually because of disputes about irrigation; raids were also constantly exchanged with Elam (S. Persia), coveted for its minerals. Sumerian sculpture shows the use of a sort of infantry-phalanx. In about 2500 B.C. one of these cities, Lagash, succeeded in forcibly forming a transient union with four others, and part of Elam was temporarily incorporated. Imports were essential for life on the alluvial plain; and imports were secured by political expansion—and also by a remarkably advanced system of letters of credit and bills of exchange. Not long afterwards King Lugalzaggisi of Umma controlled the whole Delta, and actually claimed—whether fantastically or otherwise we cannot be sure—that his power extended as far as the Mediterranean. He may well have conquered N. Iraq; at all events he was ruler of the southern part of the country.

This meant that his title was Lord, not only of Sumer, but also of Akkad.

The Akkadians were the people who came, at an uncertain date, to live just north of the Sumerians, round Babylon. Their race was perhaps 'Mediterranean', and their language certainly Semitic, though they adopted Sumerian writing and culture. They were probably at first subordinate to the Sumerians,

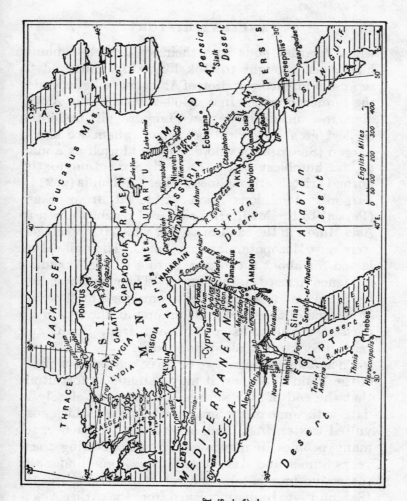

III.

THE NEAR AND
MIDDLE EAST

NOTE:
The N.W. coasts of
the Persian Gulf, as
shown here, are ap-
proximately those
of the third millen-
nium B.C.

whose bearded gods with their woollen cloth plaids have been thought to look like Akkadians and to represent an incorporation of Akkadian religion under the Sumerian rule. In *c.* 2400–2200 B.C. the Akkadians rose successfully against Lugalzaggisi, under the earliest great historical personage whom we know, Sargon (Sharrukin), who describes himself as a man of the humblest birth—an early exception to the normal aristocratic régimes of these millennia (p. 214). Sargon's dominions soon stretched from Elam (Persia) to the Mediterranean, and reached north to Asia Minor, in the eastern area of which (Cappadocia) were now Mesopotamian merchants. His unification lasted for about a century, during which Akkadian influence passed into Sumer. Then his kingdom broke up among warring units, until for a brief period at the end of the third millennium B.C. the city of Ur reasserted Sumerian control over Iraq, Elam, and central Syria; but Elam worsted it.

Then followed some two or three centuries of chaos in the Plain of Shinar; it may perhaps be fortuitous that the end of Ur's supremacy coincides closely in date with some of the great earthquakes which convulsed western Asia and, according to Schaeffer, set many peoples in movement (p. 68). During these years Sumer and Akkad may have come under the successive momentary control of Assyrians (p. 72) (Sargon I—to be distinguished from the earlier Akkadian), northern 'Manda' mountaineers (Nur Dagan, p. 72), and Elamites (p. 80). But then in the nineteenth or eighteenth century B.C., a formidable power arose in Akkad. For Babylon—perhaps throwing off Elamite suzerainty—again became the centre of a great empire, comprising the whole Fertile Crescent.

Its best-known ruler is the codifier of the law, Hammurabi. His patron-god was Akkadian, and his chancery wrote the Semitic language of Akkad in the cuneiform script of Sumer. But the rulers themselves may have been partly 'Nordic'. For they were Amorites, a people described by the Ur Chancery as 'a horde like a storm which of old knew not a city', which had descended southwards on great regions of the Syrian hinterland around the time of the earthquakes of c. 2100–2000 B.C.

These great movements towards the south had another effect too. They brought with them, from the Armenian highlands which were as great a centre of metallurgy as Asia Minor to the west of them, a large number of people who knew how to work bronze. In the Fertile Crescent the use of bronze now spread from the aristocracy downwards. For such reasons, a middle class came into existence, occupied in mercantile activity; and such a class is a characteristic feature of the empires of the second millennium B.C.

In c. 1750–1650 other great catastrophes, again centred on Armenia and Asia Minor, seem to have set the peoples in movement again; and the dynasty of Hammurabi was overthrown by a series of northern invaders. Babylon was occupied by the Kassites (c. 1600 (?)). These were peoples of a low degree of culture, though they introduced the horse into Iraq; their 'Nordic' rulers spoke an Indo-European language, but their followers perhaps some Caucasian tongue. From their time onwards, for more than a thousand years, the role of S. Iraq was usually a subordinate one. It maintained more or less independent kings, of whom one broke the power of the Elamite

Empire in the twelfth century B.C. But it was never in control—though it was often in revolt, chiefly under dynasties of 'Sea-landers', Chaldaeans. These had their brief moment of supremacy when, the Assyrian Empire having fallen, in the sixth century B.C. they established their rule as 'Princes of Sumer and Akkad' at Babylon, which Nebuchadnezzar II transformed into a truly imperial capital. For a short time this 'neo-Babylonian' empire controlled the whole Fertile Crescent; but it fell very soon to Persia.

Throughout this long period of 2500 years, and for longer still, the frequent political convulsions experienced by S. Iraq did not destroy the striking cultural homogeneity and continuity of this racially most heterogeneous area; and its successive rulers clung to the title of 'Prince of Sumer and Akkad'. Later, however, great empires based on Persia established their capital on the Tigris, at Ctesiphon: these were the Arsacid Parthians, in the second century A.D., and the Sassanid Persians, who took it from them in A.D. 224.

8. *N.W. Mesopotamia.* When a much diminished version of Hammurabi's kingdom fell to 'Nordic' (?) invaders, a further group seized upon another long-civilised area of Mesopotamia. When the Euphrates has descended from the Armenian mountains in which it rises, it turns westwards across the present Turkish border. Then it curves south-eastwards; and within the re-entrant formed by these two curves is N.W. Mesopotamia. To the east and south-east it is roughly delimited by the River Khabur which flows into the Euphrates roughly at right angles with it. The upper waters of the Khabur, on the

Turco-Syrian frontier, were an area of very ancient habitation. Its villages were making a fine pottery as early as the fifth millennium B.C., while S. Iraq was still under water.

But then its inhabitants moved south, and the area fell from view until the second millennium, when it appears as the homeland of part of the later Jewish community. Next, the same mass movements from the Armenian highlands which brought the Kassites to Babylon in c. 1600, propelled other formidable peoples in a more westerly direction to the Khabur Valley. These founded a strong kingdom called Mitanni, which might have some striking revelations for us if we could find its capital—we only know its name, Wash'shukkani. The races and languages of this State present an inextricably complicated picture. Hittites (p. 68), with their peculiar tongues, were probably conspicuous in it. It is now suggested that the rulers were 'Nordic' and spoke an Indo-European tongue,[1] but that the subjects spoke a Caucasian language; however, at least for official purposes, they —like Hammurabi the Amorite before them—took over the Semitic language of the Akkadians and the cuneiform script of the Sumerians.

Mitanni expanded eastwards, and seems to have occupied or at least invaded northern Iraq; and for about a century, notably under King Shaushatar (c. 1450–1423, according to Forrer), it may have been the most important State among the 'Concert of Powers' which is characteristic of the Near East at this period. Probably the Mitannians, like the Hittites, owed their success to their training of horses

[1] These rulers also invoked the same gods as the Indo-European immigrants to Persia and India.

and employment of the chariot. It is very likely that Mitanni was the first large State to recognise and utilise the potential value of iron—of which the cheapness was soon to make tools far more readily available, and wars even more terrible than before. As far as we know at present, the first suitable process for the bulk production of iron was invented by a tribe in the Armenian highlands north of Mitanni; and on the absorption of this area into the State, the secret of the ironworking was transferred too. This was a mighty 'secret weapon', comparable in its day to the Atomic Bomb. Its percolation into the Fertile Crescent from the north recalls the similar process by which hosts of bronze-workers had passed the same way (p. 63).

But evidently iron could not be developed quickly or extensively enough to save Mitanni. Its geographical position was too central to be satisfactory. It lay 'in an arena of constant dispute, surrounded by growing powers all hungry for territory' (Drower). The Egyptian Empire threatened from the south and west; the Assyrians of northern Iraq, separated by no natural frontier, could not be kept down for long; and the Hittites in Asia Minor were formidable and covetous. In the fourteenth century B.C.—not necessarily as a result of a great earthquake throughout the Near East in c. 1365—they brought this experimental state to an end.

Thereafter N.W. Mesopotamia played a subordinate political part. It often achieved prominence, but this was always the uncomfortable prominence of a bone of contention between great powers, like Syria to its west and south. In this respect it was particularly conspicuous towards the end of the ancient

period, when the Romans disputed it continually
with the Arsacid Parthians and then the Sassanid
Persians.

9. *Asia Minor*. The ruler in Asia Minor who helped
to squeeze Mitanni out of existence was the Hittite
Shubbiluliuma, a formidable monarch who controlled
an altogether different sort of State. Its capital,
called Hattusas (now Boğazköy) was in the eastern
part (Cappadocia) of the grim plateau which forms
one, or several, of the regions of this geographically
diversified peninsula. The Hittite kingdom, unlike its
predecessors in the Near and Middle East, was not a
riverain kingdom. It is true that Boğazköy is near
to the Halys, but the Halys is not comparable to the
Euphrates; there are no great rivers in Asia Minor.
This was the first great upland empire, based on
fortified cities in a rugged, invigorating climate, far
in the interior. It was separated from Syria and
Mesopotamia by the massive Taurus Mountains. On
three sides, the frontier of Asia Minor is the sea. But
the Hittites took little interest in the sea, and left it
to other peoples, over some of which they exercised
a loose suzerainty. The Hittites were probably dour,
vigorous highlanders, feudally organised, who derived
their strength from horse-breeding and the chariot;
from the utilisation for their army, and jealous
guarding, of the iron-smelting technique taken over
from Mitanni; and from the wealth of Asia Minor,
too, in metals.

Cappadocia had attained a high cultural and economic position early in the third millennium B.C.
The area had served as a trading outpost of successive
powers in Mesopotamia. Moreover, one of the towns
in this region, now Alacahüyük, reveals great royal

tombs which suggest that it was the capital of a powerful State. The population of central Asia Minor at that time ('proto-Hittites') was no doubt already greatly mixed, but perhaps basically 'Mediterranean'. Then, possibly from about the beginning of the second millennium B.C., there arrived in successive waves the various groups whom we know of as the Hittites.

In Asia Minor, the question of immigrations and wanderings of the peoples presents features of a very special character. C. F. A. Schaeffer has argued that these mighty movements were several times brought into being as a result of terrible earthquakes such as frequently fall to the lot of this region. At all events Alacahüyük fell, in *c.* 2100–2000—leaving the area at the mercy of the Hittites, themselves perhaps displaced from some wrecked homeland elsewhere.

Perhaps they came from somewhere round the Black Sea, or beyond it. The Hittites are represented wearing pigtails, putteed sandals, or tall boots. Their races and languages present serious complexities. Indeed this feature, a common one in the ancient world, is peculiarly characteristic of Asia Minor. 'The great civilisations that emerged from time to time . . . were none of them strictly racial, but were compounded of diverse elements fused into something recognisably new' (L. Woolley). No Hittite skulls have yet been found; but their gods are shown with retreating foreheads and chins, and great hooked noses. These are the features of the 'Armenoid' (Anatolian) branch of the 'Alpine' group. It seems right to speak of Hittite languages rather than language; for the ruling house spoke one language, and other Hittites spoke a second, related to it but distinct. These languages are of an exceptional character, since they seem to provide a blend of the two distinct families, the Indo-European and Semitic. It is disputed which of the two should be regarded as predominant in the Hittite tongues, but their debt to the former is now believed by a number of scholars to be largely one of vocabulary. Their religion of 'a thousand gods' is no less peculiar and eclectic.

During the second millennium B.C., if not before, the Hittites of Anatolia became united in one kingdom; and under Murshil I they subdued N. Syria and broke out southwards as far as Babylon. But then came a period of eclipse, due to wars of which we know little. Later, however, their most powerful monarch, Shubbiluliuma (c. 1390–1350 B.C.), after dealing with a barbarian menace from the north, very successfully adopted indirect tactics to absorb Egyptian possessions in Syria and Phoenicia; and soon afterwards we find the Hittite aegis extending almost to the Persian Gulf. As an early Chinese sage observed 'the really expert conquerors are victorious without joining battle' (Tao te Ching); but such peaceful victories were rare in the ancient world until the time of Augustus. Shubbiluliuma then went on to 'protect' Mitanni, whose secret of iron-production was utilised for the Hittite armies. A little later an Egyptian pharaoh, enquiring about the process, was put off with evasive excuses. But even before that, Shubbiluliuma suspiciously refused a marriage alliance with Egypt; and in the thirteenth century, an open clash occurred at Kadesh, in N. Syria, between the two great States, with their numerous satellites. A solemn peace followed, and a Hittite princess was sent to marry the Egyptian monarch.

But the Hittite kingdom of Asia Minor did not survive for long. All its frontiers were threatened. Assyria, to the south-east, was beginning to be a dangerous neighbour. Barbarians still pressed from the north. Moreover, in *c.* 1200 Asia Minor was experiencing the mighty movements of peoples—not all due to further catastrophic earthquakes during the previous century—which Egypt could only just hold. The weakened Hittites could not; their empire was overrun and submerged, and their political power reduced to a smaller, but still powerful succession-State just beyond the south-eastern border of Asia Minor at Carchemish in the Naharain (between Orontes and Euphrates). This lasted until it fell to Assyria in the ninth century B.C.

From the fall of the Hittites, until its absorption in the Persian Empire in the sixth century B.C., the Anatolian plateau could only muster kingdoms of secondary importance. The first of these was the agricultural kingdom of Phrygia, founded at about the end of the second millennium or a little later by rulers speaking an Indo-European tongue. They imposed this language gradually on the mixed peoples in their State, but in return adopted a strange collection of earlier religious institutions. In the seventh century, the Phrygians were overwhelmed by a huge influx of Caucasian(?)-speaking horsemen from the north, the Cimmerians. On the ruins of their kingdom rose the wealthy state of Lydia. Its eastern border was the Halys, and it controlled the Greek cities of the west coast. A bimetallic coinage (i.e. on two standards) was issued in order to encourage trade between East and West. Lydia fell to the Persians in 546 B.C.

But Asia Minor perhaps attained its highest prosperity when, in the centuries immediately before and after the beginning of our era, Hellenisation was pushed inland, first by the Attalids of Pergamum whose kingdom emerged as one of the succession-States of Alexander, and then more especially by the Roman emperors. Then, when the western part of the Roman Empire crumbled away, Asia Minor, less vulnerable from N. Europe, became the centre of a great State again. For the Byzantine Empire, though its capital was across the strait, drew its major support from the great Anatolian treasure-house of men and minerals.

10. *N. Iraq.* One of the peoples that hastened the downfall of the Mitanni and Hittite kingdoms ultimately achieved a power much greater than either, namely, the Assyrians. The home of this nation was the Upper Tigris Valley (known to the ancients as Shubartu). It consisted of undulating rain-watered pasture-land, with temperate climate but bitter winters. The people of this valley reached a high standard of culture very early. Even before 4000 B.C. there were stone houses in walled villages, and the finest pottery that we can attribute anywhere to so early a date.

But then, for more than a millennium, this area sinks from view; its people lived the lives of simple shepherds and were at the mercy of invaders from all sides. For its position is so central, and its valley so attractive to the more powerful neighbours living in mountainous, deserted, or torrid lands all round, that a quite exceptional effort was needed to meet this mighty 'challenge'; and the Assyrians were not yet ready for it. They fell successively to Sumerians,

Akkadians, Babylonians, Elamites, northerners and Mitannians. To the south only a narrow belt of desert separated them from the widely different life of hot, alluvial Sumer and Babylonia. To the west —without a natural frontier—lay Mitanni; and to the east and north lay the mountains which begin as Iraq approaches Persia and Turkey (Armenia) respectively.

It was out of Armenia, particularly, that a constant surge of roving peoples came or ever threatened to come. These roving peoples were the more formidable owing to their aptitude in metalworking (p. 66). It was probably from the north, too, that the first Assyrian attempt at large-scale invasion was crushed. According to a recent reconstruction by E. O. Forrer, King Sargon I of Assyria for a brief moment early in the eighteenth century B.C. succeeded in uniting the whole Fertile Crescent; but his government was wiped out by Nur Dagan, the leader of a great semi-barbarous horde of 'Manda' highlanders (Hyksos of Egypt (?)) who—again for the briefest of periods—prevailed from Egypt to the Indus. During most of the second millennium, the Assyrians were an independent but precarious participant in the 'Balance of Power' politics that characterised the epoch. In the eleventh century they broke out again under Tiglath-Pileser I, but this success too was only momentary.

In the ninth century we again find Assyria threatened from the Armenian mountains. This time the enemy was a ferocious people who conquered a great highland kingdom, rich in metals and metalworkers, on an impregnable fortress on Lake Van (Turushpa). This kingdom was called Urartu (Ararat).

Its rulers may have been products of the great movements of the peoples in *c*. 1200–1000; their 'Vannic' tongue, which they wrote (as well as Semitic languages) in cuneiform, may have been Caucasian. In the ninth and eighth centuries the Urartians, especially under their kings Argistis I and Sarduris III, even pushed as far as Media to the east and the Orontes to the west; and they were long a thorn in the side of the Assyrians.

Constant pressure from outside, and not infrequent incursions and conquests, had left a permanent mark on the race and language of the Assyrians, which show a pronounced mixture. Like other peoples of the time they used the Sumerian script but mostly spoke a version of the old Akkadian (Semitic) language; since this, with many variations, prevailed throughout Iraq, it is known as Babylonian-Assyrian. This is the eastern branch of the Semitic group; but the Assyrians spoke other Semitic tongues as well (at the end of their career we find Aramaic—N.W. Semitic—prevalent). However, their language shows a curious inability to distinguish and pronounce Semitic sounds; and this bears witness to the various races—to some of which the Semitic tongues were alien—that had either merged, or were still living in partial separation, on the Upper Tigris.

Finally the Assyrians profited from the hosts of metal-working peoples who had poured in on them from the north. For they accelerated the decline of the great iron-producing kingdoms, one after another —Mitanni, the Hittites, and finally Urartu as well (eighth century). Then, with such technical aids, they instituted the greatest and most terrible military power that the world had ever known. The main period of their supremacy was *c.* 883–681. In addition to Urartu and other Armenian territories, successive victims were Babylonia to the south, Syria to the west, even Egypt to the south, and vast areas of Persia to the east. The successive conquerors built themselves great new imperial capitals on the Upper Tigris, north of the ancient capital Ashur— Ashurnasirpal II at Nimrud (Khalkhi), Sargon II at Khorsabad (Dur-Sharrukin), and finally Sennacherib at Nineveh.

This unprecedented dominion was acquired and maintained by an army of unprecedented efficiency, showing only too clearly the importance of iron as an aid to slaughter. The nucleus of the Assyrian army was the infantry-bowman; there was also a most dangerous light cavalry arm, and great development of siege-craft. We have clear evidence of ruthless cruelty, mass-deportations on a vast scale, and a totalitarian régime. This régime was the first to replace the feudatory system by a division into provinces; and it ensured rigid centralisation by the construction of roads of great length and high quality.

But the constant mobilisation, garrisoning, and fighting which this ruthless organisation necessitated was in the end too much even for the vast resources of which the kings disposed. In the mid-seventh century, a further insupportable burden was imposed. The whole western half of the empire was overrun by enormous semi-barbarous hordes of Scythians, mounted archers of Indo-European speech who had recently occupied great areas of S. Russia. This weakened Assyria so much that its many bitter enemies among the middle-eastern States were able to strike; and, with Egyptian support, the Medes from N. Persia and Chaldaeans (neo-Babylonians) from S. Iraq converged on Nineveh, which fell in 612 B.C., providing many a moralist with a dramatic theme.

11. *N.W. Persia.* The chief participants in the fall of Nineveh were the Medes. This was the climax of a long process during which Assyria, having disposed of the Urartians round Lake Van, had attempted with less success to deal with various peoples near the other great lake in this highland region south of the Caucasus, Lake Urmia, in the modern Azerbaijan. This great salt lake, in the modern Azerbaijan, is the centre of a fertile drainage area, receiving, among other rivers, the waters of the Jaghati from the south. On either side of the Jaghati was a land of wooded slopes, called Mannai in antiquity. It lies at the northern extremity of the great Zagros range which separates the low country of Mesopotamia from the vast and lofty inland plateau of Persia.

Mannai lay opposite Assyria, as Susa lay opposite Sumer. But in Persia these fertile drainage areas gained political strength only by connection with the plateau beyond, when the association of mountain peoples and waterside civilisation proved irresistible. We know very little indeed of the history of Mannai during the second millennium B.C., but it does not appear that any such union was effected. It was probably one of a number of small States in the area, perhaps under the rule of mixed 'Mediterranean' and 'Alpine' people speaking Caucasian tongues, such as may have been the Elamites farther south (p. 80).

In the ninth century the country was continually attacked by the Assyrians, who could not however establish durable control of the country. The records

of the period show that at about this time the names
of the chieftains of this area gradually change from
Caucasian to Iranian (Indo-European). Early in the
previous millennium 'Nordic' invaders with an Indo-
European tongue had reached the vicinity of Lake
Urmia, and now, no doubt after considerable racial
intermixture, they were spreading (and spreading the
use of iron) into Persia. They gradually reached that
great area of the Persian plateau which lies south-east
of Urmia, and due south of the Elborz range and the
Caspian which lies beyond it. This was Media, and
here the new arrivals built their capital Hangmatana
(Ecbatana, Hamadan). Late in the ninth century,
Median chieftains still had Caucasian names, but in
the seventh century a great power arose under King
Phraortes (Khshathrita) (c. 675–653 B.C.).

At this time Mannai and Armenia were temporarily
overrun by hordes of barbarous Caucasian-speaking
(?), hard-riding robbers from beyond the Caucasus,
the Cimmerians; and the whole area was also experiencing huge incursions of the Indo-European-
speaking mounted archers and nomads from the
Dnieper and Kuban valleys, known as the Scythians.
But Phraortes succeeded in absorbing the fertile area
of Mannai, and welding the whole formidable mixture
into a coalition or empire, into which he (or a prede-
cessor) brought also, as vassals, his kinsmen the
Persians to the south. He directed the whole of this
power against Assyria; but this was still too strong
for him. Moreover, soon afterwards one of his
successors Cyaxares (Uvakhshatra) was obliged to
pay tribute to the Scythians who were breaking into
the Assyrian Empire. But Cyaxares was 'in at the
kill' at the fall of the Assyrian capital Nineveh (612),

and annexed northern Iraq and subsequently the eastern half of Asia Minor; he also extended Median territory in an easterly direction, establishing suzerainty over the country of Parthia which lay on its borders, to the south and south-east of the Caspian.

No Median site has yet been excavated: 'we may venture to hope that the mound at Hamadan will . . . permit the Medes to speak for themselves' (Olmstead). So of this great empire we know very little. We do not even know the character of their Indo-European language. The Medes appear still to have been half-nomads, wearing leather tunics and sheepskin coats, high-laced boots and round felt caps with neck-flaps. They owed their power to three newly developed types of highly mobile troops: spearmen, bowmen trained by Scythian instructors, and cavalry, equipped with the excellent horses which were the chief products both of Mannai and of the plain round Hamadan. With this mixed army they maintained their rule; and Cyaxares, we learn, was called king of 'Manda' (p. 72). But the Medes' supremacy was strongly tempered by the vesting of great religious power in the hands of a non-Median tribe, the Magi, who created a constant check on the power of the alien rulers. But the Middle East was not yet fated to remain under the control of people from this area; for the Persians, to the south, successfully revolted against Media and by 550 B.C. had added most of its empire to their own (see next section).

Much later, when the Persian Empire in turn had been divided up among the successors of its conqueror Alexander, northerners again established at Ecbatana control over a vast area. These were semi-nomads of

Indo-European speech but uncertain race who occupied Parthia (from which they took their name), and
expanded from it to rule for five centuries (second
B.C.-third A.D.) a feudal empire from the Euphrates
to the Indus. They were 'a silent and easy-going race,
fond of hunting . . . the supreme imitators' (W. W.
Tarn)—especially of the Greeks—except for an original military feature, their heavy mailed cavalry
and, later, the horse-archers that crushingly defeated
the Romans in 53 B.C. During the following centuries,
however, the Roman emperors generally succeeded in
preventing them from creating major dangers; though
N.W. Mesopotamia and particularly Armenia were
continual bones of contention. In order to deal better
with the west, they moved their capital from Ecbatana to Ctesiphon in Iraq, near Babylon. But their
administration was feudal, and central control poor;
and—like the Medes—they never succeeded in thoroughly assimilating the south-western area of Persia.

12. *S.W. Persia.* The great Zagros range, and the
mountains beyond it, stop short of the south-western
corner of Persia, and this is of totally different
character from the rest of the country. It is geographically a part of the Fertile Crescent rather than of
Persia; for like the neighbouring land of Sumer, it is
an alluvial plain. The Persian Gulf receives the
waters not only of the Tigris and Euphrates, but also,
to the east of them, the rivers Kerkha (Choaspes) and
Karun (Eulaeus and Pasitigris), coming from the
Iranian plateau. Today these four rivers are all
joined in one great channel, the Shatt-al-Arab, before
reaching the Gulf; but in ancient times (as in Sumer)
the coastline lay much farther to the north, and the
four rivers all flowed into the sea separately.

The region watered by the Kerkha and Karun consisted of a strip of sea-land (Bit Yakin, mostly not existing before Neolithic times) narrowing to a plain enclosed on the other three sides by the foothills of the plateau. In the plain, on the Kerkha, lay Susa. When the floods were controlled, the plain—desolate today—gave a hundred-fold and even two-hundred-fold return for its crops. Game was abundant; the Karun near by was navigable, unlike any other river in Persia; and in ancient times Susa had easy access to the sea. In spite of the great heat, this was one of the nuclei of Persian civilisation. Occupation and culture came early, and in some respects were parallel to those of neighbouring Sumer. A network of canals shows the effort made to harness the rivers to agriculture; and it has been conjectured that the baking furnace and potter's wheel were discovered in this area (copper was also used early).

The first known inhabitants were people from the Elamite Mountains to the north and east—such mountaineers always coveted the plains, and Susa and Elam were so continually in the same hands that the whole country was later known as 'Susiana'. However, though Susa was from the first a commercial centre, the first known capitals were in the hills, at Awan and Anshan. We do not know where they were; yet to the very end of Persian history its monarchs were 'Kings of Anshan'. Possibly Anshan lay near the Kerkha, north-west of Susa. By its discovery and excavation, archaeology could probably revolutionise our knowledge of middle-eastern history. Even at a remote oasis far to the north-east (Sialk), there was as many as seventeen successive settlements even before 3000 B.C.

The special character of the area lies in this duality between upland Elam (a land of minerals) and riverain Susa; and therein lay its strength (p. 75). The race of the early Elamites is wholly obscure, but was certainly mixed at a very remote date. 'Mediterraneans' existed among them—and comparison with the Sumerians has been suggested—but it is also believed that there was, especially in the uplands, a strong 'Alpine' element. Their social customs show that inheritance passed in the female line (matrilinear). It has been supposed, though this too is uncertain, that the early language was the southernmost example of the Caucasian group, and that this, standing half-way between Indo-European and agglutinative tongues, was perhaps the basic language of the whole Near and Middle East. But others have noted parallels with Dravidian languages (especially Tamil). The people of Elam used a linear, ideographic writing very early indeed—perhaps as early as Sumerian cuneiform and Egyptian hieroglyphic. But soon after the middle of the third millennium B.C. they adopted the Sumerian script.

Race and culture alike were successively modified by Sumerian and Akkadian influence. We hear of raids into Sumer and Akkad of Elamites and also barbarians from the north of Persia; but Elam was part of the empire of the Akkadian Sargon, and then of Ur. Elam took its revenge on Ur at the end of the millennium; and it seems to have attained great prominence in about the eighteenth century, when Genesis, Chapter xiv, tells of a great military coalition under an Elamite king Chedorlaomer (Kudurlagamar). He includes among his subordinates a king of Shinar (S. Iraq), 'Amraphel', who might be

Hammurabi. E. O. Forrer believes that at this time Elam was in league with the horde of 'Manda' northerners under Nur Dagan (=Hyksos (?)) who may have occupied vast areas (p. 72). Much of the history of the period is still lost.

It now seems that in the twelfth century B.C. early Elam reached its political climax, under King Shilhak-Inshushinak (G. G. Cameron). The brother of this monarch had driven the Kassites out of Babylon; and we learn from the inscriptions of Shilhak that he conquered 250 cities, encroached on Assyria—possibly taking Ashur itself—and extended his rule far to the north and south-east of Persia. He called himself 'King of Anshan and Susa'. Sculptural reliefs show his soldiers with long, square beards, sleeveless jackets, short skirts, and upturned boots. Immediately after his death, his empire fell to a Babylonian counter-stroke, and Elam returned to the position of a minor provincial State.

The Nordic peoples who invaded Persia from the north early in the second millennium included not only the Medes but also another group of mountaineers, the Persians, who at first seem to have settled to the west of Lake Urmia, in the north-western corner of the country. From then onwards, after 1000 B.C., no doubt after great racial intermixture, they moved or filtered south to occupy, not at first the Elamite part of the plateau around Susa, but the region east and south-east of it (Persis, or Persia proper), another plateau split by fertile valleys. From their new capital in this area, Pasargadae, they assumed power over a mixed 'Mediterranean' and 'Alpine' population. Their great dynasty, the Achaemenids, is first heard of in the seventh century B.C.

It was perhaps at about this time also that they established control over Elam and Susa, to which they moved their capital.

For some time, however, they were vassals of Media, and hard pressed by Scythians and Assyrians. But not long after the fall of Nineveh their king Cyrus I (558–528 B.C.), during an unprecedented career of conquest, revolted against the Medes, seized Ecbatana (550), and took over the whole kingdom (though trouble was long experienced from the priestly Magi). He then obliterated the Lydian kingdom in Asia Minor, and took over from its control the Greek cities on the west coast. Next he turned East and extended his control to the whole of modern Persia and Afghanistan, penetrating as far as Samarcand in Russian Turkestan (Maracanda). Finally, by the conquest of Babylon (539–8), he took over, without difficulty, the whole of the Fertile Crescent—the Chaldaean (neo-Babylonian) Empire.

His successors Cambyses and Darius I added to this unprecedented dominion Egypt and, for a time, the Scythian regions of the Russian steppes, and part of the Punjab. Darius, who brought a different branch of the Achaemenid family into power, established a great new residence in Persis, at Persepolis. His inscriptions there show in some measure the linguistic and racial complexity even of this one corner of the empire, since some of them are trilingual, in Persian, Akkadian, and Elamite; the last named is the language of the archives. The script, as ever, is the Sumerian cuneiform. But the chief language of the empire was now Aramaic, written in a modified form of the Phoenician alphabet. All these countries were only held together by an unprecedented system of roads; the Assyrian innovations in road-construction were utilised and greatly improved. To the west, however, the Greeks proved a barrier to further expansion. Darius put down a revolt of the Ionian city-states (showing a clemency which was a strange innovation in the political life of the ancient world); but he and his successor Xerxes failed to make progress on the Greek mainland and in the Aegean.

Cyrus and Darius were outstanding aggressors, but they were also outstanding men who ruled this vast area with singular enlightenment; and it remained united for two centuries until the entire territory fell, in a series of phenomenal campaigns (334–327), to the Macedonian army of Alexander the Great, trained to a hitherto unknown pitch of efficiency by the latter's father Philip. In the following century, however, much of the empire began to be won back by Parthian northerners; and after a long further period the wheel came full circle, and the Parthians gave way to a further dynasty of Persians, the Sassanians (A.D. 224–636), whose most conspicuous ruler Artaxerxes I (Ardashir) again established his dominion from Armenia and Iraq to the Oxus. He maintained friendly relations with Rome, which suffered severely, however, from his successors.

V. THE MEDITERRANEAN AREA

13. *Egypt.* The Mediterranean region in general possesses a climate favourable to people and to crops; and the Nile Valley in particular is astonishingly fertile and agreeable. Thus, except for the absence of solid architecture—not needed in this climate— Neolithic civilisation in the fourth millennium B.C.

was as advanced in Egypt as it was on the Tigris, Euphrates, Khabur, and Karun. Probably, however, it differed from these areas in the source of its wheat cultivation, deriving this ultimately not from S.E. Afghanistan but from Abyssinia.

At the earliest period of our acquaintance with the Egyptians, we already find a complex racial mixture. The 'Mediterranean' man of early Egypt is perhaps the oldest, and maybe the 'purest', of that group that we can trace. Yet the varieties inhabiting Lower and Upper Egypt (N. and S. Egypt respectively) already seem to differ. The northerners, who have smaller heads and more delicate features, probably came from the east; the southerners probably came from farther south. Nor is this all; for a round-faced, 'Alpine' (?) type gradually spread south and mixed with them. And so no doubt did other strains as well. So the race of the ancient Egyptians was far from homogeneous. The same may be true of their language, which they wrote down very early—perhaps as early as the Sumerians and Elamites—in the pictorial script known as 'hieroglyphic'. This language is described as 'Hamitic'; but it contains structural features—due no doubt to the primitive inhabitants of Lower Egypt—which enable philologists to claim Semitic influences or origins.

However, these mixtures coalesced, and Egyptian culture rapidly took on a marked degree of unity; the ancient Egyptian came into being, with his shaven head, wig, waistcloth, and white robe. This unity was made possible by political unity, which in turn was created by a geographical factor. That factor was the Nile. Egypt's dependence on the Nile is overwhelming. That is to say, its careful regulation is essential; and it was clear that this had to be directed centrally. So 'it seems probable that Egypt was the first large stretch of territory in the ancient world to be unified under one ruler' (M. S. Drower). According to recent calculations, this unification must have been accomplished as early as 3188 B.C. Previously Lower and Upper Egypt had constituted separate kingdoms, ruled respectively from Buto (in the mouth of the Delta) and Hieraconpolis (not far north of the First Cataract). The dynasty of the unifier, who is traditionally known as Menes, soon moved from Hieraconpolis to a more northerly centre of Upper Egypt, Thinis; and the whole of Egypt was governed from there. Later, the union was interrupted for considerable periods (p. 87); but it was never finally lost. 'Egypt has a unique quality . . . exhibited equally by the land itself and by the people who inhabited it, namely, a capacity for conservation exceeding that of any other country in the world' (S. R. K. Glanville).

The Egyptian system owed its longevity not only to the natural productiveness of their soil, and to its assistance in helping them to avoid natural catastrophe, but also to the geographical situation of their country. For the Nile Valley is cut off from invasion, on east and west, by the desert. This position, while ensuring Egypt a more peaceful life than the riverain cultures based on the Persian Gulf, also prevented it from expanding overland into imperial states and unions. Nevertheless, the external communications of Egypt were in another respect far easier than theirs. For the sea-board of Egypt was on the Mediterranean; and the Mediterranean provides its coasts with unique facilities for intercourse —including conquest. Yet the Mediterranean is not one sea or lake, but—despite inter-communication—several. In particular, however, the seas of the western Mediterranean are only connected by a narrow channel with those of the eastern Mediterranean. In the latter, 'the advantages common to the whole basin . . . assume an outstanding importance' (G. Glotz). So, three or four centuries after the unification, the capital was moved north to a city at the apex of the Delta itself, Memphis. By then an Egyptian navy was already sailing the eastern Mediterranean; and at least by 2700 B.C. it was fetching from the Lebanon the timber necessary for its own enlargement. Another shortage was of copper. Though this was available in Sinai, until after 2000 B.C. no extensive use was made of bronze, which thus fails, as in America, to provide an adequate yardstick of culture (iron was not in general use until after 800 B.C.).

A Sinai mine-worker, at Serabit el-Khâdem, is now believed by many to provide our earliest known example (twentieth to eighteenth century B.C.) of a discovery pregnant with political and social significance, phonetic and to a large extent alphabetic writing. 'Too ignorant to learn the complicated hieroglyphic of the Egyptians, but knowing that they employed a consonantal alphabet to supplement the syllabic and ideographic signs, he wondered why no one had realised the beautiful simplicity of a purely alphabet writing. To a few common Egyptian signs he gave a name in his native Canaanite and took the first consonantal sound as its phonetic value. He scratched a few short sentences in his Canaanite dialect on the rocks of Sinai, and the consonantal alphabet was in use' (A. T. Olmstead).

Egypt's resources, harbours, and navies had already enabled her to create the first Mediterranean empire. Archaeology has now suggested Egyptian colonisation on the Lebanon coast at the beginning of the second millennium. The capital, which (after a period in Middle Egypt) had been moved back to a religious centre of Upper Egypt, Thebes, was again moved north, now to the south-western extension of the Delta's fertility, the Fayum. But in *c.* 1800–1750 the empire was broken, and Egypt passed through a period of chaos and foreign occupation. (According to Schaeffer, this was the climax of great movements of the peoples caused by earthquakes in Asia Minor and Armenia.) The invaders of Egypt were the Hyksos or 'shepherds'. These were of mixed race (identified by E. O. Forrer with the 'Manda' mountaineers of Nur Dagan). Their language seems to have been Semitic, but may have been acquired on the long southward wanderings. Coming from the lands of metals and metal-working, they may have owed their success to the large-scale production of bronze—and also to an instrument of war new to the Egyptians, the war-chariot and its horses.

The Hyksos established their capital near the north-eastern extremity of the Delta. But they had difficulty in holding the south, and in about the sixteenth century were driven out altogether. Now the Egyptian Empire was truly established, with its capital again at Thebes. The frontier was pushed to the farthest borders of the Naharain, the northernmost extremity of Syria; and control was exercised by an impressive system of travelling and resident inspectors. In the following century Thothmes III received tribute from Babylonia and Assyria. The zenith was reached in *c.* 1400, or a little afterwards, by Amenhetep III; but his son Akhenaton, a man of extraordinary spiritual qualities far ahead of his time, was content to neglect his imperial mission, and retired to a newly constructed capital free from religious tradition (Tell-el-Amarna).

In *c.* 1320 a new dynasty, of northern sympathies, moved the capital back to Memphis, and then for a time to Pelusium, on the isthmus of Sinai itself; and it was relations with a northern power, the Hittites, which engaged its attention. The battle of Kadesh, early in the next century, left matters undecided with them. But now was coming the last of those gigantic movements affecting the Hittite dominions. These migrations brought the Hittites down, and were only very narrowly repelled from the very borders of Egypt. Despite the successful defence, Egypt had no strength left, and her days as a great independent power were over.

Only a brief, archaistic revival was apparent when Assyria weakened in the seventh century, and the Egyptian government established its capital (Sais) and a Greek 'Treaty-Port' (Naucratis) in the Delta. But soon Egypt fell to Persia; and when Persia had succumbed to Alexander (334–327), and the latter's empire was split among his Macedonian successors one of them, Ptolemy, ruled from Alexandria. In the last century B.C. the Ptolemaic kingdom became, first the client, and then the richest possession, of Rome.

14. *Crete.* Once maritime unions had been established in the eastern Mediterranean in the second millennium B.C., it was clear that Crete was a potential centre for such an empire or confederation. As

the events of the Second World War showed, its position is central and strategic. Its shape gives it long coasts facing north and south respectively. To the north it faces the Aegean (E. Mediterranean) lands and islands—'it seems made by nature to rule over Greece' (Aristotle). Its south coast is not too far, but far enough, from Egypt. 'It is thus the land nearest to all three continents' (Glotz). It has harbours; its mountains are wooded and divided by fertile valleys; it has the best climate in the Greek world.

We know of no Early Stone Age in Crete. But during the fourth and third millennia B.C., immigrants seem to have arrived from the nearest parts of Asia Miror. Conceivably their culture was influenced by the Sumerians; but this is highly problematical. As in Egypt, bronze was not used extensively until late in the third millennium, at the earliest. Towns were first built in the eastern part of the island. But in c. 2000 the balance shifted to its central area, and it was there that the astonishing cities of the 'Minoan' civilisation took root and grew, together with a delicate and elaborate art wholly unlike those of earlier civilisations and in many ways more sympathetic to modern European tastes.

The greatest of these cities was the royal capital, Cnossus, of which the population may have numbered 100,000.

This suffered damage, from causes unknown, in c. 1700 and c. 1600. But its greatest age is c. 1600–1400, and it is now that persistent Greek traditions of a Cretan naval empire 'of Minos' are confirmed by archaeology. For not only was there uniformity of culture among the cities of Crete itself, but Cretan

products are found all over the Aegean and perhaps
farther afield still; there is also talk of this people in
Egyptian records. Then, soon after *c.* 1400, the
Cretan power was blotted out of existence; the
palaces and cities were largely destroyed, and un-
ambitious small towns and villages, perhaps partly
occupied by new immigrants, took their place. Early
in the last millennium B.C., Crete became Hellenised
by Greek immigrants, and was one of the first areas
to profit by the Oriental influence which inspired the
Greeks (and may have inspired the revival of city-
life: see p. 110). But Crete rarely now exerted any
influence on the politics or trade of the ancient
world (p. 116).

We do not know how or why the Cretan cities were
destroyed. The cause may have been invasion.
There is a great deal that we do not know about the
Cretans. 'What was the science which enabled the
master mariners of Knossos, *without the aid of a
compass*, to navigate their ships to the shores of
Britain and of Norway, and whence came that
science?' (J. W. S. Sewell). Some feel that the desti-
nations reached were not quite so remote, if allow-
ance is made for middle-men and for the later
achievements of the Mycenaeans; but the problem
remains, since there is no doubt that the Minoans
did go very far afield indeed.

We have Cretan writings (of more than one sort),
but we cannot read them. However, their appearance renders it rather unlikely that the Cretan
language (if the term is legitimate) was either Indo-
European or Semitic. As regards race, we have the
assistance afforded by Cretan skulls. These are predominantly long-headed and suggest that the bulk

of the Cretans were 'Mediterraneans'. But some are round-headed and indicate that, from an early date and to an increasing extent after the fall of Cnossus, some of the immigrants were 'Alpines'. The different groups then intermarried, and no doubt intermarried again with the later 'Nordic' arrivals, as in other Greek lands. The 'Minoans' are represented in sculpture and painting as small dark men, often with long hair to their waists in fantastic knots or curls, wearing putteed sandals or high boots, and waistcloths with a short kilt.

Certain archaeologists now feel that this date c. 1400 B.C., when the Cretan civilisation fell, is in many regions of the world a decisive point. Though 'Bronze Ages' are in many parts still in effect (for the use of iron has not yet become frequent beyond Mitanni and the Hittites), now—after a pause—civilisation will soon begin to expand so much that, in contrast to what follows, several preceding millennia (Neolithic, Copper, Early Bronze Ages) can be grouped together as one (Kendrick calls them the 'Eochalcic Episode'). This epoch may be regarded as ending, and a New World beginning, with the collapse of the Minoan sea-empire.

15. *The Levant; and colonies in Tunisia.* Among the chief beneficiaries from the downfall of Minoan sea-power were the Phoenicians, living on the narrow coastal plain of Lebanon, unsuited for corn-growing. This great maritime people spoke a Semitic language not far removed from Hebrew; the north-western group of these languages is sometimes divided into two branches, of which one comprises Phoenician and Hebrew. The other comprises Aramaic, and this too is found at an early date—later it prevailed. Egyptian

monuments show them with 'Alpine' (Armenoid) noses—recalling Anatolian domination of this area; and—after the fall of Boğazköy—the proximity of Hittite communities such as the succession-state of Carchemish in the Naharain (between Orontes and Euphrates). But the Phoenicians clearly represent a strange racial mixture, including elements of Amorite (Nordic (?)) and Canaanite. They called themselves 'Canaanites'. This was also the name applied by the Jews to the peoples who reached Palestine before them. The race of the Canaanite peoples is uncertain; it was no doubt extremely mixed. By the middle of the second millennium they had achieved a luxurious civilisation, which was, however, blotted out by the strife between Egypt and the Hittites and by the Jewish invasions.

The Phoenicians were also no doubt (like the Jews) descended, in part, from early colonists from Mesopotamia. One of the peoples who had provided these were the Semitic-speaking Akkadians. For the Greek historian Herodotus regards the Phoenicians as immigrants from the Persian Gulf, in the third millennium when Sargon of Akkad was active far outside that area.

The ports of the North Syrian and Lebanese coast were busy from that time onwards. Byblus achieved early significance, and later Arvad (Aradus) and Ugarit (Ras Shamra) became important. These cities provide rich archaeological material since their wares and cultures are no less mixed than their populations. For long they achieved no political unions and were often more or less subject to Egypt or the Hittites. Were they too racked by the successive earthquakes believed to have devastated Asia Minor and Armenia

during the second millennium? At all events the
most important achievement of the Phoenicians during this period was the adaptation of the Sumerian
'cuneiform' script to represent not syllables but
letters of the alphabet (Ugarit, *c.* fourteenth century);
later we find at Byblus the number of letters reduced
from 30 to 22, constituting the true Phoenician alphabet. There seems much to be said for the view that
this was ultimately based on Egyptian hieroglyphic,
though 'the Egyptians never discerned the great
advantages of an alphabet unmixed with other
graphic elements' (A. H. Gardiner). This simplifica-
tion caused a vast increase of literacy. More than
one system was initiated, but the principle was the
same, and a great step towards co-operation had been
taken. It was from this source that the Greeks
derived their alphabet.

The maritime activity of the Phoenicians was
stimulated by the fall of Crete (and perhaps by the
arrival of Cretan refugees); and before long the
Phoenicians entered into, and greatly extended, the
Minoan heritage, and planted important 'colonies'.
They did not, however, achieve unity at home, but
remained divided into powerful city-states. These,
unlike the Hittites and others, did not succumb
finally to the great movements of the peoples. First
Sidon (*c.* 1250–1000) and then Tyre (*c.* 1000–550), on
its island, took the lead. During the former of these
periods colonies were founded at Utica (in Tunisia)
and Cadiz; during the latter period (*c.* 814 (?)) was
established Utica's neighbour which was before long
to overshadow it, Carthage.

In the tenth century, King Hiram of Tyre looked
for backing in Phoenicia's own neighbours of the

Levant, with whom she was accustomed to have a local trade. Syria must defeat any attempt to generalise. It repeats on a vast and complex scale the racial mixtures that have been noted in the Phoenicians. Unlike every other part of the Fertile Crescent, and despite a certain uniformity of its languages (which were mainly Semitic of its two north-western branches—Phoenician-Hebrew and Aramaic), it hardly ever achieved any degree of political unity, except as the appendage of great States elsewhere. Typical of its history is the coalition of small Syrian States which in the fifteenth century had faced Thothmes III at Megiddo; for it was routed and dispersed. Only for a brief period thereafter did one man unite the territories on either side of the Jordan, join with them the great Aramaic-speaking city of Damascus, and ally his union with the Phoenician sea-power of Tyre—as well with Egypt, whose pharaoh's daughter he married. This unifier was David's son Solomon, King of the Jews (*c.* 975–935 B.C.), who thus momentarily plays a part in world politics.

Some of the ancestors of this race—as mixed as any other of the Levant—had been 'Mediterranean' Aramaeans, semi-nomadic peoples who throughout the second millennium had filtered into Syria from the Arabian desert. The branch described in the Old Testament had lived on the outskirts of Ur in Sumer until *c.* 2000–1800, when the decline of that power had caused them to seek a new home in N.W. Mesopotamia; but the influence of Hammurabi is seen in the legal code of Deuteronomy. Not long afterwards some of these tribesmen moved south, perhaps as part of the great ethnic movements which brought the partly Semitic-speaking Hyksos (perhaps Nur-Dagan's 'Manda') into Egypt. Of their gradual passage through the Levant there is anthropological evidence in the nose regarded as characteristic of the Jews today, for this they acquired through contact with the Hittite ('Alpine'-Armenoid) 'colonies' of N. Syria.

The Book of Exodus also bears witness, with some basis in fact, to Egyptian elements in the Jews; and other parts of the Old Testament show signs of Egyptian divine kingship. Possibly some of the southward migrants had entered Egypt. At any rate, later on, disturbed conditions in Egypt expelled large hordes of people through Sinai to the Levant—either in c. 1570–1500, or in c. 1400–1300, or (less probably) after c. 1200. In the course of their long wanderings mixture may have occurred with the 'Nordic' (?) Amorites. Intermarriage must also have taken place with the already racially mixed Canaanite population (p. 34). The Canaanites had suffered a cultural decline, and in the latter part of the second millennium B.C. archaeology shows Canaanite and Jewish culture as one. 'Their cultures were indistinguishable as, probably, in reality the peoples were also' (H. P. Hall).

The Jews were an inland people like the Hittites rather than a seafaring people like the Cretans or Phoenicians; and alliance with the Phoenicians was a master-stroke of policy for them, as well as being welcome to Tyre owing to the requisitioning on their behalf of Jewish forced labour on a great scale. But after Solomon's death the alliance lapsed, and his dominions split up; and in the next century we again find a coalition of Jewish and other Levantine princes being defeated by a great power (by Assyria at Karkar).

This time, and from this time onwards, the Phoenician cities, too, were hard put to it to maintain their independence. Finally, in the sixth century, they entered a most profitable vassalage of the Persian Empire, for which, when it fell, they fought vigorously against Alexander the Great.

But long before this, the centre of Phoenician influence had been transferred to Tyre's great ninth-century 'colony' in Tunisia, Carthage, which gradually asserted its independence. Carthage owed its success to a balanced constitution and to its excellent seamen. Many of these were products of intermarriage between the settlers and local 'Mediterranean' populations, the latter being akin to the earliest Egyptians and perhaps originally speaking a 'Hamitic' tongue. Carthage established a fair-sized land empire; but her main effort was at sea, where in alliance with the Etruscans she checked Greek colonisation off Alalia in Corsica (*c.* 535 B.C.). Carthage revived Tyrian claims in Spain, and dominated Sardinia and W. Sicily; but the western Greeks successfully defended E. Sicily at Himera (480 B.C.). It was not until over two centuries later that the same island brought Carthage into contact with Rome. Against Rome, despite invasion of Italy by Hannibal (218–206 B.C.), Carthage lost three wars which resulted in the destruction of the city itself (146 B.C.). On the centenary of its destruction, its refoundation as a Roman colony was announced by Caesar.

16. *Greece and the coast of Asia Minor.* The sea-power of Crete, on its mysterious eclipse in *c.* 1400 B.C., found an inheritor on the Lebanese coast. But

an area no less likely to share in the inheritance was
the north-east corner of the Mediterranean, the
Aegean Sea—with its many islands, the Greek
peninsula to its west, and the coast of Asia Minor
to its east. For this area, though accessible to the
Anatolian plateau, is markedly different from it,
and belongs geographically and climatically to the
Aegean area. The coastline of these elaborately
carved shores is enormous, and endowed with a
sufficiency of harbours. Every important point on
these gulfs and promontories lies on a marine or
'amphibious' highway. Inland communications, however, were too difficult to invite neighbourliness or
unification; the sea was an inevitable medium. And,
though the climate was usually temperate, the soil
was not so extensively fertile as to keep people
satisfied within their small plains and valleys.

Here, in a dramatic form, were the same conditions
as prevailed in Phoenicia; and on a dramatic scale
they produced similar results. Racially, too, the
people who produced them were as mixed as the
Phoenicians. They were also mixed with the same
basic ingredients; to speak of the ancient Greeks as
'Europeans', with 'Asiatics' starting to the east of
them, is misleading. The Greeks were 'basically
"Mediterranean", with a strong admixture of "Alpine", and no doubt some "Nordic"' (C. G. Seligman).
Joining the Neolithic 'Mediterranean' population,
short-headed 'Alpine' peoples early reached other
islands as well as Crete; while from c. 2000–1000 there
were gradual or repeated infiltrations of 'Nordic'
peoples, speaking Indo-European tongues, who had
intermingled with 'Alpine' and other strains in the
course of their long journeys.

One such infiltration, known as the 'Achaean invasion', is detectable at the beginning of this millennium, perhaps as part of the same great ethnic
movement as blotted out the first Hittite kingdoms.
Mycenae, in the north-east of the Peloponnese, became one of its headquarters. Another important
centre was Orchomenus in Boeotia (north-west of
Athens). But there were many cities scarcely inferior; another was at Troy, across the Aegean, near
the strategic narrows at the north-west extremity of
Asia Minor, the Dardanelles. Troy's classic struggle
with peoples of the Greek peninsula, told in the *Iliad*,
was perhaps an important incident in the wanderings
of the peoples; but it was not a struggle between
Europe and Asia in any facile modern sense.

The archaeologists tell us that one of the many
successive settlements at Troy was destroyed in
c. 1200; and this coincides with Mycenae's greatest
magnificence. The Mycenaeans imitated Cretan culture to some extent, but their dress and appearance
were quite different. The men were bearded and
wore short trousers, and instead of leaving the upper
part of their bodies bare they show short-sleeve tunics
with belts and stiff, 'flared' skirts reaching half-way
down the thighs. In general, the Mycenaeans were
less sophisticated than the Cretans; for example,
the latter would not have allowed food-remnants
to pile up on their floors. Mycenaean splendour
was a splendour of size and semi-barbarous gold, of
a great and well-armed king like the slightly later
'Chou' in N. China. The cities were on hills, and, like
those of the contemporary mainland empire of the
Hittites, were endowed with mighty fortifications.
Mycenae, too, 'predominates by virtue of the proper

organisation of force' (S. Casson). We find roads
radiating from Mycenae to lesser centres of a uniform culture at many points on the mainland, and
it is legitimate to accept Homer's general picture
of a more or less loose feudal supremacy.

But the Mycenaeans did not just rule a mainland
State like the Hittites. They reflect the geographical
difference between Greece and Anatolia, which (despite the lengthy coastline of both) makes the former
but not the latter a maritime country. Mycenae was
not on the sea but near it—near both eastern and
western seas—and the sea-power displaced to Crete
passed there even before Phoenicia had its share;
though the two sea-powers had many contacts.
Mycenaean goods are found in Rhodes, Cyprus, and
the coasts of Syria and also of Asia Minor, which
thereby again assert their Mediterranean character.
But, perhaps because of Phoenician superiority in
the E. Mediterranean, the Mycenaeans were before
them in reaching the west. It has been suggested
the Cretan ships did so earlier still, but the Mycenaean links with S. Italy, Sicily, and Spain are close
and important; and a link also exists with England,
but it may have been provided by Spain.

The great movements of the peoples, at the end
of the second millennium, which were staved off with
difficulty by Egypt and obliterated the Hittites and
Troy, took Mycenae and its dependencies as further
victims. In c. 1200–1150 Mycenae was destroyed by
fire, presumably by a new wave of more barbarous
invaders of much the same racial mixtures and Indo-
European tongues as their own. This was the
'Dorian invasion', which completed the elements that
created the Greeks of classical times, and brought

with it the loose cloak (*himation*) that is the characteristic feature of Greek dress. Further waves of invaders or refugees, or probably both, moved—perhaps in part from near Athens, which later claimed to be their homeland—to the area later known as Ionia, the central part of the west coast of Asia Minor.

All these invaders brought iron with them, or it followed in their wake; but the splendours of the Bronze Age courts were obliterated. Now, if not earlier, the Indo-European speech prevailed, and from it emerged three main dialects of Greek—Attic-Ionic, Achaean (including Aeolic) and West Greek (including Doric). But when they came to be written, they were written in adapted forms of one of the alphabets which the Phoenicians had used for their own Semitic tongue. Herodotus expressly states that the Ionians took their alphabet from the Phoenicians.

Indeed, after the fall of Mycenae, the only unifying agency that remained in the eastern Mediterranean was that provided by the Phoenician navies. It was, perhaps, partly due to them that the Greek mainland (like Crete) did not suffer a total breach of cultural continuity. However, life was now poor and austere; the village had again become the normal political unit; and there was a pause before the new Iron Age of Greece revived civilisation in new forms. Meanwhile, the final constituents of that classical culture were now assembled.

17. *Italy.* By the time that the constituents of the later Greek civilisation were assembled in Hellas, the second great peninsula of the inner Mediterranean, Italy, had also received the ingredients of its classical culture. In some respects Italy was even more likely

than Greece to attract and civilise invaders and immigrants. For it possesses plains that are much larger, and so encourage attempts at a wider degree of unity.

One of these plains, the Po Valley to the north, was—despite the Alps—not easily defensible. But, just south of a further barrier, the Apennine chain, lie two further plains; and they face towards the west coast, which is less vulnerable to invasion than the shores of the narrow Adriatic. The southern one of these two plains, Campania—behind the modern Naples—is a volcanic territory producing three, or sometimes four, corn crops annually, and rich also in the vine and olive. The northern plain is bisected by the navigable River Tiber into a northern half, Etruria, and a southern half, Latium. It is just fertile enough to provide the challenge from which, as Toynbee has shown, many of the greatest civilisations arise. 'By dint of careful draining and persistent labour it can be made to grow good harvests, and even when partly submerged supplies good pasture in winter' (Rostovtzeff).

In the greater part of the second millennium B.C. Latium was apparently uninhabited; but other parts of N. and S. Italy were occupied by Neolithic 'Mediterranean' (?) peoples who are apparently those known later as the Ligurians and Sicels respectively. The Ligurians (who later gave their name to the region round Genoa) are believed to have reached Italy from Spain—via France—and to have come originally from N. Africa owing to the drying up of the Sahara. Of their language only a few place-names have survived; but these confirm that it was not Indo-European. The Sicels, who occupied large parts

of southern Italy, likewise came from N. Africa, presumably by way of Sicily, in the eastern part of
which they remained in historic times. Their language, again, was not Indo-European; it has been
suggested that it may have been Hamitic. These
Neolithic peoples buried, and did not cremate, their
dead.

Between 2000 and *c.* 1500 B.C. copper- and bronze-
using immigrants from across the Alps, known to
scholars as the 'Terramaricoli', joined these and
other earlier populations and dwelt in villages in the
Po Valley and (as we have now learnt) in various
other parts of Italy too, though still not in Latium.
The race of these 'Terramaricoli' is obscure; but it
appears likely that they spoke an Indo-European
language. Unlike their Neolithic predecessors, they
were accustomed to cremate their dead. The waves
of immigration may have continued throughout the
millennium. Then, in about the twelfth or eleventh
century B.C.—at the time of the great movements of
the peoples in the Near East also—a fresh wave of
immigrants or invaders entered Italy, again from the
north. These are known as the 'Villanovans'. They
again cremated their dead, and their language was
again Indo-European, but unlike their predecessors
they were familiar with the use of iron. Their race
was probably mixed, more 'Alpine' than 'Nordic'.

Their principal area of settlement, as far as is
known to us at present, lay to the south of the Po
estuary, between Bologna and Ravenna. But outlying groups of these peoples, the 'Southern Villanovans', pushed south-westwards and occupied
Etruria and Latium. They may not have been the
first people to reach Latium, for there are signs of

inland occupation from *c.* 1150 B.C., and tradition reports that the earliest occupants were Sicels; a Ligurian element has also been tentatively traced. The 'Southern Villanovans' no doubt mixed with these, and the descendants of this blend (after several further racial admixtures) were the Latins—one of the ingredients of the ancient Roman. In this conglomeration of peoples and cultures the language which prevailed was that of the most advanced community, the 'Southern Villanovans'; and the result, eventually, was Latin. This is the only member of its group of Indo-European tongues (the 'Italic' group) of which we have knowledge; it is akin to Greek but seems of somewhat later origin.

A further subdivision of this linguistic group is often described as the 'P Group', as opposed to the Latin 'Q Group'. The 'P Group' was represented by a second great wave of invaders during the same epoch. These were a number of tribes known collectively as the Umbro-Sabellians. They occupied a large area of central Italy. Unlike the 'Villanovans' and Latins, they buried and did not cremate their dead; and their 'P Group' of Indo-European tongues apparently contained strong alien elements. These are quite likely to have come, in part, from yet another principal element in the populations of pre-Roman Italy—the Illyrians. These were also immigrants of the Early Iron Age, and buriers, not cremators; but, whatever their race—and this has been much disputed ('Alpine' (?))—their language was evidently not Indo-European. They came across the Adriatic. A northern group, the Veneti, occupied the fertile coastland north of the Po; a southern group, the Messapii, occupied the opposite extremity of the

Adriatic coast, in Calabria; and it is now believed probable that a central group landed in Picenum, opposite Etruria, and mixed with the Bronze Age 'Mediterraneans' there, creating a society of markedly warlike character. Gradually the Picenians coalesced with the neighbouring Umbro-Sabellian tribes, and adopted their language, though apparently with infusions of their own. It is also suggested that the Latins of historical times contained a Picene and so an Illyrian element.

Tradition related that the Illyrians had originally come from Asia Minor. So, it was said—and is now believed again by many—did another people who played a great part in the early civilisation of Italy and Rome, the Etruscans. Early in the first millennium B.C. (some say rather earlier) the Etruscans imposed themselves on the populations inhabiting that half of the Tiber plain that lies north of the river; and they established a formidable and pugnacious group of city-states, and rapidly expanded into Umbria and Latium. The question who these people were is as great a mystery as any of the numerous unsolved problems that have been mentioned in this brief survey. Their language, with its harsh groups of consonants and nasal vowels, is incomprehensible to us, but it is believed not to be Indo-European; possibly it was Caucasian.[1] Skulls show a predominance of long-headed people, but a proportion also of round-headed; thus here again we have evidence of a characteristic racial coalescence. Further evidence of fusion is the retention, alongside each other,

[1] According to one theory, the Etruscan language was a survival of a linguistic group which had earlier been predominant in the Mediterranean. Traces of a similar tongue occur on inscriptions of the N. Aegean island of Lemnos.

of the two customs of disposing of the dead, the burial that prevailed among the Neolithic, Umbro-Sabellian and Illyrian peoples, and the cremation of the 'Terramaricoli' and 'Villanovans'. The Etruscans were early and strongly subjected to Greek influence. Indeed, it has now been established that from at least the eighth century B.C. this influence was strong throughout central Italy; it was no doubt spread by the Greek colonies which lay not far to the south.

The main constituents of the ancient Italians had now arrived. Umbro-Sabellians, probably partly Illyrianised, and later Etruscans, joined Latins on the site of Rome, and out of the blend came the Romans. The story of the *Aeneid*, with its immigrants from Troy, was a later patriotic myth designed to link Rome with a heroic but non-Greek antiquity; but it had this much of truth in it, that out of the three main ingredients of the Roman, though the Latin predominated, the other two—the Umbro-Sabellian and the Etruscan—had brought in Eastern elements.

Of the ancient Roman, as well as the ancient Greek, the chief components were now present. But the principal theme of this study is political, and in this theme unification plays a great part. So it remains to say that the Greeks 'colonised' a vast area of the eastern, central, and even western Mediterranean; but that—except perhaps unions in Sicily and S. Italy—never succeeded in forming a durable unit of any size, until Alexander of Macedon conquered the Persian Empire; whereas Rome gradually increased her power until she ruled from Mesopotamia to the Atlantic, and beyond the Rhine and Danube.

CHAPTER III

THE HISTORIES
OF GREECE AND ROME
(Maps IV and V)

EVEN in this abbreviated form, the story of the ancient world is a complex one. It is also a somewhat monotonous one. I would not, therefore, suggest that either the general historian or the teacher should necessarily consider each and all of these geographical areas with approximately the same degree of emphasis. Although it is important that he should appreciate the historical claims of more than a few of them, he may be allowed, and even expected, to turn the limelight on to some of them more than to others.

In Western Europe, by long tradition, the recipients of this limelight have been Greece and Rome. Indeed, in most British universities today, 'ancient history' means the history of Greece and Rome and of nothing else whatever. This concentration on Greece and Rome *to the exclusion of all other ancient history* is clearly an archaism. It goes back to times when the Greek and Roman classics played a predominant part in education. It also goes back to times when only a very little was known about other ancient civilisations. Both these situations have now radically changed. It has also been suggested that the time has gone by when the historian could indulge a sense of European superiority by ignoring Oriental regions generally (p. 2). All the earlier *raisons d'être* for *exclusive* concentration on Greece and Rome have gone.

106

It is unfortunate that some classical scholars have not accepted this position more readily. For, by tending to ignore it, they have distracted attention from the great claims to our interest that Greek and Roman history still possesses. That is to say, the demolition of its claim to a monopoly of our time is very far from demolishing its claim to a large proportion of it; and this has been obscured owing to the equally uncompromising attitudes of these classics on the one hand, and of the protagonists of more recently developed historical disciplines on the other.

For, in spite of the much larger picture which ancient history nowadays presents, it still remains true that the student of the subject is entitled to focus a large proportion of his interest on the classical world. This is not only because we still have most information about these parts of ancient history. Nor is it because we in the West are naturally disposed to admire their art and literature more than those of any other ancient countries. Both of these have been shown to be considerations to which the historian should not attach excessive weight (p. 9). There are better reasons than these why he should still, even nowadays, study the ancient history of the Greeks and Romans in greater detail than that of other ancient peoples.

The first reason lies in our choice of politics as a central theme, the choice dictated by the central problem of today. For the history of the Greeks and Romans provides a more valuable storehouse of political systems, development, and happenings than does the whole of the rest of ancient history put together; and this is due not only to the brilliance of its political histories that have survived, but to the

actual wealth of events. Not all of these developments were new, though many of them were; but the
remarkable feature lies in the concentration in the
histories of these two peoples of so wide a variety of
political experience. This particularly applies to the
aspect of politics to which our present circumstances
attach particular importance—political unity. For
Rome created unity on entirely new and unprecedented, indeed unparalleled, dimensions. Here indeed is an appropriate study for 1951, as L. Waddy
emphasises in his book on *Pax Romana* published last
year. Rome's own historians noted correctly the
epoch-making character of the innovation; one of the
greatest of them, Polybius, a Greek of the second
century B.C., observed that this great enlargement of
the world's horizon by Rome marked an altogether
new stage, because it meant that henceforward
history was no longer a disconnected subject. But
this theme of unity is vividly perceptible, in advance
or in decline, throughout the histories of the classical
peoples: indeed it may be considered their keynote.

So Greece and Rome are more relevant to our
modern problems than are other parts of the ancient
world; therefore they deserve the special attention of
its general historians. They deserve it for another
reason too. They are the nearest to us, in three
senses of the word—in two cases perhaps equal
nearest, but in the sum nearest of all. They are
nearest geographically; they are equal nearest in
time. Most important of all, they are nearest, or
equal nearest, in culture. There are, it is true, many
different elements in our Western civilisation. 'If our
own culture can claim to be on the main stream, it is
only because our cultural tradition has captured and

made tributary a larger volume of once parallel traditions' (Childe). But the two traditions that are, for
us, the most important are those of the Jewish and
Graeco-Roman worlds. The Jewish influence lies not
so much in the history of the Hebrews as in their
thought; but the significance of the Greeks and
Romans to the modern world lies as much in their
history as in their thought. Moreover, their thought
often expressed itself in their history (p. 205); and
their history possesses a nearness and relevance to
our own times that can be attributed to the history
of no other people. Greece has been described as
'proto-Europe' (G. de Reynold).

This special *proximity* of the Greeks and Romans
makes it even more imperative to study the lessons
and warnings in politics and political unity that they
have to offer. It would not justify us in forgetting
the other ancient civilisations, for that, as has been
suggested, would be to lose sense of proportion; but
it is more important to know about one's parents
than about one's grandparents and great-uncles,
especially when the former are no less remarkable
than the latter.

So for these reasons Greece and Rome deserve a
more detailed treatment, in proportion to other
ancient civilisations, than has so far been given them
here. A brief summary of the form that this expanded
treatment might take will now be suggested. It may
be added that here the Greeks and the Romans are
considered, not as forming a single civilisation (a view,
revived by Toynbee, which seems to force the facts),
but as two civilisations possessing common features.
Though they are closely related to each other—
in many ways more closely than any preceding

civilisations—they remain separate until, at the very end of the ancient period, they merge into the Byzantine Empire. However, their resemblances and overlaps with each other make it convenient to group them within the same chronological scheme.

1. *Period of Settlement*, ninth and eighth centuries B.C.

In Greece the Iron Age took unstable shape in poverty-stricken villages, bound together in loose and warring tribal organisations under hereditary kings advised or directed by councils of nobles. But continuity had not been completely broken, and recovery seems to have begun in areas where the past had most instruction to give, the neighbourhood of Mycenae and the island of Crete.

The region of Mycenae maintained, or soon resumed, its political ascendancy. Though reconstruction soon began at Mycenae, the latest immigrants were based rather on neighbouring Argos, which became dominant in the Peloponnese. Such domination was accompanied by the transformation from village to town and to city-state. The reappearance of cities as normal units, however, may have occurred at about the same time or even a little earlier in Crete —again facilitated by the surviving remnants of a great urban life there. There were other places, too, in which similar revivals were encouraged by strong earlier Bronze Age cultures. One of these was Boeotia (north-west of Athens), in which the lake-side city of Orchomenus, formerly a lesser Mycenae, figures in Greek traditions of very early political groupings. Another such place was Corinth on the isthmus, now known to have been reoccupied—at least to some

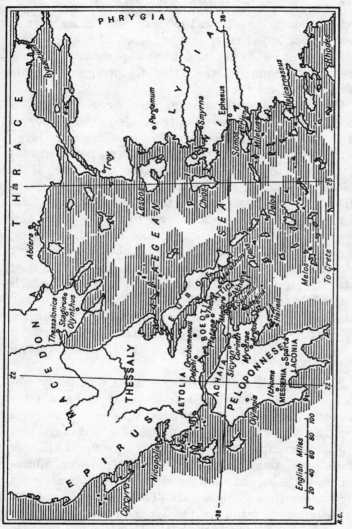

IV. GREECE AND THE AEGEAN

extent—not long after *c.* 1000 B.C. Such cities were at
first under royal rule; but in most, the kings were
before long weakened and then superseded by their
aristocratic councils, which then formed governments
of the hereditary few.

When cities were thus created or re-created, a
former tribal area was usually divided among several
of them. But occasionally the new cities were large
enough to absorb the villages (or even petty towns)
of a whole tribe, or even of more than one. This
joining together of different communities to form a
city-state was described by the Greeks as *synoecism.*
Sometimes the absorptions were merely political and
did not involve the physical uprooting of the villages;
in such cases the latter were not urbanised but
became part of the rural territory of the new
city. Such a process took place in Attica, of which
the whole territory (1000 sq. m.) passed into the
hands of Athens. The same happened in the south,
at Sparta, which thus began in the eighth century
to supersede Argos as the dominant power of the
Peloponnese.

Elsewhere, however, villages were physically absorbed or amalgamated to form parts of a new city.
Sometimes a single village grew into a city through
the transfer of a rural population within its fortifications. Sometimes the inhabitants of several villages
abandoned them in order to live together. Sometimes, without abandoning them, they joined them
together within a single wall. This is what happened
in Italy on the banks of the Tiber. First, the Latins
had established a village on the Palatine hill near its
ford, while Umbro-Sabellians (Sabines) had other
villages on the hills near by to the north and east.

Then these neighbouring villages gradually coalesced to become the city of Rome.[1] The tradition that this (like the Greek, and Etruscan, cities) was originally ruled by kings is a probable one.

2. *Expansion, Evolution and External Threats*, eighth to fifth centuries B.C.

(a) *Expansion*

Partly owing to political troubles at home in this transitional stage, but more particularly because of the Greek mainland's barren soil and a new spirit of enterprise engendered by strong Oriental influences on Greece, many groups of emigrants now began to leave the country and to establish new city-states (called 'colonies' but usually independent) in a vast area from Spain and S. France (Massalia) to Cyrene and the Black Sea. Among the great 'colonisers' were Chalcis (on the island of Euboea), Miletus (W. Asia Minor), and Corinth.

The most important areas in which new city-states were thus formed were Sicily and S. Italy, which thus form an integral part of 'Ancient Greece'. In the latter area, the earliest northernmost 'colony' was at Cumae, little more than 100 miles south of Rome, and largely or at least partly responsible for the early Greek influence which that city is now known to have experienced. Greek influence was also strong among the Etruscans. These were now grouped in powerful fortified cities. They obtained minerals from Sardinia and Corsica, and ruled the mainland from the Apennines in the north to

[1] According to recent theories, this development cannot properly be said to have taken place until the seventh century B.C.

Salerno in the south: in the sixth century an Etruscan
dynasty ruled Rome and caused it to grow and
prosper.

(b) Evolution

Before this Etruscan domination, Rome may well
have joined one of the religious confederations of
neighbouring city-states, the Latin leagues, based on
venerated shrines in the area. In Greece, too, a loose
confederation of States for religious purposes was
based on one of the great centres of worship, Delphi;
and the Delphic oracle was habitually consulted
before colonies were founded. The advice of the oracle
was likewise taken before the codifications of local laws,
of which the pioneer attempts represent the greatest
internal achievement of this period. The earliest
known instance of such a codification is traditionally
attributed to a city as far afield as Locri (Epizephyrii),
a mixed colony in S. Italy. Such codifications may
often have been gradual, but ancient traditions
always believed them to be the single acts of great
lawgivers; this earliest one of all was called Zaleucus.

The lawgivers concerned themselves with economic
questions; thus the Athenian reformer Solon later
(c. 594–3) revolutionised agricultural technique by
directing a switch from mixed farming to specialised
production for export. The growth of trade that
accompanied such developments, and the 'colonial'
expansion in general, created a mercantile class;
coinage in various forms, bullion and specie, came
into existence. The new class supplied the new
'hoplite' infantry which henceforward began to replace the aristocratic cavalry as the basis of Greek
armies. In some leading cities, the new class of
merchants replaced existing governments by 'tyrants'

V. ITALY

(dictators), of an efficient but often bellicose character. This movement seems to have been initiated by a group of neighbouring cities near the isthmus, namely, Argos (under Pheidon), Sicyon (Orthagoras, *c.* 660 B.C.), and its great mercantile neighbour Corinth. Corinth was the first city-state since Mycenaean days to become a naval and commercial sea-power on a large scale (though it was rivalled by Miletus in Ionia).

Meanwhile in Sparta—perhaps therein imitating the cities of Crete—the State took on an even more markedly totalitarian character than the tyrannies, in order to maintain in subjection a large part of the Peloponnese. This was principally achieved by the First and Second Messenian Wars, after which large populations were reduced to permanent serfdom (the Helots).

The Spartan system remained, but elsewhere, before 500, these 'tyrannies' mostly gave way (except in Sicily) to plutocratic administrations ('oligarchies'). In other cities these 'oligarchies' developed direct from hereditary 'aristocracies'; but sometimes the latter persisted unchanged, as in the loosely knit confederation of Thessaly, which was a strong power in the sixth century. Across the Adriatic at Rome, perhaps in the following century, another aristocratic system (with a Senate presided over by two annually elected magistrates later called Consuls) was introduced in a State much changed and weakened by the elimination of the Etruscan régime.

(c) *External Threats*

The period 500–470 B.C. was one of external dangers. The Achaemenid Persian Empire absorbed the

Greek city-states of W. Asia Minor, but failed to conquer the mainland in the face, first, of resistance from Athens (Marathon, 490), and, then, of a momentary coalition led by Sparta (Salamis, 480: Plataea, 479).

The history of Carthaginian and Etruscan encroachment in the West followed somewhat similar lines. In the sixth century Carthaginians and Etruscans defeated the fleets of Ionian and Massalian Greeks, and the former established possessions in W. Sicily. But they were driven from it, at the battle of Himera (480), by Gelon, 'tyrant' of Syracuse, who had established by a system of alliances the greatest Greek power of the time. His successor, Hiero I, defeated the Etruscans at sea off Cumae in Campania (474)—perhaps a cause of their fall at Rome, now in an isolated position as neighbour of powerful Umbro-Sabellian tribes. New political significance was now given to her association with the Latins, and encroachments were successfully resisted.

3. *Climax of the City-State*, fifth and early fourth centuries.

In Athens, during the fifth century, the government became vested in the large citizen-assembly ('democracy'). Elsewhere, notably at Corcyra, this class-issue caused serious bloodshed. During the same period the relation of plebeians to patricians became the centre of attention at Rome also, where a long series of legal adjustments and some disturbances took place.

During these years Rome also made good her superiority over her neighbours. To her south, Syracuse re-founded a short-lived supremacy over the

Western Greeks; and in the Aegean Sparta's leadership fell to Athens. The Athenians enlarged the original coalition at Persia's expense, and converted it into a confederation (the Delian League). This, however, rapidly assumed an imperial character.

Later in the century more truly federal institutions, though accompanied by the same tendency towards domination by one member, were exhibited by other leagues, such as those of Athens' northern neighbour Thebes, and Olynthus on the southern borders of Macedonia. This latter part of the fifth century was mostly taken up with the Peloponnesian War between the Athenian and Spartan groups, in the latter of which Syracuse was for a short time included owing to a disastrous Athenian invasion. The war was won by Sparta in 404 B.C.

Soon after 400, however, Sparta lost its dominant role. This was for a few years assumed by Athens' northern neighbour Thebes; then Athens made a second, equally transient, attempt to form and control a combination of city-states (the 'Second Athenian Empire'). Meanwhile Dionysius I of Syracuse was more successful in establishing his predominance over the Western Greeks (mass-production now appears in Sicily); and to their north, Rome—after a set-back due to Celtic invasion—broke the power of the Latins, while continuing a moderate broadening of her constitution which gave some power to the Assembly.

4. *Macedonia and the large States*, later fourth and third centuries B.C. (overlap with 5).

The 'Second Athenian Empire' was swept away by a great organiser and general from the fringes of Hellenism, Philip II of Macedonia. Most Greek city-states on the mainland and in Asia Minor now ceased to possess any true independence, though they continued to retain a measure of self-government, nearly always under oligarchic control.

Philip's son Alexander III (the Great) turned East and altered the face of the world by annexing, after a series of unparalleled campaigns, the whole Persian Empire. After Alexander's early death in 323, his enormous empire broke up amid the bloodshed of the 'Hellenistic' age. By the next century several large and frequently warring kingdoms took shape under his Macedonian generals and their descendants. The Seleucids (based on Syria) controlled most of his Asiatic dominions (later the Attalids formed a separate kingdom based on Pergamum in western Asia Minor); the Ptolemies ruled Egypt and surrounding territories; and the Antigonids reigned in Macedonia and parts of Greece. In the rest of the mainland the old city-states were eclipsed by new confederacies in formerly backward areas, the Achaean and Aetolian Leagues on the south and north coasts respectively of the Corinthian Gulf. Spartan history of this period is chiefly noteworthy because of drastic but unsuccessful attempts at social reform. Economic collapse begins (p. 228).

Farther north, Epirus was unified into a looser confederation; and the rulers of this intervened in the West, thus giving Rome her first contact with mainland Greeks. For several decades at the turn of the fourth and third centuries Rome had been locked in a struggle with the southernmost and most formidable of the Umbro-Sabellian groups, the Samnites. The successful conclusion of these wars brought Rome into close proximity with the Western Greeks.

Pyrrhus of Epirus intervened in their favour against Rome. But he was obliged to retire and to leave Rome as mistress of central and southern Italy.

5. *Rome an Overseas Power, c.* 264–133 B.C.

This southward move towards Sicily led Rome into sharp conflict with Carthage, which she defeated in two successive wars (the First and Second Punic Wars), in spite of Hannibal's twelve-year invasion of Italy during the second. These wars resulted in the Roman annexation of overseas provinces, Sicily, Sardinia, and Spain. Rome also secured her northern frontier against Celtic incursions, and her east coast by establishing a base in Dalmatia.

This brought her into opposition with Antigonid Macedonia; and from *c.* 200 the history of the Mediterranean becomes the story of Roman conquest. In less than a century the Macedonian and Seleucid powers were shattered, the Aetolian and Achaean Leagues dissolved, Carthage and Corinth destroyed, and Attalid Asia Minor annexed.

This growth of the empire caused great changes, not least at home. Greek literature and philosophy began to take strong effect. In particular, some members of the Roman governing class began to be influenced by the enlightened doctrines of Stoicism, introduced by the philosopher Panaetius of Rhodes in the second century B.C. Also, conquests caused the rise of a wealthy mercantile class; and serious unemployment was caused by the supersession of peasant farming in Italy by capitalist ranches using slave-labour on a large scale—a practice perhaps introduced from Carthage.

During this period the oligarchic administration of

Rome began to show itself seriously incapable of dealing with its increased commitments.

6. *The Roman Crisis, c.* 133–30 B.C.

The two last-named dangers now took effect. During these years there were formidable slave-wars, especially in Sicily; and the two Gracchi drove a wedge into the monopoly of senatorial government, starting a struggle that lasted for a century. The equilibrium was further disturbed by successful generals. Wars were won in Africa, southern Gaul, Asia Minor, and Italy itself—against revolted Italians to whom concessions had to be made. The victorious commanders, such as Marius and Sulla, controlled private armies and in turn asserted autocratic rights at Rome, under the threadbare cloaks of Traditionalism or Democracy.

In the fifties B.C., three potentates of this sort formed a dictatorial coalition (the 'First Triumvirate'). One of them, Crassus, in search of military glory, was defeated and killed at Carrhae in N.W. Mesopotamia by the recently risen power of Arsacid Parthia. But his colleague Caesar, on a similar mission, conquered with great cruelty and then annexed the greater part of Gaul. Then, as a climax to mutual suspicions and constitutional propaganda, he broke with his remaining colleague Pompey, suppressed him in a terrible civil war spreading throughout the empire, and established dictatorial rule. His murder in 44 B.C. was followed by a further fourteen years of civil strife. The first contestants to be eliminated were the two anti-Caesarian factions, the 'Republicans' (Brutus and Cassius) and Pompey's sons, one of whom had mobilised slaves to form a naval force.

Caesar's lieutenant, Antony, holding the East, and allied to the last Ptolemaic monarch of Egypt, Cleopatra VII, succumbed after Actium (31 B.C.) to Caesar's youthful grand-nephew Octavian.

7. *Augustus*, 30 B.C.–A.D. 14.

Under Octavian, who took the name Augustus and became absolute ruler of the whole Roman world, a new epoch started. The entire machinery of the government was overhauled to fit it for governing the empire. Every branch of the administration was improved out of all recognition. The political power of the Assembly, however, was terminated for ever. But the traditional oligarchic institutions of the State, such as the Senate, were at first enabled to collaborate with the emperor without total loss of prestige. This was achieved, under Augustus and to some extent under his successor Tiberius, by an ingenious system according to which the ruler (*princeps* —the First Citizen) exercised much authority by indirect means (*auctoritas*); thus, while retaining complete control in practice, he avoided the appearance of undue interference, and was able to call his imperial régime the 'Restored Republic'.

Augustus regarded peace as only attainable by further conquest. In spite of the size of the empire, the northern approaches to Italy were still in the hands of lawless tribes, and these were now eliminated. The territory of the empire was extended by the annexation of central Asia Minor (Galatia), Palestine, and a chain of provinces north of the Alps. Augustus also intended to annex Bohemia and to extend the Rhine-Danube frontier to the Elbe, but these projects—which might have had incalculable effects on modern history—failed. The immediate causes of failure were a revolt in the Illyrian provinces and a German ambush respectively, but the real cause lay in the economical military budget of Augustus which left an inadequate margin for emergencies.

Thus diplomacy was preferred to arms whenever possible—notably in dealing with Parthia (p. 78). The common lot of most of the vast population of the empire became peace instead of war. Trade prospered accordingly, in an unprecedented fashion. The successes of the government were exploited by propaganda of an unprecedented efficiency and intensity. Inscriptions, sculpture, architecture, all played their parts in this; and so especially did the coinage—now planned to cover the whole empire— whose constant changes of type show it as to some extent a substitute for government-controlled press and radio. The régime was further supported at one end of the intellectual scale by hitherto unequalled expenditure on games, and at the other by the astonishing galaxy of literary talent—including Virgil and Horace—who, by good luck or good management, included in their writings the praises of the régime.

By such means, determined attempts were made to secure the position of Italy and Italians as the centre of the new system. But there was also intense activity in reorganising the provinces, notably Gaul and Spain. These were linked together by a network of roads which borrowed the best features of the Assyrian and Persian systems, and greatly exceeded them in size and technique.

Under Roman auspices, many Greek or Hellenised States survived on the borders of the empire as 'client kingdoms', e.g. the Bosphorus (Crimea). The limited

self-government of city-states was retained, still
under Right-Wing rule; and a further great expansion of Hellenism took place through the creation of
new Greek cities, many of them in areas of alien
culture (e.g. Phrygia in central Asia Minor; cf.
Augustus' foundation Nicopolis in W. Epirus). Many
existing city-states flourished as never before, notably
in Ionia (e.g. Ephesus and Smyrna), some receiving
a new element and a privileged status by the settlement of Roman colonists. Caesar had occasionally
settled civilians (e.g. Corinth), but the colonists of
Augustus were ex-soldiers (e.g. Berytus (Beirut) in
the Lebanon; and garrison towns in the Pisidian
district of central Anatolia).

8. *The Pax Romana.*

During the first century A.D. the greatest successors
of Augustus were Tiberius—to whose reign the
Mission of Christ is attributed—Claudius and Vespa-
sian. These, almost as much as the lurid autocrats
like Caligula and Nero with whom they alternated,
proved unable to maintain the pretence of avoiding
monarchic rule, and the result was a gradual diminu-
tion of self-government in the provinces and of
senatorial initiative at home.

But in general the policy of Augustus was maintained (it received continual lip-service), and much
was done to stabilise the system he had founded.
The frontiers were adjusted by further annexations
(e.g. Britain) and by the absorption of client kingdoms. Peace was maintained in most of the vast
territories of the empire, and trade continued to
flourish, Campania now eclipsing eastern markets as
a world centre.

In spite of the ostensible 'Restored Republic', Augustus had attempted to secure continuity of power within his own house; but each of the first two dynasties failed (in one case in serious civil wars, A.D. 68–70) owing to the weaknesses of this method of selection by heredity. The great emperors of the second century, however—Trajan, Hadrian, Antoninus Pius, Marcus Aurelius—were provided by a system of adoption. This was the climax of the Roman World Peace, which continued unbroken throughout most of the century. The peculiar contribution of the Roman government during this period was its great development of law and humanitarianism, logical conclusions of the Stoic doctrines that had been implicit in the philosophy of the principate since the start. In this period, too, was the climax of economic development, and in industry as in agriculture the provinces began to eclipse Italy.

9. *The End of the Pax Romana*, second to fourth centuries A.D.

Late in the second century an ominous sign was provided by the appearance of Germanic tribes within the Danubian provinces and even raiding Italy. Civil wars, too, resulted from Aurelius' abandonment of the adoptive principle and the subsequent murder of his son. As winner of these wars (A.D. 193–6) emerged Septimius Severus, an African, who militarised the government. His half-Syrian son officially confirmed the abolition of distinction between Italians and provincials; and the Roman religion was now competing increasingly with eastern creeds. Early in the third century, the external threats to the empire were redoubled. Encouraged by constant internal struggles between claimants to the Roman imperial throne, an aggressive new Persian dynasty, the Sassanids, prevented the Romans from adequately facing the Germanic threats on the Danube. The failure of law and order throughout large parts of the empire caused a strong tendency towards local separatism under local generals to assert itself. The currency collapsed into disastrous inflation, and the greatly increased cost of an over-elaborate administration led to terrible poverty, economic chaos, and the final ruin of self-government.

The complete disintegration of the empire was arrested by the almost superhuman military efforts of a series of emperors from Illyricum (the modern Yugoslavia)—Claudius Gothicus, Aurelian, Probus, Diocletian (A.D. 284–305) and Constantine (306–337). But Diocletian, regarding the task as too great for one man, established a dual principate, himself ruling from Asia Minor and a colleague in the West. He also set a twenty-year term to the tenure of emperors, and provided for the nomination of successors. This last arrangement rapidly became a dead letter; but some measure of economic recovery was achieved, at the price of an increasingly oppressive bureaucracy, under monarchs of an Oriental absolutism.

Constantine pursued these tendencies; but he reversed the recently intensified policy of contesting the spread of Christianity by persecution, and grafted it on to the traditional Roman ritual as the official faith. He then reunited the empire with its capital on the Bosphorus at Byzantium—now re-named Constantinople or 'New Rome'. The unity of the empire was not maintained; until 476 a Western Empire lingered on with capitals at Milan and

Ravenna. But henceforward Constantinople permanently replaced these, and Rome itself, as the chief centre of the empire. It owed this supremacy not only to its remarkable convenience for maritime communications, but also to its proximity to Asia Minor; for that country had now superseded the more vulnerable European territories as the chief imperial reservoir of manpower and resources. The Western provinces, and Italy itself, became detached piecemeal from the empire; Latin gradually gave way to Greek as the official language; and the East Roman or Byzantine Empire, though it did not restore the *Pax Romana*, conserved the classical traditions and resisted obliteration until 1453.

The distinction between 'ancient' and 'medieval' history is an artificial one, and we can take our choice of dates for the transition. Those selected by historians have ranged between the fourth and the sixth centuries. It was early in the fourth century that East and West first were separated, and that the empire became Christian; it was in the fifth century that the last 'puppet' emperor of the West was deposed; it was in the sixth century that much of Western Europe abandoned the town-life which had been initiated in the Middle East at the outset of the period with which this survey began.

But there is much to be said also for the suggestion of F. Lot that we should think of the ancient and medieval epochs as separated from one another by another period (*c.* second to eighth centuries)—a 'repetition' (though history does not precisely repeat itself) of the great Wanderings of the Peoples with which the history of Greece and Rome had started.

CHAPTER IV

THE CENTRAL THEME: WAR

THE last chapter has focused the attention particularly on Greece and Rome, and has dealt with their histories, still in extremely general terms, but none the less in a little greater detail than it was possible to devote to other parts of the world. Let us, then, consider this story of Greece and Rome, and endeavour to see whether it reveals any dominant, guiding theme—any thread which runs through the whole complex fabric and knits it together. It has been suggested that the 'philosophies of history', postulating cycles, progress, or retrogression, cannot, from the evidence that we possess, be said to provide any such unifying or organic element (p. 13). It was concluded, with H. A. L. Fisher, that there was only one uniformity to be discerned: 'I can only see', he observed, 'one emergency following another as wave follows wave.'

This conclusion is abundantly confirmed by the course of events in the ancient history of all lands. It is even possible to be more specific, and for the word 'emergency' to substitute the word 'war'. *Far and away the most important and frequent events in ancient history are wars.* It is not necessary to illustrate this point in detail. It is clearly illustrated by the survey that has just been attempted. It is true that in a minority of cases the great events cannot certainly be traced to wars; but even when this is so, it may well be because of deficiencies in our information. However, in the majority of cases this difficulty

does not exist. Under the majority of headings wars
are frequent if not continual, and the most significant
events consist of them or are caused by them.

This, again, can most clearly be seen in the histories
of Greece and Rome. For the sake of convenience
this was here divided into nine periods. In the vast
majority of these periods the major developments
were wars and the immediate results of wars. Indeed,
this is true of as many as seven of these nine periods
—all except periods Nos. 7 and 8 of the Roman
Empire, representing two centuries out of fifteen. The
evidence from this particular section of ancient history is especially illuminating. It is true that wars
predominated equally in such other parts and periods
of ancient history as have left us any record. But
their evidence is perhaps less unequivocal, owing to
mighty accidents such as the earthquakes of the
Middle East, and the flooding of great rivers; for in
some cases these may have created impossible conditions in which war was the only means of survival.

For Greek and Roman history, however, no such
excuse could be offered. Earthquakes continued in
Asia Minor, but they only affected the fringes of the
Greek world (with one or two exceptions), and they
did not damage them very severely. Nor were Greece
and Rome at the mercy of great and unpredictable
rivers. Yet, if we take, as regards the former, the
words of one of its most discerning students, G. B.
Grundy: 'Wars! Wars! Wars! Nothing but wars!
some little, some bigger. . . .' 'War was as natural
a part of Greek city life as games and recreations are
of our own' (A. E. Zimmern).

Nor can this ineluctable conclusion be qualified or
diminished by attempts to belittle the horrors and

upheavals caused by ancient Greek or other ancient
wars. When Zimmern suggests and elaborates on the
theme that war 'was simply an exciting and not
unusual way of spending some weeks in early
summer', an admirable writer is suffering from a
serious misconception in favour of a people he would
seek to praise and to excuse. Greek warfare was
attended by fundamental consequences of misery and
disintegration. We are apt to think back to our own
eighteenth century when war was sometimes carried
on in a comparatively 'gentlemanly' and sporting
fashion (cf., earlier, Bacon: 'a foreign war is like the
heat of exercise and serves to keep the body in
health'), and to imagine that this state of affairs was
characteristic of epochs earlier than our own. But
nothing could be more erroneous (Toynbee); the eigh-
teenth-century gentlemanliness was a flash in the
pan. Ancient war (at least from the epochs in which
weapons first became formidable) 'was waged ruthlessly. The persons and property of the conquered
were at the mercy of the victors, and the religions of
the period usually urged the extermination or enslavement of defeated peoples. The bodies of the slain
were often mutilated, captives were subjected to
horrible tortures, and the victors carved boasting
records of their atrocities upon the monuments'
(Gettell). Most, though not quite all, of this applies
to the Greeks and Romans as well as the other
peoples of the ancient world. Roman wars were
ruthless, and Greek ones 'carried on with the bitterness of almost personal hostility' (E. A. Freeman).
And what even Gettell's description does not begin
to describe are the more indirect, but equally fundamental, dislocations of political and social life caused

by the constant warfare. 'In small states a disastrous war meant ruin not for a few, but for the majority, if not all . . . and in Greece . . . this danger was never far away' (F. R. Earp).

All these lamentable results were completely appreciated by some of the most thoughtful people of the time. This is particularly true of the fifth century B.C., that great period of almost every sort of civilisation except the all-important political sort. There are terrible indictments of war in the Athenian drama, which reached its climax at this time. 'War the madman,' Aeschylus calls it, 'mocker of the ways of God.' Even more conclusive are the implicit denunciations of Euripides, who, in the more sophisticated and disillusioned days of the *fin de siècle*, analysed the human sufferings caused by war. The historians of the same century are no more backward in seeing the implications of the greatest problem of their time. Herodotus, whose special study was the Persian Wars, sums them up in terms differing widely from the romantic assessment, the concentration on glorious aspects, that are too common today. 'In the three generations', says Herodotus, 'of Darius, Xerxes and Artaxerxes, *more woes befell Greece than in the twenty generations preceding Darius*—woes caused in part by the Persians, but in part by the contentions among the chief men of Greece itself concerning the supreme power.' But far the most searching commentary on Greek wars is the coldly scientific analysis of Thucydides, the historian of the Peloponnesian War between Athens and Sparta that brought the fifth century to a disastrous close. This has been described as 'one of the most devastating indictments of war ever penned' (Cochrane). More

will be said of it later; meanwhile, it is enough to note
that, for this acute observer and critic, war was
'unrelieved and ever-deepening gloom'.

There is a curious parallel to these protests against
unending warfare in another part of the world at
much the same period. For in China too there were
constant wars, and in China too there were constant,
eloquent but unavailing criticisms of this state of
affairs. The personal tragedy of Confucius in the
sixth century was his failure to set it right. But
even before his day, we read in the *Book of Odes*:
'For a long time no peace has been our lot: heaven
grinds us on this whetstone.' Indeed, in China, there
was continual popular indignation against war, which
by ancient tradition the Chinese mentality does not
regard as glamorous. But nevertheless, in China too,
there were continual wars. War is the dominant
feature of ancient Chinese history—and of all ancient
history.

But this is only part of a larger and even more
painful fact. War is the dominant feature of all
history. It has always been 'one of the most prominent phenomena in man's dealing with man' (C. W. C.
Oman). Now Gordon Childe remarks: 'the profes-
sional historians have absorbed from their masters
and models the conviction that war should form a
central theme in history, and have nearly persuaded
their shy patrons that they should be interested in
it'. This implies that the allocation of so prominent
a place to war is a misleading and subjective decision
of the historian. But unfortunately this is not so.
This prominence of war is an authentic, observable
phenomenon. This degrading conclusion is concisely
stated by Winston Churchill. 'Battles are the principal

milestones in secular history. Modern opinion resents this uninspiring truth.' It is, indeed, a fact to be resented; but it is true. The proper approach to such an overwhelmingly important fact is neither to adopt an 'escapist' attitude, nor to miss the wood for the trees by nibbling away at dreary and insignificant military details in Livy and Caesar. Nor is it of much assistance to erect the alleged inevitability of war into another 'philosophy of history'. G. N. Clark has interestingly described how this view, 'the Cycle of War and Peace', arose in the sixteenth and seventeenth centuries. War and Peace are only parts of a repetitive process in the sense that (leaving aside such intermediate refinements as 'Cold War') we have always had one or the other. It is true, then, that an alternation, a repetition, does occur. But it by no means follows from this that such a repetition is bound to occur in accordance with fixed rules, as inevitable as the sequence of night and day. By knowing the causes of night and day, we can do nothing to eliminate either; but the alternation of war and peace rests with human decisions and efforts. There is no reason to accept the cyclical view of war and peace, or its deduction 'we will never get rid of war' (Creighton) (cf. pp. 12f.).

The historian may advise regarding the future, but he is not entitled to foretell it in this way. His duty is to explain how the past has led up to the present. If Creighton's observation had been couched in the past tense, it would have been both legitimate and accurate. For it is true—and this is seen with extreme clarity in ancient history—that, hitherto, wars have followed one another with only brief periods of intermission. And since this is true of history in general, it has to be emphasised with especial care by that historian who is concentrating on the subject which, in the light of today's problems, must be regarded as central—politics (p. 20). For wars are declared, directed, and terminated by governments. Indeed, the *chief* function of governments throughout the ages has been war-making; or, as Russell puts it— and an investigation of ancient history confirms this —'the chief activity of the State is preparation for large-scale homicide'. Thus it is quite right to consider military history as a part of political history; but a still more vital part of the latter concerns the actions that begin and end wars, that cause and follow them. The alternation of war and peace is the dominant theme of history; so it is all the more the dominant theme of political history. The greatest political problem is the keeping of the peace (D. Thomson). Everything depends on a true understanding, and so control, of the factors which direct the movements from war to peace, and from peace to war.

Yet, curiously enough, this central and topical theme in ancient history is hardly ever treated as such in our text-books. This may seem a strange statement when they are full of wars—like ancient writers before them. It is perfectly true that they repeatedly give us arid stretches of unimportant war narrative, obsolete tactics and so on, which possess hardly a minimum of modern interest. 'It is the reproach of historians that they have too often turned history into a mere record of the butchery of men by their fellow-men' (C. W. C. Oman). This 'Drum and Trumpet' school, exemplified by those who still choose the military books of Livy as the principal Latin texts for school-children, is not the answer to our problem. What are far less frequent, and indeed are almost unheard of, are attempts to consider the subject of war or of ancient war *as such*; to look at it firmly as the dominant and pre-eminent subject that it is, and to devote to it that analysis on broad lines which *would* be, and is, of vital modern significance. In fact, it is our duty to consider how and why, in general terms, ancient wars came into being; whether there were any general principles governing these processes; and why the wars could not be prevented. The almost total absence of such discussions—not least by the 'universal' historians— may, as Churchill diagnosed, be due to people's resentment of the prominence of war in history. For resentment causes realistic discussion to be spoilt, or, as in this case, suppressed.

Suppression is one principal form of that universal historical phenomenon, bias. Bias in itself, so long as it does not pervert and distort, is a thing that it would be waste of time to deplore. 'A mind devoid of all bias', observed Eduard Meyer, 'is likely to be devoid of all other mental furniture also.' It is therefore not rude, but polite, to assume that we all have bias. Indeed, if we say that we have not, it only means that our bias is unconscious. But it is not very efficient to allow our conscious mind no control over this inevitable bias, so let us make it a conscious one. 'The main thing is to be conscious of one's point of view' (Popper). This point of view, this bias, will be more interesting and relevant if it is concerned with a central and topical subject. In our field the most central and topical subject is war; so let our bias concern war. That is to say, let us, in our teaching and writing about ancient history, adopt and seek to propagate a bias against war.

It should be made clear at this point that the course which is advocated here, and which (it is suggested) should be advocated to the historian's readers and hearers, is by no means what is ordinarily described as 'pacifism'—absolute rejection and refusal of war in any circumstances. The latter does not seem a logical procedure. If oneself or one's vital interests are really attacked or threatened, it seems, as the Renaissance jurist Grotius saw, irrational not to defend them or prepare to do so. The vital interests of most people would be infringed if their country, or the larger political unit or group to which it belongs, were attacked. When Hobbes expressed the view that *any* rule would be juster and happier than war, his mistake was to leave out the word 'almost' (Locke; cf. Carritt). 'War is a desperate remedy only to be used in cases otherwise hopeless' (G. Unwin). The pacifism of Tolstoy would be tantamount to an invitation to aggressive wars—since it is not, and will not yet become, world-wide: 'pacifism can only work if and when it becomes universal' (W. Brown).

Thus war *in self-defence* is logically required. But any such assertion as this is liable to a strong objection. It may be condemned as wholly abstract and theoretical, since it does not even touch on the fundamental difficulty of deciding which wars are fought in self-defence and which are not. Self-defence has been defined above as the defence of oneself or one's vital interests, and the latter have been defined as very often including the integrity of the political grouping to which one's country belongs as well as of one's country itself. But even so it will be objected

that the historian will incur a serious difficulty, and
risk of arbitrariness, if he endeavours to determine
which wars have been fought in self-defence and
which have not.

But this objection is not, *in practice*, a very formidable one. It is true that the difficulty will sometimes occur; but in ancient history, at least, it will
not occur very often. Opinions to the contrary are
likely to be based on one or two notorious cases in
which the responsibility is doubtful, such as the
Peloponnesian War, or the Civil War between Pompey
and Caesar. These have attracted particular attention from the very fact of this piquantly disputed
responsibility. But they remain exceptional. In the
great majority of ancient wars it is clear enough
which side was the aggressor. In some wars both
sides fought from predominantly aggressive motives.
In a very few—the conflicts between right and right
studied by the Greek tragedians—this can be said of
neither side. But it remains true that distinction
between defensive and aggressive wars is a criterion
which can be used by the historian in the vast
majority of cases.

It is a criterion which we constantly try to apply
in thinking of the wars of the twentieth century; and
there is no reason whatever why the historian should
convict himself as a schizophrenic by applying one
set of standards to the present day and a wholly
different set to the ancient world. War occurs in
both; let it be subjected to the same judgments in
both. At present this is by no means customary.
Kindly people who deplore aggression in the modern
world feel and express either positive approval, or at
least no disapproval whatsoever, when they write or

teach about equally naked aggression in the ancient
world. This phenomenon is particularly conspicuous
in our educational system. For quite small children,
one of the principal text-books is that brilliant but
immoral work Caesar's *Gallic War*. These same
children are, or should be, taught to deplore the
aggressions of Hitler; but their text-books and
teachers express no disapproval of Caesar's blatant
aggressiveness, due almost entirely to an ambition for
personal glory (p. 233) and accompanied by atrocities which shocked even the Roman senate. Presumably the *Gallic War* found its way into curricula
partly because of its alleged linguistic simplicity and
partly as an aid to the inculcation of manly virtue in
the young; but the source is tainted, and the account
is by no means a propaganda-free, straight-from-the-
shoulder statement of a simple officer.

Let our ancient history, then, like our discussions
of current affairs, endeavour to observe a sharp
distinction between truly defensive warfare on the
one hand and all other sorts of warfare—i.e. aggressive warfare—on the other hand. As regards the
former category, H. M. Last defines the process
'which makes men stand up for themselves when
they are wronged' under the general heading of sentiment. Probably this is a correct definition of the
motive which actuates many people in such circumstances; and it is true that sentiment, emotion, can
be directed into suitable channels like these (p. 185).
But it is only part of the truth; and this is fortunate,
since it is very easy in public life for a sentiment
however noble in origin, to degenerate into evils such
as aggressive nationalism (p. 180). If people were
wholly *rational*, they would stand up for themselves

when threatened by destruction, just as effectively as they could by the inspiration of any sentiment. And, owing to the dangers of sentiment, it would be less hazardous if their self-defence were prompted by this equally efficacious alternative, reason, since in the latter there are no such dangers. Self-defence may, indeed, sometimes require to be spurred by emotional appeals. But it is none the less a reasonable, sensible action in itself, and the less of that explosive quality, glamour, which is attached to it the better.

For glamour easily leads to forgetfulness of the defensive aim. The ancient historian will need to be very careful not to extend the aegis of respectability and justifiability beyond self-defence (as interpreted on p. 136). For example, he should not widen this latter conception to include the 'preventive war' and the 'crusade'. The historian of the ancient world is recommended not to allow his broad distinction between the two categories of war to be smudged by any such refinements. The 'preventive war' is usually a thin disguise for an aggressive war, unless it is absolutely certain that the enemy was himself wholly decided upon aggression; very few, if any, ancient cases of war-making can fairly be defended as 'preventive'. With 'crusades' the ancient historian has no business. No wars were fought for Christianity until the fourth century A.D.—the very end of ancient history (p. 126). It is not legitimate to extend the conception of a crusade in order to justify ancient aggressive wars fought in other causes. H. M. Last seeks a moral justification for Roman expansion in the principle enunciated by Gibbon: 'the savage nations of the globe are the common enemies of civilised society'. Toynbee includes among justifiable wars those undertaken 'in the pursuit of an aim recognised to be of transcendent moral worth and social value'. Recognised by whom? Such 'recognitions', in which not everyone has shared, have caused many wars. But it is enough for the ancient historian to observe that the ancient world provides no such transcendent causes.

The purpose of these last paragraphs has been to attempt to give the teacher or general historian a definition of the limits in which he should adopt and deliberately communicate a bias against war. The conclusion is, emphatically, that he should not extend this bias to peoples who seem to him, after as careful an investigation as possible, to have entered wars in self-defence. But it should be the guiding principle that wars on any other pretext whatever should be regarded with the strongest possible condemnation. For all of them are liable to the strongest possible censure both from the rationalist and the moralist.

It has been pointed out that war in *defence* of oneself, one's vital interests, or one's political unit is defensible on rational grounds. The same cannot be said of any other sort of war. Elsewhere, it is true, we have suggested that, as far as can be seen, the sinner does not always do so badly (p. 26). But he also does not always do too well. This is a fact which is habitually obscured by the form which our general histories, and particularly our political histories, are obliged to take. For it is inevitable that they should to some extent adopt 'the happy artifice of Condorcet' (p. 29), and stress the communities which achieved most importance, paying particular attention to the climactic periods of that importance. But these

apogees were usually created by aggressive war; so
history-books mostly have the effect of indirect, but
none the less powerful, propaganda in favour of
'paranoiac ambition' (Aldous Huxley). This is misleading, since it concentrates the floodlight on the
successful war-criminals and wholly ignores the very
numerous aggressors who came to grief. Indeed,
owing to the necessary artifice of Condorcet, these are
easily forgotten. But if the facts could be hunted out,
one could write as long a book about them as about
their successful counterparts. And even from our
present survey it can be seen with great clarity that
many *successful* aggressions were exceedingly short-
lived (pp. 243f.).

The aggressors who failed, failed partly because of
sheer stupidity—for ancient governments were full
of this (p. 232)—but partly also because of the
notorious *unpredictable* quality in wars. This totally
defeats rational calculation and very often indeed
produces results wholly different from those intended.
Men 'pursue the ruin of others in ways that lead to
their own ruin' (Rivers). This was a vital point
which Thucydides saw particularly clearly. 'Consider
the vast influence of accident in war', says one of his
spokesmen, 'before you engage in it. As it continues,
it generally becomes an affair of chances, chances
from which neither side is exempt, and of which both
sides must risk the effects in the dark.' For 'war of
all things proceeds least according to definite rules,
but draws principally upon itself for contrivances to
meet an emergency . . . it forces men to do things
which they never meant or wished to do'; it tends to
produce conditions in which rationality can have no
place. 'War is an operation performed by the patient

on himself while in a state of delirium' (G. Unwin).
Because of this unpredictability, 'for those who have
a choice and whose fortunes are not at stake . . .
war is the greatest of follies'. Add to this that
'the perversity of peace settlements is proverbial'
(Toynbee); for even if the original purpose of the
war seemed defensible, this is likely to be lost sight
of before its termination. That is one of the reasons
why wars, other than unavoidable wars in self-
defence, are wholly at variance with rational conduct
—because they do not proceed in accordance with
any possible rational prediction.

That is to say, even the winner may very well
suffer too severely for the effort to have proved worth
while. This aspect is stressed by Toynbee, who finds
militarism a symptom of suicide and decline. It was
clear enough in the fourth century B.C. to the Confucian Mo Ti (Motse), who concluded that 'to put the
affairs of state right in this fashion is directly counter
to the interests of the state'. 'From war proceed
slaughter, solitude, and the want of all things'
(Leslie Stephen). Or, even if apparent benefit to the
conqueror results, very often it is limited to a small
clique of what used to be called 'profiteers'. This too
was as true in ancient times as it is now. For wars,
though they might benefit the slave-dealer (p. 227),
nearly always resulted in the dissipation and destruction of real wealth; 'the destruction of houses . . . is
the reverse of wealth-production' (Childe). This is
only one of certain automatic and fatal regular
economic consequences of war, which governments
have tried to conceal (G. Unwin). For example, war
diverts men from useful employment, and perverts
enterprise (T. R. Glover). Its biological consequences,

which used by poisonously false arguments to be
regarded as eugenic (Karl Pearson), are the very
opposite to this (A. Keith, D. S. Jordan). Many of
those who lose their lives are the members of the
community who can least be spared. Waste and
misery are 'intrinsic and inevitable' in war (Toynbee).
Again, to regard the matter from another point of
view, war must inevitably mean intellectual retrogression. For the intellect relies on the truth. 'At
ordinary times the truth is only thought ill-mannered,
but in war-time it is thought criminal' (Rivers). 'War
and Culture are incompatible' (W. Brown). All these
are reasons why the launching of non-defensive wars
is irrational (Kolnai); and it is the urgent task of the
historian—one of the most useful tasks that he can
perform—to remove the glamorous haloes bestowed
upon them and their instigators.

This irrationality applies in full measure to the
inter-city wars of the Greek world—'all of them
ruinous to the states that made them', said G. B.
Grundy, who is not wide of the mark in ascribing
this persistence in suicidal pugnacity to 'childish
perversity'. A famous inscription tells us that within
a single year (459–8 B.C.) Athenian lives were lost in
various enterprises (some of them disastrous) 'in
Cyprus, Egypt, and Phoenicia', on a Greek island
(Aegina), and at two points on the mainland (Halieis
and Megara). It could not be argued that many of
these men lost their lives in *defence* of themselves, of
Athens, or even of any larger unit to which Athens
belonged. It is not therefore enough to comment,
with Sir E. Barker, that they are signs of 'unbounded
and unstinted political energy'.

War belongs to the sphere of politics (p. 134); and

there can be no more serious indictment of any political institution or development than to assert, as is here asserted of non-defensive war, that it is irrational. For 'a wider diffusion of the specific virtues that flow from a due respect for reason is an absolute precondition of any measures for civilisation's survival proving effective' (C. A. Campbell). Quite early in the Iron Ages of societies, if not earlier, thinking people began to appeal to what they believed to be reason. The appeal was strongest in Greece. But among the Greeks, as elsewhere, the appeal was unsuccessful; and the failure to listen to it was the principal cause of the failure of their and other civilisations. The great duty of political humanity was, and is, to build up a respect for reason—'a scientific habit of mind in forecasting the effects of our actions; the habit of taking account of all relevant evidence in arriving at a belief' (Rivers). Throughout history there is only one way to avoid the worst political disasters: 'through acts of free-will on the part of morally enlightened, intelligent, well-informed and determined individuals, acting in concert'(Aldous Huxley). It is true that 'reason', as well as anything else, can be distorted by propaganda into seeming to be what it is not at all; but it is also true that most people who are really guided by reason do not generally think so very differently from one another in connection with each individual crux as it appears (H. G. Wells).

Reason, then, deprecates nothing more strongly than all wars, other than those of a truly defensive kind. So does morality. Here we have no need to consider the question whether the ultimate sanction of morality is rational or whether it is not; for in this case reason and morality point in exactly the same direction. In his disapproval of non-defensive wars, the teacher or writer of ancient and modern history is supported not only by reason, but also by morality, however defined. Even at first sight it seems clear enough that aggressive war is morally wrong.[1] But it is always worth reasserting, since the edges of this truth have been misleadingly smudged by certain irrelevant objections. Four of these deserve to be mentioned.

(1) One is little more than a 'red herring'. It is the 'dilemma' of Athenian behaviour. We are said to owe much of the brilliance of Athens to her deliberate breaches of faith with her allies in the fifth century B.C. (p. 118). This point was explicitly made at the time. In the Funeral Speech of Pericles, transcribed by Thucydides, the imperialism of Athens is defended on the grounds that she was 'the school of Hellas'. It is perfectly true that architectural and sculptural works of art at Athens were paid for by funds extorted from the allies by wars. But this has no bearing on the *moral* aspect of such wars; it is a point of aesthetic, not of moral interest. (Nor, incidentally, are we in a position to judge what Athenian art would have been like without all this money; it might have been just as good.) National culture cannot be held to depend on national power (F. Kuhn). It is again perfectly true that in many respects Athens deserved to be called 'the school of Hellas'. But scholastic tasks, self-imposed or otherwise, should not need to be accompanied by force.

[1] This was also perfectly clear to many enlightened people in the ancient world (cf. p. 131); this is not a case of unfairly judging one period by the standards of another (cf. Preface).

(2) A second difficulty that has been raised in connection with this condemnation of war is that of distinguishing between defensive and other wars. This is, occasionally, impossible or at least difficult (p. 138). This has led some thinkers on the subject to see in war 'a clear case of ambiguity and conflict in the moral sphere' (A. Robertson). It is true that such ambiguities sometimes occur. But they form only a small proportion of those with which the ancient historian has to deal. Often the motives of neither side are defensive. In such cases there is an ethical ambiguity of a sort, but it does not disturb our main thesis that war is evil. The instances that do not seem to harmonise with it are merely the border-line cases, inevitable in every historical study, which remind us that 'nature never draws a line without smudging it' (Churchill). They do not invalidate the general truth of the thesis.

(3) The third objection to it is equally immaterial. This is the assertion that war cannot be immoral since it brings out in people a moral fervour that cannot be brought out in any other way. Now it is perfectly true that war induces a moral fervour, and this is one of the things that have tempted rulers to enter wars. For a foreign war is wonderfully effective in making people forget their material troubles and rally round their government, however bad (indeed this is merely an illustration of the general truth that in times of acute crisis political affairs are more important than economic affairs, p. 20). This, no doubt, is one of the chief reasons for supremely immoral remarks like that of Mussolini: 'war alone ... puts the stamp of nobility upon the people who have the courage to engage in it'. Mussolini was

practically quoting Bismarck's description of war as the 'noblest and holiest expression of human activities'; and Bismarck in turn was echoing an ancient Dorian and Spartan view. Fichte and Treitschke underlined the advantages for the *State*. The feeling is epitomised by Nietzsche: 'the good cause hallows war? The good war hallows every cause!' So 'it merely matters how, not for what object, we fight' (W. Best).

Many of these sentiments were induced by the moral fervour that a war rapidly creates in individuals, thus strengthening States. This effect of wars is undeniable. But it is by no means equally true that the same degree of moral feeling cannot or could not be brought out in other ways; and to assume the contrary is a dangerous form of *laisser aller*. Indeed, far from it being invariably true that 'martial merit is real merit' (Bagehot; cf. Ruskin), such moral fervour in support of any but defensive wars is wholly misapplied. It is 'a sinister perversion of a noble spiritual force' (Toynbee). It is rather true to say that 'only in peace can the virtues of a nation achieve their rightful reward' (Laski). A book by James is significantly entitled *The Moral Equivalents of War*. The 'military virtues' are virtues which, unless displayed in defence, should and can be displayed in other walks of life. It is one of the greatest tasks of society and States to ensure that this is done; or at least that the combative instincts are diverted to a harmless channel (p. 185).

(4) For the remaining objection to the description of aggressive war as essentially evil, the responsibility lies with those who have suggested that governments need not obey the same moral rules as persons. 'We

deny', said Bosanquet, '. . . that someone is guilty of murder when a country carries on war, or of theft when it adopts the policy of . . . annexation.' But if we do, then we should not do so: Bosanquet's assertion is a *reductio ad absurdum* of the dangerous doctrine of sovereignty (p. 154). The only possible conclusion that is not of a highly anti-social character is that there must be no division between the ethics of the State and of the individual: 'the principles of true politics are those of morality writ large', said Burke—and he was echoing the words of the Athenian statesman and philosopher Isocrates in the fourth century B.C.

For this to become a reality, criminal responsibilities must be extended from persons to States; and in this extension the past five years, with its trials of war-criminals, has seen some progress. All the same, for many years assertions like Burke's were seriously discredited; and it is not difficult to see why. The assertions were true enough, but they were sometimes based on an ancient view of society which is hardly tenable. According to this view, society is an exact replica on a larger scale of a human being. This analogy was familiar to the Greek philosophers and was already implied in Egypt as early as the second millennium B.C. Such a theory, like others comparing society to different organisms and mechanisms, is too simple, and was brought into disfavour through its exaggeration by historians and philosophers. Moreover, its practical efficacy seemed to vanish when the Church assumed control of ethics, so that political leaders no longer seemed responsible for morality. However, it remains true that a society or government bears more resemblances to a person than to anything else (G. D. H. Cole); and one of those resemblances lies in the morality which it should practice. By making war, except in self-defence, a State is acting as evilly as a man is acting when he commits a murder. To judge from the trials of 1945–51, this has now been accepted by international lawyers; and it is a conclusion which the teacher and writer of ancient history cannot ignore. If they would feel an obligation, in their exposition, to speak of murder as a bad action, then they are under the same obligation with regard to non-defensive wars.

A perusal of text-books, as has been suggested, shows that, far from this being put into effect, a bloodthirsty bellicosity or at best callousness (which has the same effect) is much more common. Striking examples are discoverable in accounts of the atrocities of the later Roman Republic. The avoidance of such attitudes is a necessity. It is also very far from meriting the charge of what is known as pacifism (p. 136). Nor is it so revolutionary as our text-books might lead one to think. Already in the time of Thucydides the morally debasing effects of war were as clear as its irrationality. 'In peace and prosperity', he says, 'both States and individuals are actuated by loftier sentiments because they do not find themselves suddenly faced with imperious necessities. But war takes away the easy provision of daily wants, and is a violent teacher: *it brings most people's characters down to the level of their fortunes.*' In another passage one of his speakers, the Syracusan Hermocrates, puts forward the view that the evil nature of war is so familiar a proposition to everyone that it would be tedious to develop it. If it is tedious, this is not due to any over-familiarity, for the conclusion in question has singularly failed to impress itself on the course of events or on those seeking to describe them. Later, again, one of the first great Christian writers of the Roman Empire, the North African Tertullian, argues that the true ethical bases of war are fraud, cruelty, and injustice.

In more modern times, the same has often been said again, though still without effect on many of those who teach and write history. Spencer cautiously but correctly observed: 'an ethical sentiment, rightly so called, produces repugnance to war'. Aldous Huxley conveys the message more strongly: 'man is unique in organising the mass murder of his own species'. This is 'the greatest evil of the modern world' (Hankins)—'nothing but an unmitigated disease of civilisation' (Malinowski). And of particular relevance to historians (even if they disagree with some of his other views) is this assertion of J. B. S. Haldane: 'a book glorifying war may be quite as anti-social, and to my mind quite as obscene, as one glorifying illicit love, but it is never suppressed, and seldom publicly denounced'.

Now if, in teaching and writing to the young, all wars other than defensive ones are not spoken of with the moral and rational disapproval that they deserve, the teacher or writer is half-way to this anti-social obscenity. It is true that earlier it was suggested that history should not be regarded as conveying moral *lessons* (p. 27). But that does not mean that undoubtedly immoral actions need be treated, at least by the 'universal' historian and teacher, as morally colourless. 'It is no proof of impartiality to treat wickedness and goodness as on the same level' (Theodore Roosevelt). Croce today still holds that history always registers a moral decision; and Acton observed: 'it is the office of historical science to maintain morality as the sole impartial criterion of men and things'. One feels now that Acton was presuming too much when he aspired, or directed the historian to aspire, to apply his yardstick to everyone and everything. Yet in certain matters it remains possible to do so by virtue of a clear-cut issue. Among those matters are all wars that are not undertaken in *defence* of oneself or one's vital interests or the political unit to which one belongs. It is not always possible to say whether a war falls into this category; but it very often does (p. 137). Against aggressive wars it would be insincere not to show 'that legitimate, honest advocacy which a good cause deserves' (G. N. Clark).

J. R. M. Butler points out that the historian is entitled to pronounce moral judgments if he dares, but does so as moralist rather than historian. It may be suggested that the 'general' historian and teacher of history do, in this respect, to some extent partake of the qualities of moralist. The 'general' historian is writing for people who are unfamiliar with the subject and so have not the opportunity to derive from it, for themselves, these important decisions. The teacher has the still heavier responsibility of at least refraining from doing propaganda in favour of unreason and evil. But if he does not label aggressive war with these words when he sees it, he is *implicitly* doing this propaganda. *If he is not explicitly a moralist, he is implicitly an immoralist.* In regard to war, this hazard has not been sufficiently avoided. But it is possible to do so without in the smallest respect sapping the will to self-defence, which does not in the least depend on the attachment of glamour to aggressors.

For the whole of this subject, ancient history provides uniquely valuable material. The 'general' historian and teacher will be doing a disservice if they judge it by rational and moral standards other than those which they apply to issues of war and peace today. Indeed, if they do so, they will be neglecting the means by which they can be of the greatest assistance in the modern world. That is not to say that they must indulge in propaganda without regard to the facts (p. 18). But it does mean that they must treat aggressive war as a phenomenon which is of the utmost importance owing to its supreme frequency throughout history, its supreme relevance to the present day, and its supremely irrational and immoral character. It is therefore clearly of the highest importance to determine why wars have occurred. Ancient history provides a remarkable field for the study of this subject; so the task will now be attempted of determining the causes of ancient wars.

PART II

THE CAUSES OF ANCIENT WARS

CHAPTER V

INTERNATIONAL ANARCHY

ONE of the chief causes of war, in ancient as in modern history, may be defined as *international anarchy*. By this is meant the simultaneous existence, within reach of one another, of separate States bound by no compact sufficiently pressing to prevent wars, which thus become very frequent and hard to avoid. This, rather than any more ephemeral occurrence, is the fundamental expression of human bellicosity. Those who have stressed this include Lord Lothian, Thomas Mann, Sir N. Angell, and Lord Beveridge—like Washington, Lincoln, and Elihu Root before them. 'The fundamental cause of war is neither unjust treaties, nor racial or religious or cultural differences, nor maltreatment of minorities, nor need of raw materials and markets, nor imperialist ambition, nor strategic considerations, nor those broad-shouldered scapegoats, capitalism or nationalism. The cause of war is the anarchy of sovereign States' (Beveridge).

This is as true of the ancient world as it is of today. In substance, the situations of the world today and of, say, ancient Greece differ only slightly. In both there was this international anarchy—the risk, indeed the strong probability, of the highly unstable equilibrium being hopelessly upset at any moment owing to the desire of some State or other for aggression. This equilibrium, such as it is, is traditionally known as the 'Balance of Power'. Gibbon, it is true, felt happily able to remark 'the balance of power will continue to fluctuate . . . but these partial events cannot essentially injure our general state of happiness'. How obsolete that is today!—even if the 'Balance of Power' is likely to remain our lot (E. L. Woodward, E. H. Carr). In the ancient world, too, no balance of power was ever stable enough to create a *modus vivendi*. 'When States talk about the balance of power, they profess the first and mean the second.' But whatever their professions and aspirations, in any case 'the frontier—even if unintentionally—creates the enemy' (H. Freyer).

Today the problem is defined by the term 'sovereignty'. Sovereignty is the condition of States today, and has been the characteristic feature of international politics ever since Bodin and Grotius prepared the way for the conception in the sixteenth and seventeenth centuries. Every sovereign State has the perpetual, inalienable, and *absolute* control of all its own affairs and all its own subjects. The events of the mid-twentieth century give us more than a hint that this idea does not suffice to deal with our chief problem—the avoidance of destruction. This inadequacy is, perhaps, well enough illustrated by the following declaration of the American Senator Borah: 'There are some things in this world more to be desired than peace, and one of them is the unembarrassed and unhampered and untrammelled political independence of this republic.' But there have been cases in history of States feeling politically hampered and trammelled owing to the possession by others of things that they would like. According to this definition, it would be legitimate to go in and get them; but that is precisely the supreme egotism which we most need to render impossible.

This danger is clearly seen in the extraordinary conclusions that have been derived from this doctrine of sovereignty. Machiavelli stressed the powers which the State, thus untrammelled, possessed. Richelieu regarded it as the pattern of God's will. Hobbes drew from it the natural deduction that the individual must be sacrificed to the State. This opened the way to further enlargements on the theme of the essential subjectivity of the individual as opposed to the true, objective reality alleged to be incarnate in the State. It is well known to what lengths this attitude was carried by the German philosophers in the nineteenth century and German men of action in the twentieth. Hegel saw the State as the only standard both of morals and of reason: 'the State is the realised ethical idea . . . the State is absolutely rational'. So to Treitschke: 'the State is the highest thing in the eternal society of man' (the opposite view is that the State is a mere convenience, like a lavatory). This throws the door wide open to wars undertaken for the aggrandisement of the State, and the Nazis who recently unleashed such wars are in the direct line of descent from Treitschke, Hegel, and Hobbes. But they in their turn directly and logically deduced their theories from the Renaissance conception of sovereignty. Treitschke and Hitler have shown us some of the false positions into which this doctrine leads us; and they are positions which invite aggressive war. The same doctrine of sovereignty invites aggressive war in another way too —by preventing the taking of adequate precautionary measures against it. For example, there can be no doubt whatever that a good many of the defensive measures that are today indispensable precautions against destruction impose certain limitations on the political sovereignty of individual States. Here, then, is a second way in which national sovereignty is inadequate and obsolete. Yet, unfortunately, it remains with us today. It remains with us, too, in the shape of the formula 'sovereign equality'—the 'equal rights . . . of nations large and small' (U.N. Charter)—though this 'superstitious respect' for sovereignty is hardly fair to individuals, of whom (quite apart from the equivocal nature of the term 'nation', p. 34) 100 million in one State will thus have no more say than 1 million in another.

Here, then, is a third reason why the principle of sovereignty in which we were all brought up is anomalous. Toynbee describes it as emanating from a 'spirit which makes people feel and act and think about a part of any given society as though it were the whole of that society'. Moreover, he acutely defines the old-fashioned, obsolete quality of this conception. Looking at the present situation with a historian's detachment, he observes that sovereignty may well prove to have been a luxury 'during a brief "modern age"—now ancient history—in which we were enjoying an exceptional spell of freedom from external pressure'.

But the ancient historian must take note of the fact that something, which for all practical purposes resembled this doctrine of sovereignty, prevailed throughout the ancient world. It is true that, legally speaking, the doctrine was not yet in existence. The Greeks, for example, did not think in terms of the ties binding people to sovereign. But they came to much the same practical conclusions by stressing the ties of the individual to the community. Plato and Aristotle show very clearly indeed, however, that by the community they mean the State. Aristotle, for instance, stresses the essential identity of the individual with the State: man 'gives up his will to a will in the formation of which he participated' (Gettell). When Aristotle says 'man is by nature a political animal', what he means is 'apart from the State, man has no meaning' (Barker). It is easy to see that Hobbes, Treitschke and the rest had not very far to go. The Greeks too (except Socrates) had failed to distinguish between conscience and public duty (Zimmern); and, among them too, this failure was a powerful and permanent incitement to let loose their combative instincts in national wars. Indeed, Aristotle was only formulating in philosophical form an attitude that, before his time, was universal in the ancient world. National war, in whatever cause, was considered justifiable— as a glance at our survey of ancient history immediately shows.

His formulation was not forgotten when Rome developed her legal system: the theory of State sovereignty as we know it is a product of the law of classical Rome. But other civilisations of the ancient world, too, had by now transferred their practice of State-worship into theory. Among these were the Indians. They did not, it is true, feel so much that the individual was *identified* with the State, which they regarded rather as a force external to him. Nor were they so interested in doctrines of the State as in the art of government. But one of the principles of this art which they evolved (*artha*) may roughly be translated as 'expediency', and has often been compared to the points of view of Bodin, Machiavelli, and Hobbes. In China, too, similar theories emerged in the fourth century B.C. from the minds of the great Legalists, of whom the first was Shang Yang; and these theories bore terrible fruit in the following century, for the totalitarian Ch'in régime was conducted on closely similar lines (p. 52).

So modern doctrines of the separate, self-sufficient, sovereign character of the State have their roots very firmly in the ancient world. This, indeed, is one of the chief reasons why the central theme in ancient history was almost always war. For every word of the strictures of Lothian and Beveridge on international anarchy is applicable in equal degree to the ancient world. Indeed, it is perhaps not until the twentieth century that we have reached a degree of international anarchy equal or comparable to that which prevailed during almost the whole course of ancient history.

Roughly speaking, ancient political history can be divided into two sorts of period—those in which the most highly civilised States were large, and those in which some of them were large but some were also small. Thus in the third millennium B.C. we hear much of city-states as well as of fairly large empires. The second millennium, on the other hand, was preeminently an epoch of large States (Egyptian and Hittite empires, Shang China, etc.). In the last millennium B.C. we begin by returning to the former situation: we have to consider the Greek and Indian city-states (and soon the break-up of Chou China

into smaller units) as well as the great empires of
the Middle East. Then, with Alexander the Great,
Chandragupta, and Rome, we return to an epoch
comparable to the second millennium B.C., in which
the civilised world was divided among great States
again.

Here this distinction is only worth making because,
often enough, historians have exalted the one type of
period at the expense of the other; and because it
needs to be pointed out, from the point of view of
international relations, any such preference is illegitimate. For, during both sorts of period alike, international anarchy prevailed and continued. During
the periods of great States, force was at most times
the sole criterion. During the second millennium B.C.,
it is true that diplomatic relations were also much
employed. But they were employed, as so often
today, as an adjunct to force; any doubts on this
point may well be illustrated by the continual military upheavals and chaotic political changes in areas
not strong enough to stand alone, such as Syria. The
great Hellenistic States, again, possessed no equilibrium other than that which was bloodily but
precariously afforded by force. None was strong
enough to overwhelm the others, but international
anarchy continued. 'Sovereign' States provide the
prototypes of George Orwell's terrible vision of a
world of three great States permanently at war.
Moreover, when 'sovereign' States achieved this large
size, there were, in ancient times, additional factors
of a technical nature which added to the risk of disturbances. 'When nothing could move faster than
a horse it was difficult for the central government
to keep a firm hold upon outlying satraps or

pro-consuls, who were apt to rebel, sometimes succeeding in conquering the whole Empire . . . it took a long time to move an army from one part of the empire to another, and . . . the civil government had not discovered ways of preventing military insurrection' (Russell). This was one of the principal causes of the forcible dissolution of the Roman Empire (p. 241). In the case of earlier States, similar weaknesses had led to the encouragement of external as well as internal wars, for they had invited neighbouring powers to intervene.

Thus at periods when the civilised world consisted of large States the international anarchy caused by the ancient brand of 'sovereignty' was very severe. But it must not be thought that, when some States were small, conditions were any better. One of the most characteristic forms of small State in the ancient world (as in medieval Italy, etc.) is that described as the 'city-state', and this particularly deserves consideration. The term 'city-state', however, is misleading (Wilamowitz). It is true that these States contained a city—or rather, in most cases, a small town, for we use the word 'city' in these cases where we should not use it today. It is also true that they were ruled from that town. But they did not consist only of it. There was practically always a strip of country as well, and this formed an integral part of the community. The German word *Kleinstaat* represents the conception better than 'city-state' (A. W. Gomme), especially as the Germans have the additional convenient word *Kleinstaaterei*, which, relevant also to the German principalities of former days, emphasises the minuteness of scale.

It is this smallness of scale which is the most

striking feature of the ancient city-state. In the first
place, it almost invariably comprised only *one* town.
Secondly, the total area of these 'sovereign', independent, political units was often very small indeed.
They were sometimes larger, it is true, in India and
China, where there is much more room. But among
the Sumerians of S. Iraq, where the earliest city-
states known to us were situated, these independent
political units were extraordinarily close together and
so extraordinarily small. And the same is true of
Greece, which—though not the founder of the city-
state as is far too often believed—has produced by
far its most famous examples. The Greeks lacked the
sense of the political significance of territorial extent
(F. Ratzel). Athens is quite exceptional in possessing
an area as large as 1000 square miles. On the other
side of the balance we may place the Aegean island
of Ceos, which, though only 65 square miles in area
(one-quarter of the size of Rutlandshire), possessed
four 'sovereign' States using three separate currencies.

But that degree of particularism is only a very
slight exaggeration of the situation existing throughout the wide areas in which Greek culture prevailed.
Geographical barriers encouraged this particularism,
and the three ideals of the Greek city-state were all
directed towards maintaining it. In order of praise-
worthiness these ideals were liberty, autonomy (the
right and possibility of using one's own laws and
constitution, and great care was taken to ensure that
lesser loyalties of tribe, clan, etc., should not com-
pete), and autarky—the fatal self-sufficiency. This
combination of ideals, naturally enough, led to international anarchy in its acutest form. Where States
were so very numerous and closely packed, the

danger of war was clearly serious; and from very early on it was felt that the best and easiest way of achieving self-sufficiency was by stealing land. Nietzsche was not far wrong in seeing the 'Will to Power' as the dominant theme in Greek history (A. H. J. Knight). So unfolded the story of wars that has been recounted in our brief survey—'a degree of anarchy which to a modern mind would seem intolerable' (Russell). This led directly and inexorably to the annihilation of the very liberty which the system was intended to maintain. These disputes positively invited annihilation; thus the cities of Sicily were always willing to call in Carthage against each other. The Greek, despite the extraordinarily elevated standards of his art and literature, 'failed where failure is irremediable—in politics' (Grundy); and he paid the inevitable price by undergoing political extinction.

This is only part of a wider charge against the city-state—the inefficiency that has so often been described as its curse. This extends to matters other than politics. For example, its persistence in politics had most damaging economic results. If the city-state was to prosper, it needed to develop specialised farming for purposes of export; but this required a measure of understanding between cities which the prevalent doctrine of autarky prevented from ever coming into existence. This autarky stood in direct contradiction to 'an economic system based inexorably on an international trade on at least a Mediterranean scale' (Childe). Moreover, this inefficiency which hindered co-operation and thus caused wars, also prevented the wars from being well conducted. In spite of their extreme bitterness (p. 130), the retention

of man-power was continually hindered by the
needs of harvesting and by bankruptcy, and the
operations of shipping were hazardous and precarious.
'The ancient State was . . . chiefly a killing machine
and a weak one at that' (Gilbert Murray). But any
cruelties which this weakness may have spared the
Greeks were supplied, in good measure, by another
of its effects—the indecisiveness of wars, and their
consequent renewal and repetition, often amounting
to semi-permanence.

These are all results of the jealous particularism of
the small Greek States. Athens, the most conspicuous
of these States in its aesthetic and literary achievements, is also the most conspicuous in its 'inveterate
self-stultifying egotism' (Toynbee). As regards politics, at least, 'nothing cures one so thoroughly from
the miserable beautification of the Greeks into an
ideal as Thucydides'—who understood the whole
tragic situation (A. H. J. Knight). We must not read
the glories of Greek art, literature, and philosophy
into Greek politics, which were, during the classical
period, warlike, aggressive, and debased. As H. P.
Hall remarks about an earlier period of anarchy, 'it
has usually been so in the history of the world.
Periods of unintelligent and barbarous petty quarrel-
ling, killing and absence of controlling authority have
generally been transfigured in legend as days of
romantic chivalry.'

This is of extreme importance to us, because 'the
Greek civilisation broke down in the fifth century B.C.
through failing to find a successful response to the
very challenge which is confronting our own Western
civilisation in our own lifetime' (Toynbee). This
analogy is one which the teacher or writer of history,

whose aim it is to find what is most topical in the
ancient world, will need to stress most earnestly. It
has often been said that the weakest point in a
modern democracy is foreign policy. Precisely the
same was true of the ancient city-state (T. R.
Glover). No one (with the partial exception of
Isocrates in the fourth century) devoted attention to
foreign relations; no Greek thought in terms of
co-operation between cities (Zimmern). Autonomy
and especially autarky made this impossible. This
is strikingly noticeable in the Greek political thinkers.
One of the first of these, Phaleas of Chalcedon (on the
Bosphorus), is recorded as having concentrated on
home affairs and totally ignored foreign policy. We
learn this from Aristotle (fourth century B.C.). Yet this
was precisely Aristotle's own weak spot too; for he
stresses that a government must aim exclusively at
autarky, and steer clear of attempts to secure the
assistance or goodwill of other city-states.

Both Aristotle and his master Plato regarded it as
inconceivable that the Greeks could live on any basis
other than that provided by the city-state. Indeed,
'perhaps its greatest efficiency issued from its part in
Greek philosophy' (V. Ehrenberg). Aristotle was
quite unconscious that the city-state 'did not work'.
He does not argue, but assumes, the superiority of the
small State. Yet he was a client of the Macedonian
court (he came from Stagirus on its southern borders),
and it was in his day that the strength of the Macedonian monarchy showed up the fundamental weakness
of the city-states—their inability to live in peace
with each other, and consequent inability to face a
shock from outside.

This crisis is presented to us in the most dramatic

possible form by the two Athenian orators Isocrates and Demosthenes. For Isocrates saw the writing on the wall, and urged the acceptance of Philip's leadership; while the speeches of Demosthenes fight a gallant, uphill, losing battle on behalf of the free, autonomous, autarkic city-state. Controversy has raged in modern times as to the 'rights' of this dispute; and there is no need to enter into it, for 'rights' can be variously defined. W. Jaeger sums up the case of Demosthenes as follows. 'His resistance', he says, 'to the forces moving his age was a fulfilment of a supra-personal law—the law by which every nation tries doggedly to maintain the pattern of life moulded by itself, founded on its own natural disposition, and responsible for the highest achievements in its history.' But it is legitimate to add that the same pattern was also responsible for the eternal blot on its history, the unending warfare which must outweigh almost any advantages; and that so great a desire to avoid change can also be described as 'the extreme deadliness of an infatuation with some past institutional or technical achievement' (Toynbee).

Thus in the ancient world systems of small States, like systems of large States, produced unending international anarchy and warfare. For the combative instinct in human nature was given a lethal outlet by those principles called by the Greeks autonomy and autarky, which thus had precisely the same practical effects as the principle of 'sovereignty' has had in modern times. That is to say, the existence of these many, independent, self-sufficient States caused and causes war. None of them felt able in any way to modify their self-sufficiency, what we should call their sovereignty. They were, therefore, unable to live together, in much the same way (to use the hoary analogy of the human being) as individuals are unable to live together if they are prepared to make no concessions. So there were incessant wars, leading directly and inevitably to total collapse, and to the complete elimination of the Greek civilisation as a political force. So much has often been said; and we may again emphasise how close the analogy is—closer than most analogies comparing the ancient and modern worlds—between the destructive self-sufficiency of the city-states and the same quality in the sovereign nation-States of today, the 'age of international anarchy'.

This analogy would seem to make Greek history a matter of peculiar interest to the student, because of this poignantly similar situation and its obvious instructiveness. So it is surprising to find that relatively little attention has been focused on the most constructive and least discouraging part of this story, namely, the remarkable endeavours of those prolific thinkers the Greeks not only to diagnose this disease but to overcome it, by breaking down this fatal unco-operativeness in favour of combination. I do not refer to mere temporary alliances, either for fighting or political purposes. Shortlived military alliances like those of the Greeks against the Persians were nothing new. They went back far even beyond Troy —witness Genesis, Chapter xiv, with its large-scale alliance mobilised by Chedorlaomer of Elam in the eighteenth century B.C. Such unions may be gallant, or they may be merely violent, but in any case they are transient; after the war they vanish. For similar reasons it does not seem that the teacher or writer of general history, faced with the necessity for rigorous selection, needs to say too much about the usual sort of political alliances. These are merely hit-or-miss expedients to preserve that inevitably precarious thing the 'Balance of Power'; and they have throughout history proved unable to guarantee peace. This is because their members are unrestrictedly sovereign States, and are therefore automatically unable to live together in peace for long.

On the contrary, what should excite the historian, and should be made to excite the student, is the sort of measure intended to break down this bad-neighbourly quality, and so to reverse this constant destructive and suicidal trend. This type of endeavour is notably exemplified in the Greek and Roman world, firstly, by the great initial advances in law, and secondly, by the various kinds of political union transcending mere alliance. Nothing could be more inspiring than to trace back great ideas which marked a determined step away from international anarchy. Thus a vital part of ancient history is the history of ancient law, and its gradual advances towards rational principles of international relations. An impressive legal system, strongly directed against extortion, is already found in the Sumerian State of Urukagina in the middle of the third millennium B.C.; and in the eighteenth century B.C. such reforms were incorporated in the great legal codification of Hammurabi. But this, and the more developed Assyrian code which followed, were chiefly concerned with law as a means of keeping a just order. It remained for the Greeks to fasten the law to an absolute standard of morality, thus setting it above the lawgiver —where it remained for centuries, with occasional reversals, notably under the Greek 'democracies' in which, instead, numbers, as represented in the Assembly, were regarded as sovereign (p. 200). Here I am indebted to my colleague P. B. R. Forbes, who points out that this conception of *Eunomia* is one of our most important and characteristic inheritances from Greek thought; it held the field throughout medieval and modern history, until the French Revolution revived the 'democratic' conception. Forbes also points to a passage in the very early poet Hesiod which stresses the special significance of *Eunomia* for our present study. For Hesiod recognised that this absolute morality was the opponent of war. There are three sisters, he says, who 'mind the works of men'—Justice, Peace, and *Eunomia*.

Here, then, is one of the leading ideas which mark resistance to international anarchy. Practical expressions of this supra-national morality are found in the adumbrations of international law which already appear in the Greek and Roman world—notably arbitration of disputes, commercial treaties, exchange of 'consular' agents, and at Rome the *fetial* code which (at least in theory) required that wars should be just. Most important of all was the Greek philosophical doctrine of the Natural Law. This was a principle, derived from the Stoic Brotherhood of Man (p. 209), which recognised 'the law imposed on mankind by common human nature, that is by reason in response to human needs and instincts' (F. de Zulueta). This was combined, at Rome, with native Italian conceptions such as the *ius gentium*, which covered rules applying to citizens and noncitizens alike. Such enlightened ideas, and others such as the moral purpose of law, the validity of

common-sense standards, and the idea of giving each
man not equality but *his own*, all play their part in
the remarkable legal system which is Rome's greatest
gift to the world. Among the most distinguished
jurists of the empire were Salvius Julianus (d. *c.* A.D.
169), Papinian (d. 212) and Ulpian (d. 228). It is
regrettable that owing to a modern dichotomy of
studies their names are rarely heard from teachers or
writers of general history.

Another topic scarcely accorded in text-books,
though one of the most important governmental
developments of all time, is the Greek and Roman
experimentation in dual citizenship, that is, in the
possession by one person of more than one citizenship. It is not an easy subject (though an untechnical
formulation of it should be attempted), and this is
not the place to discuss it in detail, either in its Greek
formulations or in the great part which its modifications played in the Roman State. But its essential
feature may be described as a deliberate attempt to
create an institution which will allow the member of
a small State to rise above its fatally narrow limits,
by possessing other actual or potential citizenships
as well. This other citizenship, granted either to
individuals or to whole communities, may take either
of two main forms. Either it is simply that of another
State—in which case here at least are two States that
have finally become much less likely to go to war
with each other, and so have begun to solve their
greatest historical problem; or it is that of a union
or league transcending single States altogether. In
the latter case one is on the way to an even greater
and more inspiring possibility, the elimination of war
over a much larger field.

Here, too, one is in the presence of that great subject which may roughly be described as Federation. This is a comprehensive term under which may be included every sort of inter-State combination surpassing mere alliance, that is, every sort which achieves the indispensable sacrifice of some sovereignty (by every participant) to the common good. Here is a strikingly topical and important subject for the student of history. For everyone today needs to consider most urgently, with every scrap of evidence that can be collected, the possibility that our annihilation can only be avoided by unions of this degree of closeness. There was a terrible accuracy in Lord Lothian's prophecy sixteen years ago: 'While public opinion today may be far from thinking in these terms, events are driving the issue to the front with tremendous speed.'

Whether we like it or not (and many people are instinctively opposed to such a conclusion, p. 22), this is the burning question of the mid-twentieth century, because it is the question on which hinges our survival. It receives remarkable and illuminating documentation from the ancient world, and particularly from the history of Greece. Yet, for reasons which will be suggested on the next page, this information has been gravely neglected (Halecki). Not long after the middle of the nineteenth century, E. A. Freeman wrote an account of ancient Greek federations which is the classic study of the subject. It is a brilliant book. But even since the latest of its editions, research has advanced greatly. Yet it has had no successor.

One principal reason why it has had no successor is very illuminating for the historian today—namely,

the intensive feeling and prejudice engendered by
questions of sovereignty and of its mitigation. Sovereignty is so jealous and sensitive a subject that the
words federation and federalism are always tending
to go the way of all political terminology and become
charged with emotions that impede understanding (p.
212). The present writer, for instance, feels obliged
to anticipate all sorts of suspicions and to stress that
he is not canvassing here for or against this or that
particular form of inter-State union advocated or
deprecated today. He is urging, in general terms and
without entering into modern partisanships, that the
subject is an important and burning one.

This *caveat* is not so far-fetched as it sounds. For
it is certain that such readings of modern antipathies
into historical studies have directly cramped the
study of ancient federalism. Already in 1862, Freeman observed that research on this topic had been
discouraged owing to disillusionment caused by the
American Civil War. Soon afterwards it was discouraged again by the federation of Germany.
Research in many countries found that it could not
survive the uncomfortable fact that a government
which they did not favour happened to have become
the most conspicuous federation; and certain historians, on the other hand, allowed German institutions to flavour their study of ancient federalism.

It may be objected that, earlier, it was said to
be desirable that a modern tone should be given
to ancient history (p. 17). But it is one thing to
stress ancient federations as a subject deserving
modern study, and another to allow one's thoughts
concerning them to be perverted by modern prides
or antipathies. It is to some extent because of

such irrelevances that E. A. Freeman's fundamental work on the subject has not had the successor which has for many years been needed.

Freeman was keenly interested in the Achaean and Aetolian Leagues of the third century B.C., and he concentrates on them almost exclusively. But this means that he says much too little about far earlier federal experiments that possessed even greater political significance. Our information about them is hard to come by; but it is now clear, for example, that the federations centred on Thebes (Boeotia) and Olynthus (not far from Salonica) as early as the fifth century B.C. include features of a most original and noteworthy character.

Moreover, a study of the coins now suggests that there may well be equally early origins of the Lycian League (S. Anatolia). Montesquieu recognised this to be the most perfect of all federations in form, because it incorporated the true representative principle which the constitutions of ancient national governments were never able to achieve (p. 199). The Lycians were not always regarded as Greeks—even in the Hellenistic and Roman times in which their League achieved maturity—but here, as so often a more important factor than their race, was their acquisition of the Greek culture which lay at their borders. They acquired it, and added to it their own specific achievement, a truly representative federal government. This achievement on the frontiers of Hellenism reminds us that, at the other periphery, the Leagues of the Latins may well prove to have reached quite a high degree of political maturity even as early as the sixth century B.C.; and that these precedents, and Greek advances in federalism, dual citizenship and the like, all later played their part in the imperial Roman capacity to combine central control with local self-government. While the Roman Empire did this, it enjoyed the only lengthy period of peace which the ancient world ever knew.

These movements towards combination and co-operation comprise a subject which is highly relevant to the chief problems facing mankind; and it would be amazing that it should be so neglected were it not for the fact that 'with incurable obstinacy modern writers on the growth of mankind and the development of civilisation ignore co-operation and emphasise competition' (p. 182). General histories of antiquity could, with benefit, be rewritten around this and kindred topics. Moreover, federalism is one of the subjects which most strongly justifies the historian's allocation of more space and time to the Greeks, Romans, and Italians than to other parts of the ancient world (p. 108). For these were the peoples responsible for its vast progress and development: here is the topic which is truly classical. The rest of the world provided comparatively few preliminary or competing attempts. China, it is true, in the ninth to sixth centuries B.C., shows unions that might almost be called federal; but it is suggested by a covenant of 652 B.C. that their organisation may have been too vague and loose fully to deserve such a designation. The ancient history of federation is almost entirely Greek and Italian.

Unfortunately, however, it is on the whole a record of failure rather than success. However, even these failures were epoch-making; and even the experiments and 'blue-prints' are extraordinarily instructive, not least because of the nature of their failure.

In Greece, federalism succumbed repeatedly to the marked preference of the Greeks for international anarchy. In Rome the contributions of federalism to political history were real; but they were before long overshadowed by the great predominance of the central power. Thereby, Rome for a time, in the end, eliminated international anarchy. Yet the price was a high one; for the means was force. Anarchic violence was eliminated by violent methods. Here, in a word, is the paradox of ancient history. There was only one way of removing international anarchy by non-violent methods, and that was federation; but it failed, and so the way was left open for the more forcible method. For us today this is a most relevant and poignant situation. Are we, unlike the ancient Greeks, going to co-operate enough to achieve survival? If not, then we too will succumb to force, for ours too is an age in which political units cannot exist for long in self-sufficiency and anarchy.

So the Roman solution was a second-best one. Yet, with that ruthless immorality which history some-times shows, it scored a remarkable measure of success—not so great a success as federalism might have scored (p. 212), but a remarkable success all the same. For it did, for a time, genuinely succeed in abolishing international anarchy. It did so for a very simple reason. It occupied such a vast region that there was no people on its frontiers which could seriously contest its power or revive the anarchic struggles of nations. Thus, during most of the first two centuries of our era, peace reigned. The Arsacid Parthians did not control their own realm strongly enough to cause the Roman emperors anything more than purely local disturbances; and the Han Empire was too far away to have direct relations with Rome. So the *Pax Romana* reigned, and Rome's earlier violence had ended with a solution of the age-old problem of the ancient world.

It is not the sort of solution which we can envisage today—and we shall be assisted to do so if we note the lessons of ancient history. But none the less it was a solution, and it is therein that the greatness and importance of the Roman Empire lies. It does not lie in any major improvements in imperial organisation. Just as the Greek city-state was not an original political form, so we can trace in the Near and Middle East, and a very fascinating process it is to do so, a continual series of improvements in imperial administration throughout the last three millennia B.C. In this respect at least, there was Progress (p. 12); though the first empires were not the cruellest. Here were some of the lessons that Rome could learn, directly or indirectly. Already in *c.* 3188 B.C. Egypt, with its riverain communications, had joined two States (inhabited by two or more races) within a single nation, united by divine kingship. By the middle of the next millennium Lugal-zaggisi of Sumer, another river country, controlled many more peoples, and did so by indirect (feudal) rule. Soon afterwards Sargon of Akkad pursued similar methods on a greater scale, and instituted trading outposts beyond his borders. Then Ur-Engur of Ur paid tribute to the principle of universality (p. 209) by his title 'ruler of the Four Quarters of the World'. The Sumerians and Akkadians also stressed the importance of law.

In the second millennium Egypt replaced feudal by imperial organisation, by establishing commissioners in the conquered Levantine territories. Hammurabi codified the existing laws, and he and other Babylonians caused great financial improvements. The Hittites created a new form of empire, the first great upland, continental State. The Cretans, on the other hand, instituted the first known example of a maritime empire; and they, and the Mycenaeans and Phoenicians, showed the true potentialities of the Mediterranean as a medium of trade. The Assyrians next demonstrated the great powers that a truly efficient army and administration can give; they were the first to divide a huge multi-national empire into provinces, to link it by roads and to obliterate lesser frontiers by mass deportation. The efficiency was maintained over a much greater area still, and the administration humanised out of all recognition, in the great Persian Empire of Cyrus and Darius. This incorporated all the merits of past systems, along with a novel tendency to peace and a toleration under which, for example, Ionian Greek philosophers enjoyed an unparalleled freedom of speech, contacts, and original thought. After this climax the Roman achievement in administration, at most, was to combine a not inferior system with the federal experiments of the Greeks, dual citizenship and the like, and of the Latins themselves.

The real Roman achievement was the creation of a State which, owing to the lack of any truly formidable neighbours, possessed all the essential qualities of universality: which could—if some of the means of acquisition were forgotten—be linked with the Stoic idea of the brotherhood of all mankind (p. 211). For the best part of two centuries the Roman Empire may justly be described as such a universal State.

Toynbee uses the phrase 'universal State' to denote one of his 'societies' in its imperial stage. It should, perhaps, rather signify a world-State. But there has never been a world-State so far. However, the great Han Empire took the official name 'all that is under Heaven', unconsciously reviving an antique Sumerian claim to universality. The vast size of the Chinese Empire and its formidable land-barriers made this claim seem really true until at last an envoy of the emperor, after twelve years *en route*, brought back news of what lay to the west.

Neither the Han nor the Roman Empire was a world-State; but in those days of less than world-wide communications we are entitled to regard as a universal State something which, though smaller, offered the same guarantee of peace—namely, a State so large that it had to fear no serious competition on any of its borders. The Han Empire failed to achieve this stability: from the beginning it had terrible troubles with the Hsiung-nu to its north. But the Roman Empire was allowed a considerable breathing-space (until near the end of the second century) before it too had really serious trouble in the north; and it was likewise not until the third century that, to the east, the dangerous Sassanid Persians succeeded the less formidable Arsacid Parthians. During this breathing-space, Rome achieved the unique *Pax Romana*, a second-best to the federal union that might have been, but still an achievement that has never been equalled before or since.

The reason why it has not been equalled is simple. It is because, during that period, the Roman Empire was, by the present definition, a universal State—it was, as no other State has been, so big that for a time there was no danger beyond its frontiers. So there was no serious war. Today, the only organisation that can likewise prevent war must, owing to modern communications, be really world-wide. We also must, today, reject the view that it can or should be created by conquest. So we have to try to improve on the ancient world. Meanwhile the Roman Empire is highly instructive to us. For, though created by conquest, it attained a point much nearer to universality than has any other political unit before or since. This was the practical precursor of the universality claimed by the Christian Church (p. 213); but the Church has not yet ever renewed the cessation of international anarchy which ancient Rome for a time achieved.

CHAPTER VI
NATURE AND NATIONALISM

IT has been suggested that the first cause of ancient wars was institutional—that is to say, that it was the international anarchy created by the existence of separate, self-sufficient, States. But institutions were created by the minds of men; and it is in the minds of men that a second great cause of ancient warfare lies.

This, too, is singularly relevant today. For this too is a period when men's minds often seem dangerously unsuited to the task of dealing with the appalling problems that threaten them. 'Twentieth century political thinking is incredibly primitive' (Aldous Huxley). 'In ninety per cent of Europeans, malevolence overbalances shrewdness' (Rivers); and, unfortunately, as C. D. Broad points out, the pace is so largely set by the most backward and evilly disposed individuals and communities. This has a marked bearing on the causes of wars, ancient and modern. For, in addition to the institutional cause, a great deal depends on this question of people's sentiments and opinions. A great cause of war is psychological (C. A. Campbell). Yet, as J. C. Flügel has recently pointed out, politicians, except for certain astute but generally evil rulers of totalitarian States, make little salutary use of the findings of psychology. He rightly deplores the fact that there is, as yet, no 'political psychology' comparable to the well-established branches of medical, industrial, and educational psychology. 'Our so-called social psychology has still as yet only superficial contacts with the stern political realities on which our civilisation may so easily be wrecked.'

The sternest of these political realities is, and was, war. Wars are very largely due to the combative element in human nature. 'Instinctively we divide mankind into friends and foes', says Bertrand Russell. But this does not mean either that we ought to regard our combative instinct as inevitably leading to war, or that we ought to try to stamp it out altogether. It has been usual to exaggerate either in one direction or the other. It has been customary either to hold the comforting opinion that reason is dominant in man, or to take the contrasted view that man is and was, originally and fundamentally, bellicose and destructive. We now find it impossible to share with William Godwin and others the former of these opinions. H. M. Last writes as follows of his first reading of *Human Nature in Politics*, by Graham Wallas, with its criticism of rationalist theories: 'I shan't forget my own excitement at being invited to admit that man is not a wholly rational animal, that his conduct is strongly influenced by sentiment, and that some notorious parts of the political philosophy of the nineteenth century rested on assumptions not all of which were sound. . . .'

The opposite view belongs to the tradition of the early pre-Socratic thinkers. Bias of Priene (in Ionia) observed, 'most men are bad'. In its modern form it is summed up by T. H. Huxley's 'gladiatorial theory of existence'—'nature is red in tooth and claw', and so man (far from being the rational being of Godwin, etc.) is under the same ineluctable necessity of practising internecine warfare.

This view was very early extended from individuals
to States. Hobbes is the notorious exponent of this
analogy. Indeed, we find the process already fully
completed in the ancient world. Early Hindu thought
was close to Hobbes in this respect. Again, a great
Ionian philosopher of the sixth century B.C., Heraclitus of Ephesus, called war 'the father of all and
the king of all'—strife, he said, was the underlying
principle of life. Plato, too, who devotes a wealth of
detail to internal political affairs, shows that as far
as external politics goes he is quite resigned to the
inevitability of war. So are the great orators,
Demosthenes and Aeschines, whom Athens produced
in the days just before her eclipse by Philip of
Macedon. They, like many other Greeks, merely
regarde l war as a normal incident of political life—
war and peace were like sunshine and rain. Indeed
this has been the general opinion until quite lately
—that war did not need justification but was a
natural, normal happening.

An easy corollary of this view was the theory that
it was natural for some to rule over others by force.
This idea appears prominently in ancient Greek literature. The poet Pindar was one of the first to put it
forward. Then Thucydides puts it into the mouth of
a spokesman of imperial Athens, lecturing a recalci-
trant minor subject (Melos) before its destruction
(416 B.C.): 'of the gods we believe, and of men we
know, that by a necessary law of their nature they
rule wherever they can . . . all we do is to make use
of it, knowing that you and everybody else, having
the same power as we have would do the same as
we do'. It is true that the 'liquidation' of Melos
shocked even Greek feeling profoundly; but in the

next century Aristotle returns to the theme. 'The art of war', he says, 'is a natural art of acquisition, for it includes hunting, an art which we ought to practise against wild beasts and against men who, though intended by nature to be governed, will not submit; for war of such a kind is endorsed by nature.' This is the doctrine later put forward by Machiavelli, that it was natural for States deliberately to seek expansion.

All these theories consciously or unconsciously proceed from the assumption that man, like nature, is naturally 'red in tooth and claw'. But, even if we accept for this particular purpose the analogy between individual and State on which this is based (p. 148), modern anthropologists such as Elliot Smith, Perry, and Rivers, have cast grave doubts on the basic assumption regarding man's original nature. It has been decisively shown that methods of evolution are not always, and have not always been, so bloody (C. H. Waddington). Primitive man did not and does not always love fighting, and his early weapons were not well suited to it. Evolution includes not only a Law of Mutual Struggle but also a Law of Mutual Aid (Kropotkin). This was partly explicit in Darwin (and even Protagoras in the fifth century B.C.); but Thomas Huxley and Herbert Spencer, true to the character of nineteenth-century individualism, emphasised the former law and minimised, or even omitted, consideration of the latter (S. Casson). It cannot be said that all mankind is and was, originally, fundamentally, and wholly, bellicose. Thus it is clearly illegitimate to argue, from mankind, that States *have to be* bellicose.

Yet, as we know, both men and States have so often been bellicose. This was already true by the time our epoch of historical study begins. 'The enlargement of the social unit must have been mainly the result of war' (Russell). Indeed, war has proved to be a special feature of these 'civilised' centres— 'where populations are sufficiently dense and culture sufficiently advanced' (J. C. Flügel). Since this point was reached, there have been very numerous wars. Even though it is not necessarily true or the whole truth to describe human beings as naturally bellicose, it has become true to say that man, since his earliest political organisation, has proved himself to be a 'fighting animal. If you train him well and lead him well he will nearly always fight, if necessarily until he is killed' (W. McDougall).

Yet, as has been suggested, unless the purpose of his fighting is the *defence* of threatened interests—as it all too rarely has been—this only means that men or their leaders, or both, have continually acted against the most solemn warnings of their reason and their morality. Why has this been so? Neither of the two theories just quoted can explain this. But it is explained perfectly by the *Dual Code* propounded by Keith and others. This may, in a sense, be called a compromise view; but it does not possess any of the disadvantages which often appear in compromises. According to this hypothesis, man has inherent in him *both* a rational, ethical, sensible, code of behaviour, and also a 'cosmic' code of savage, pugnacious behaviour—or, as J. McMurray puts it, a dualism of intellect and emotion. This was appreciated by Plato, who appoints to look after his Utopia philosophical rulers to correspond to men's rational element, and guardians to represent his 'spirited element'.

Both the spirited element and the rational element

are natural to man, though both are only fully developed by suggestion or education. His propensity to war is part of the 'cosmic' code.

What are we to conclude from this? Our conclusion cannot be too easily optimistic; but equally it cannot be wholly pessimistic. It cannot be too easily optimistic because it now appears that no amount of training and rationality will do away wholly with man's 'largely unconscious primitive ferocity' (Russell). A new theory even goes so far as to regard this as no less essential to man than the sexual instinct, and closely comparable to it. However this may be, it is undoubtedly true that people want glory and violence despite all rational forecasts of the results; and they will try to get them. 'We can debate and scheme and organise and plan for peace; but we can only act for war . . . reason is no match for passion in the practical field' (McMurray). We may recall Kant's comment: 'How can pure reason become practical? . . . if anyone could answer this question he would have discovered the philosopher's stone. . . . Man desires concord; but nature knows better what is good for his species; she desires discord.'

At first sight this might seem to confirm the gloomiest possible pessimism, such as that of Bergson who, in old age, concluded that the chasm from primitive discord to peaceful civilisation was utterly impassable. For there is no longer any hope that *completely* rational behaviour can be inculcated (cf. p. 180). We cannot any longer see any complete solution in Aldous Huxley's panacea of 'checking the cosmic process at every step and substituting for it . . . the ethical process'. This can and must be done up to a point, and any successes that it registers deserve, and must receive from historians, the highest praise (p. 151), but in the end the cosmic process will, we now see, reassert itself. Psycho-analysis has shown that natural impulses cannot be altogether denied. When reason overdoes this business of trying to stamp them out, 'nature takes her revenge by producing either listlessness or destructiveness . . . it is to be supposed . . . that our congenital mental equipment . . . is not so very different from that of Palaeolithic Man' (Russell).

But, in reality, these conclusions do not justify such black pessimism as they might be thought to. For, as Russell goes on to point out, whereas it is true that human nature possesses combative impulses, *it is not true that these combative impulses need to be expressed in war.* Some people are happier in war, but this—unless the occasion is self-defence—is an anti-social outlet that cannot be allowed: innocent outlets can and must be found. Such outlets may perhaps be divided into two categories—those that are of positive value, produced by the successful direction of the martial virtues into peaceful uses or defence, and those that are of negative value, that is to say, those which are of no particular importance to the community in themselves, but which at least succeed in canalising the combative instinct into harmless channels (p. 147). Sport comes into the latter category; though in ancient Greece, at least, the great Games played a positive role in inter-State co-operation.

Neither process is easy; for emotions with desirable or even harmless social consequences are, unfortunately, harder to generate—as history shows—than hate and rage and fear. On one occasion, at least, the alternative thus generated has been hardly better

than war. This is the case in regard to the appallingly
cruel Games of the Roman amphitheatres. The
emperors, who spent enormous sums on these Games,
used psychological skill in thus diverting the people
from warlike policies (and from political strife), but
the alternative that they provided was terrible. But
this is wholly exceptional. Almost any other outlets
for the combative instinct would be easily preferable
to aggressive war. And such outlets can and must be
found; for 'there is nothing in human nature that
compels us to acquiesce in continued savagery'
(Russell).

Moreover, here the analogy between human beings
and the governments which make wars (p. 148) seems
to serve It is true that governments often behave
appallingly, more appallingly, it would seem, than
any human being could. But that is either because
of mass hysteria (p. 203) or merely because governments, being more powerful, have greater means of
evil at their disposal. It is not legitimate to deduce
from either of these considerations that governments
are automatically wholly lacking in the ethical-
rational process which is present in each of their
members. Max Nomad wrote 'there are only two
principles governing all politics. First—to get power
by all means, even the vilest; and second, to keep
that power by all means, even the vilest.' It cannot
be agreed that all governments are by nature as
unethical as that, any more than it can be agreed
that all human natures are wholly unethical or irrational. Indeed, the evolutionary methods of societies
may possibly even prove less wasteful than those of
individuals. In any case, just as there is no reason
to suppose that individuals are under an inescapable

necessity to fight, so equally there is no reason to
suppose that governments are under any such
necessity.

Human nature, then, does not make it inevitable
that anyone should fight aggressive wars, and that
is a fact which teachers and writers of history should
bring to the attention of their hearers and readers as
an antidote to the apparently inevitable succession
of wars of which history seems to consist. These
make it clear to us that, though not inevitable, wars
have so far been abundant throughout history. That
is to say, our combative instinct has continually led
us into wars. This direction has always lain open to
it, and it has been helped to take it by the emotional
attractions of autarky and sovereignty (pp. 154, 161
ff.). Concerning the situation of our own people (as of
other peoples) today, E. M. W. Tillyard comments:
'that they should learn—and not too late—to miti-
gate *their emotional hostility* to any surrender of
national sovereignty is what matters most in world
politics just now'. The italics are put there by the
present writer, because the key to the difficulty is
not so much the juridical institution of sovereignty
as the emotional quality of nationalism which fiercely,
though not always consciously, operates against the
modification of sovereignty.

It has already been observed that war induces the
fires of nationalism to burn most fiercely in the
human breast (p. 147); but they burn pretty fiercely
at other times too. They are not rational or ethical,
but form part of the 'cosmic' process which rules
alongside, or in alternation, with reason and morality
(p. 183). H. G. Wells, who fought against this for a
quarter of a century, concluded: 'nationalism is in

our bones—in our tradition, in our habits, in our blood'. As Archbishop Lang rightly observed, 'nationalism feeds on the most primary and still untamed instincts of the human race'. We have all seen in Nazi doctrine to what lengths this emotional projection of sovereignty can go. For militant nationalism is emotional; it is only rational (or can be rational) on the rare occasions when the forcible defence of one's vital interests or political unit are required (p. 136). The other sort of militant nationalism, the aggressive sort, is irrational. For attempts at warlike expansion very often do not turn out according to plan; non-defensive war is a supremely irrational as well as an unethical procedure (p. 142).

Nor can there, for example, be any logical reason to use force in order to include members of the same 'race' within one's national frontiers. For, apart from the fact that races are inextricably mixed (p. 35), racial and national units are commonly far from coincident; often they cut right across each other (p. 34). 'We are told that patriotism is the outcome of common ancestry. How absurd!' (A. Forel). 'Nations' and 'cultures' are also far from being invariably coincident (p. 31); so are 'nations' and 'languages' (p. 39). The idea of innate national 'characters', national 'geniuses', is discredited. The term nation is of practical assistance just as our own nation is of great practical value to us, but neither must necessarily be identified with any racial, cultural, or linguistic conclusions. Sir Ernest Barker rightly defines national character as 'the sum of acquired tendencies built up by leaders in every sphere of activity'. Words like English, Scottish, British, French (or Hittite, Roman, or Greek) 'serve to denote a people or group of peoples bound together by tradition, or history, or language, or religion, or geographical contiguity, or united by cultural affinity of political usage (or misusage), even if diverse in origin' (Julian Huxley and E. C. Haddon). One sympathises with the difficulties that Woodrow Wilson experienced in connection with this term 'nation' in 1919 (these difficulties have recently been analysed by E. H. Carr). Misapprehensions concerning the character of nations are what cause aggressive wars—and frequently caused them in antiquity; and they too are the causes of the 'emotional hostility' to the modifications in national sovereignty which alone could prevent war.

So that is why, when militant nationalism is not devoted to the *defence* of one's vital interests or political unit (p. 136)—and even then reason will prompt one to effective action, just as much as sentiment (p. 138)—it is 'probably the most widespread and the most dangerous of modern vices. It can hardly be doubted that it does vastly more harm than all the other vices put together' (W. B. Curry). It is, in fact, except on the rare occasions of its legitimate use, one of the most terrible of those 'cosmic' forces in human nature which need harnessing in useful, or at least unharmful, channels (p. 185).

These are matters which ought to be ever-present in the mind of the teacher and writer of general history, and particularly of ancient history. There are the same two reasons as before why this should be so (p. 17). Firstly, it is his duty to concentrate on those aspects of his subject which are of importance at the present day; and no theme could be more topical than aggressive nationalism. Secondly, it is a theme in which the ancient world, too, is singularly rich. Almost all the unending wars of the ancient world were fought under a strong spell of nationalist feeling. 'It is a commonplace that this played a larger part in ancient life than in modern' (F. R. Earp). In general, the aggressive nationalism of the ancient world is closely linked with the attitude to the State that has been described. But it took several forms at different times and in different places, and these varieties are significant since each of them has contributed largely to the modern situation. Perhaps it is easiest to regard the militant nationalism of the ancient world, wherever and whenever it is found, as containing some or all of three principal ingredients—the religious, the racial, and finally the purely patriotic or political ingredient which follows most naturally from exaggerated reverence towards the State.

The religious element in militant nationalism is prominent when different political units honour different gods and pit them against each other. This is a powerful incentive to aggression since it is only 'natural' to regard one's own god as better than the next one and so entitled, from the highest motives, to overcome him. This tendency is clearly seen shortly after 3000 B.C. in the Sumerian city-states —as elsewhere in Mesopotamia, S. Persia, and Syria— where great play is made with these local patronages. It is true that the various city-states sometimes honoured each other's gods as well as their own (though they were often known by different names in the different cities); but this more liberal attitude pales beside the vigorous worship of the local patron. Thus Elamite invaders of Sumer consider it advisable to take the gods of the cities that they have sacked back home with them; and they do. We hear also of the nationalistic hatreds personified by the god Enlil and the goddess Nidaba, patrons of the cities of Lagash and Umma respectively. The men of Umma 'have shed blood in the shrine of Enlil . . . as for Lugalzaggisi, ruler of Umma, may his goddess Nidaba bear this sin upon her head'.

She could do this, because that is why she and Enlil were there—to act as the focus and figurehead of nationalist feeling. This sort of religious national-ism attains dangerous lengths when communities positively refuse to have any truck with deities other than their own, i.e. are 'monolatrous'—when the sphere of the deity is identical with the borders of the nation. Such a doctrine is known as *henotheism*. Whether or not it occurred in Sumerian times, it is found among the Jewish tribes towards the end of the second millennium B.C. The tribal chieftain Jephthah appeals to his Ammonite opponent in these terms: 'Wilt not thou possess that which Chemosh *thy god* giveth thee to possess? So whomsoever the Lord *our God* shall drive out from before us, them will we possess.'

For a short time in the tenth century the Jews, united under Solomon and in alliance with Tyre, formed an important State (p. 94). Solomon diplo-matically recognised a considerable array of deities. But when, after his death, the kingdom split up into two small States, Israel (Samaria) and Judah (Jeru-salem), there was a reaction under the prophet Elijah in favour of a militant henotheism. Jehovah is the only God with whom Israel may have dealings, and woe betide all others. Israel fell to Sargon II of

Assyria in the eighth century, and Judah to the
Chaldaean Nebuchadnezzar of Babylon in 586 B.C.;
and it was not until towards the end of these small
kingdoms that this henotheism gradually gave way
to *monotheism,* the view that there is one supreme
God for all the world (p. 208).

During the intervening period, despite backslidings
by individual monarchs, a pugnacious henotheism
prevailed. The effects of this religious particularism
in stimulating hostility to other peoples is left in no
doubt. Jehovah becomes 'provoked to jealousy with
strange gods' (Deut. xxxii, 16); that is to say, the
Jews attack their Canaanite neighbours. These, with
the support of the religious sanction, are spoken of
in the most ferocious possible terms (Deut. vii, 1-3;
xx, 10-17). Strange lands themselves had long been
regarded as unclean (Josh. xii, 19), an idea which
we also find in early Roman religion.

We are here in the presence of extreme religious
nationalism, and this is of profound importance to
the historian. J. B. S. Haldane gives food for thought
when he observes that religious intolerance is one of
the very few really important discoveries made between 3000 B.C. and A.D. 1400. 'A more or less
intense exclusiveness pervades the Biblical narrative'
(S. A. Cook); and that is why the Biblical narrative,
in the Old Testament, is so largely a record of international anarchy and aggressive war.

Indeed, this nationalistic exclusiveness long out-
lived even the States and henotheistic doctrines
which had originally bred them. It somewhat ana-
chronistically survived both the introduction of
monotheism and the destruction of both Jewish
states (Ezekiel, Haggai, Zechariah). In the ancient

world, the Jews were never again to play an important political part (though the rigorous Maccabee régime of the second century B.C. achieved some importance); but this nationalistic spirit lived on. For it possessed features which did not directly depend on political circumstances.

Of those features *the most significant is the racial.* This is a factor which needs to be observed very closely by the historian. Racialism, such as that of ancient Jews, is based, biologically speaking, on a series of thoroughly exploded fallacies (p. 38). It is, therefore, wholly irrational, and so naturally are the theories—deduced from it—concerning the alleged superiority or inferiority of this or that race (De Gobineau, Rosenberg). But it would be very wrong for the historian to conclude from this that the matter has no interest for him or his readers or students. While it is of vital importance to them that the doctrines are wholly fallacious, it is of no less importance that these fallacies have exercised an overwhelming effect on historical events. Racialism is one of the dominant factors in history. It is also extremely widespread today, so it is a topical as well as an ancient subject.

Since, however, it has no correspondence with reality or rationality, it is very important to discover to what it does owe its predominance in ancient and modern history. There are two reasons for this situation. The first is the extremely easy development of racialism from the combative instinct which is innate in the 'cosmic' part of human beings. A nation has been defined as 'a society united by a common error as to its origin and a common aversion to its neighbours'. That is unfair, but it truly implies that the first of the two unifying factors mentioned, racialism, is continually associated with the second, aggressive nationalism. Aggressiveness both causes racialism and is fostered by it. Racialism comes from the 'cosmic' feeling that the outsider is an enemy. For he is best combated by forming a close-knit group of all who are not outsiders; and that is best united by the assumption, however erroneous, that its bonds are fundamental, sealed in 'blood'—in fact that it is an extension of that natural unit, the family. 'To forget and—I will venture to say—to get one's history wrong, are essential factors in the making of a nation', says Renan, perhaps too pessimistic about its inevitability. Thus grouped into hypothetical 'races', peoples and societies are emotionally equipped to exercise their combative feelings to the full; and the result, more often than not, is aggressive war.

It was suggested that there are two main reasons for this predominance of racialism in history. One reason is this convenient adaptability to the 'cosmic', combative element in human nature. The other reason is the influence of the Jewish attitude that has been outlined. Our society has taken over from the Jews not only the great monotheistic ethics which they eventually evolved (p. 208), but also the race-feeling which was the product of their earlier henotheistic nationalism. The latter very early and indeed almost automatically assumed a racial character, more artificial even than usual owing to the extremely mixed race of the Jews (p. 95), but none the less exceedingly potent. The message which Abraham was said to have received was this: 'I will establish my covenant between me and thee *and thy seed after thee in their generations* for an everlasting covenant' (Gen. XVII, 7); and of this covenant we hear much more. The Jews regarded themselves not only as the Chosen People but as the Chosen *Race*; conversions to Judaism were a much later development. This, then, was a particular reason for the aggressive wars which abound in the Old Testament, just as racialist feeling (largely directed against the Jews) has played a great part in the most terrible of all wars in our own day.

The Jewish form of religious racialism, though virulent, is only one of several forms found in the ancient world. Another form is centred on the king: the king is a god or the son of a god. This is limiting the 'racial' supremacy to one man; but, as regards him, it is going further than the original Jewish view, for now the divine sanction for royal leadership rests not merely in a covenant but in actual divine origin. The most characteristic early manifestation of this divine kingship is in Egypt. The early kings were Horus, Sons of the Sun. Sons of Amen. Such a phenomenon does not occur in Assyria, or Babylonia, or Persia (A. H. M. Jones). Its effect on international relations, and on the sentiment of Egyptians towards them, is easy to see. Here it is not so much *their* race, as their king's race, which justifies nationalism and, where necessary, aggression. Here again a combination of religion and racialism justifies hostility; and this combination played a large part in the creation of the Egyptian empires of the third and second millennia B.C. Similarly, Ion, the founder of the Ionian 'race', was called the son of Apollo; and in the latter part of the Roman Republic it was convenient and encouraging to believe that the founder of the city, Romulus, had a descendant of Venus as his mother, and as his father the war-god Mars himself.

The divine origin of one's rulers and founders was a cast-iron excuse and justification for any sort of conduct. But the Greeks and their contemporaries carried matters one degree further. Whole governing groups and peoples claimed that they were descended from the heroes and gods who were believed to have walked the earth before men. One of the most popular of these deified heroes was Heracles (Hercules). Several attempts were made to annex him as an ancestor; one of the most successful was that of the Dorian invaders who alleged that he had adopted an ancestor of theirs as a son. Much use of this divine link was made later by city-states whose governing classes were, or said that they were, descended from the Dorian invaders; thus the racialism of Dorians and Ionians plays its part in history, though it is not so great a part as that played by racial caste in India (p. 214).

A closer contact with the supernatural was claimed by the Thebans,[1] whose ruling class were of a purely miraculous origin, sprung from dragon's teeth planted by divine advice. Other peoples felt it a better encouragement of nationalism to assert that their people were indigenous in another sense, namely that they had always been there (the Greek word is *autochthonous*). For if they had always been there, then they had been there when the gods walked the earth. This was a frequent claim, and by no means only among people of wholly Greek culture. For example, the Carians in S.W. Asia Minor, and the Sicanians

[1] Thebes, the capital of Boeotia, lies some 35 miles to the north-west of Athens.

in W. Sicily, claimed to be autochthonous. But this sort of origin was particularly asserted by the Athenians. Like the Carians and Sicanians, Athens could point to the fact that the invasions and immigrations that heralded the beginning of the Iron Age had made little impression on her; Attica's geographical seclusion had caused most of the new arrivals to 'bypass' it.

This 'autochthonous' myth became an article of faith to which frequent reference was made by writers. It is not fortuitous that the word appears three times in the most ironical play of the first tragedian to question the old order searchingly, Euripides. Nor is it fortuitous that this play is the *Ion*, named after the mythical ancestor of the whole Ionian 'race' (really an extremely mixed collection, p. 100), of which Athens claimed (mistakenly) to be the mother-city. Ion was the son of Apollo, but 'Euripides treats the story as if Apollo were just a lawless ravisher, utterly selfish . . .' (Gilbert Murray). Euripides was writing in the middle of the harrowing Peloponnesian War. He knew well, and analysed as carefully as Thucydides, the forces that create arrogant and aggressive nationalisms. And high among these he placed autochthonous and divine origins and other perversions of religion into racialism.

The Greek was also a racialist in his opinion that non-Greeks were barbarians (p. 207). However, in the nationalism of the Greek city-states religion and racialism played a proportionally much smaller part than they did in the nationalism of the Jews. It does not follow, however, that Greek patriotism was a weaker force than Jewish patriotism. This was not the case. The fellow-feeling of the Greek city-state was very strong. Indeed, 'the world has seen nothing comparable to it before or since' (A. E. Zimmern); and this applies to aggression as well as to defence. But the ingredients of this nationalistic feeling appeared in different proportions in Greece and Palestine. In Greece the religious and racial stories were merely trimmings or frills. They played their part admirably in propaganda, and such propaganda is a very important subject to study (p. 16). But the main part of Greek nationalism is more directly political. That is to say, it depends directly on the Greek conception of State which has already been outlined (p. 161).

'The chief thing of general interest in a small simple-minded community with a settled climate is not the weather, or money, or marriages, but the State.' The result was an extraordinarily high development of nationalist sentiment. It receives its classic expression in the Funeral Speech attributed by Thucydides to Pericles in one of the early years of the Peloponnesian War. Pericles claims that in the service of his city, the Athenian spends his body as though it did not belong to him, and that he counts his mind mostly truly his own when he is employing it on his city's behalf. This is a very true description of the position; and often indeed we find that the standard of virtue is limited to public service. Unfortunately, however, this public service was more often than not performed in wars of a more or less aggressive character.

There was a special reason why in cities like Athens, wars should have been especially frequent. War, as has been, is usually irrational, and thrives on the emotions. Now the system of government

which prevailed in Athens during the classical period
was one in which particular opportunity was given
for the predominance of the emotions. For this was
the system which the Greeks called 'democracy'.
Democracy is a word which is given a bewildering
number of different meanings today. The Greek form
is of importance to us because it has greatly affected
modern thought through having aroused the enthu-
siasm of Rousseau and Locke. Nevertheless, Greek
'democracy' differed fundamentally from what
Britain, or indeed any other country, understands
by the word today. For it was not representative.
That is to say, those who were enfranchised were
entitled to attend the Assemblies or parliaments
themselves; they did not elect people to represent
them there. The latter sort of arrangement is partly
of medieval and partly of more recent origin. In
ancient times, an isolated case of it occurs in the
semi-Hellenised Lycian federation of S. Anatolia
(p. 172); but neither the Greeks nor the Romans
introduced it into their States.

It is clear to us that the representative system, for
all its faults, is indispensable; but the Greeks and
early Romans, with their smaller populations, would
not have regarded such an arrangement as truly
democratic. For they would not have considered
that it gave possessors of the franchise a large enough
'say' in affairs; for example, the choice of Cabinets
without consulting the citizenry would not have
seemed proper.

So every enfranchised person was a member of the
Greek Assemblies. And, in 'democratic' states, it was
with these Assemblies that the ultimate responsibility
for the government, as well as a great deal of its

business, rested. The Assembly was sovereign: the Greek 'democracies' (therein wholly unlike our own) were governed by what are known as 'primary' Assemblies. This was the practice in the 'democratic' constitutions which Athens and other Greek city-states possessed in the later fifth and fourth centuries B.C. Not every member of the Assembly attended it regularly, but many did—the more since payments for attendance were introduced in the last quarter of the fifth century B.C.

Such payments were new, and the dangerous doctrine of the Assembly's sovereignty was new, but it was not new that the business of a State should be discussed by large gatherings. Indeed, this is a somewhat rudimentary and primitive arrangement which it is not surprising to find in less developed communities. The direct ancestor of Athenian 'democracy' was perhaps the Spartan system. There too the enfranchised body enjoyed great equality one with another, and this helped to change Athens in the same direction (p. 217). This seems paradoxical, since the Spartan system was later regarded as highly undemocratic owing to the vast masses of ruthlessly controlled non-citizens. But in Athens too there were non-citizens who took no part in the Assembly (p. 216). The essential feature of the Assembly was the participation of those who *were* citizens. Plato said that he regarded 5,040 as the ideal number. This reminds us of the Lichchavi State on the Ganges which had 7,707 senators, members of the upper castes (p. 214) meeting 'democratically' one with another. These big meetings (though not necessarily as big as this) probably go back very far in date. We may suspect that they occurred in those communities in which archaeology

reveals that there was no royal or outstanding house-
hold—notably Mohenjodaro in the Punjab, or
Gournia in Minoan Crete, or perhaps even in big
Neolithic villages such as Köln-Lindenthal on the
Danube.

At all events this institution is not necessarily a
sign of very advanced culture. Its important feature
for our present purpose is this. In Athens, as in India,
the Assembly was habitually attended by well over
a thousand people. Even juries numbered 500. This
is highly relevant to the question of emotional
nationalism. For nothing could be more strongly
conducive to emotional nationalism, to aggressive
passions, and indeed to passions of all sorts, than a
very large sovereign Assembly of this kind. This was
clear enough to certain ancient observers. It was
always a source of amazement to the Persians; thus
we find one of their princes confiding to a Spartan
his contempt for 'those who meet in the *agora*[1] to
cheat each other with lies and false oaths'. Another
Persian is reported as remarking that a large gathering of this kind 'rushes wildly into State affairs with
all the fury of a stream swollen in winter and puts
everything into confusion'.

We owe this observation to Herodotus; and indeed
there is ample evidence that the Greeks themselves
were aware of the dangers of these large gatherings.
Thus even the strongly democratic politician Cleon
saw that the Assembly was not fitted to govern.
Plato, listing ancient forms of government, places
what the Greeks called 'democracy' very low in his
order of merit; for he stresses the danger of its getting

[1] The Greek market-place and centre of public and social
life (somewhat like the Roman *forum*).

into the wrong hands. Greek States tried to safe-
guard against this by the creation of a smaller
Council which discussed all business before it reached
the Assembly. But the sovereignty and control, as was
often proved, remained with the Assembly—which
was so large that in most respects it must be regarded
as a crowd, manifesting the behaviour of crowds.

Modern psychologists have analysed more precisely
the close connection between these large gatherings
and the more inflammable emotions such as those of
extreme nationalism. Though their approaches differ
in many respects, they have mostly come to the same
conclusion as Lord Chesterfield: 'mere reason and
good sense is never to be talked to a mob. Their
passions, their sentiments, their senses and their
seeming interests are alone to be applied to'. As
Zimmern puts it, the psychologists have shown that
men are not able to transact business in hordes. A
large conglomeration of people does not merely
behave as the average of the individuals who compose
it. This is well explained in a recent book by R. West,
whose conclusions may be repeated here. In brief,
the standards of judgment and morality shown by a
crowd or large gathering are *lower* than those of its
individual components. 'We all reach our best in
different ways, and the emotional unity of a crowd
can only be achieved on a lower level' (Russell).

A crowd falls into simple uncritical attitudes. It
shows all the signs of irresponsibility; and everybody
feels absolved and safe because of the presence of the
rest. Prudence is forgotten. Elemental emotions,
ordinarily latent or repressed, come to the fore. And
what is particularly relevant to our present study is
the great strength which these tendencies gain from

a common 'axe to grind'—a common hatred. Rage,
intolerance, and aggressiveness are the qualities which
a crowd best germinates (there is that much truth in
Plato's description of the masses as 'concupiscent').
Speakers as well as hearers readily fall a victim to
this irrationality; 'for many men the presence of an
audience acts very much like wine' (W. B. Pillsbury).
Hence emerged the 'demagogue', that parody of the
democratic statesman of which Athens produced
numerous examples. This phenomenon is less apparent in representative assemblies, since speakers are
responsible to their constituents.

Not every large gathering degenerates into hysteria.
Nor even did every Assembly of the excitable Athenians; but a great many of them did. Terrible errors
of judgment were made, many of them under the
sway of the aggressive nationalism induced by crowd-
psychology. The same applies to the large juries—
'about the worst legal system ever invented' (Tarn).
Such matters are of great importance to the historian.
As Russell remarks, nothing could be more instructive
for a student than to concentrate on the emotions
that are the basis of collective hysteria; and many of
these emotions are detectable in the proceedings of
the Athenian Assembly.

The patriotism of the ancient Greek has been
greatly admired. Zimmern, for instance, asserts that
'the greatest legacy which the Greeks have left to the
after-world is their city-state patriotism'. But patriotism that serves aggressive war does not come into
the same moral or rational category as patriotism in
self-defence (p. 136). From the former, we must withhold admiration. If we did not, there would have
been no Nuremberg Trials. We did not and do not

admire the servants of aggressive war who were condemned there. It would therefore be illogical for the historian to express, or seek to instil, admiration for such Greek patriotism as likewise manifested itself in aggressive wars.

Unfortunately, that applies to a great deal of patriotism both in Greece and in the Roman Republic. Very many wars were aggressive, and we find that a high proportion of patriotic feeling and activity was devoted to the preparation of these wars and, in general, to hostility towards other States. *The citizen was always in training for war,* and the spirit in which he trained was far from defensive. For patriotism was, as so often, accompanied by a very strong feeling of national exclusiveness, which was readily transmuted into war regardless of the justice of a cause. This emotional and psychological situation, so analogous to one of our great problems today, is well analysed by F. R. Earp: 'though the number of acknowledged ties gradually increased . . . even the Greeks of the fifth century had not quite outgrown the stage at which men not bound by any tie are naturally hostile . . . the frame of mind that belongs to the member of a small tribe living among other tribes, all potentially, and in fact normally, hostile'. Patriotism expended, in accordance with such sentiments, in attacking a neighbouring city (as opposed to patriotism expended in defending one's own) is the very opposite to praiseworthy, and would indeed rightly have reserved its more eminent possessors places at Nuremberg. But it was for such actions, unfortunately, that a great part of the patriotism of Greeks, Romans, and other ancient peoples was reserved. It therefore forms a close parallel with the

aggressive nationalism which is one of the chief
causes and accompaniments of the international
anarchy of today. This is a parallel which teachers
and writers of history are under some obligation to
point out. For if they praise the aggressive national-
ists of antiquity, they are praising the criminals of
the Nuremberg Trials. And it would not be true to
say that there was no awareness among the Greeks
of their evil situation (p. 131).

So if the first cause of ancient war was the international anarchy due to self-sufficiency—what we
should today call 'sovereignty'—the second was
aggressive nationalism. But in both cases the picture
has to be completed by a brief reference to the more
hopeful aspect—that is to say, to the strivings of the
ancient peoples to overcome the fatal defect. In the
case of international anarchy, it has been pointed out
that this obverse side of the coin is provided by a
series of unsuccessful but none the less highly significant experiments in federation (p. 172). In the case
of aggressive nationalism, it is provided by a series
of brilliant philosophical advances. These had a
direct effect on events, and so they are part of history
as well as of philosophy. There is nothing unusual
about this. Despite all that the materialist view has
to teach us, thought, however abstract, does continually influence history. J. B. Bury went so far as
to say: 'thought is the characteristic and guiding force
of history'. It may or may not take a long time to
work its way through; and then suddenly, even
'speculation that seems airy may bring down an
abundant rain of events' (E. Barker). This, incidentally, should be an encouragement to the writer or
teacher of history, or to anyone else endeavouring to

impart information. For history shows that there is not necessarily an insuperable gulf fixed between himself and the men who decide whether wars are to happen.

So, too, it was in the ancient world. Efforts were made to combat, by rational and moral means, the evils that caused wars. Efforts were made, that is to say, to supersede aggressive nationalism by arguments tending to more liberal beliefs. For example, much of the thought that led to experiments in federation was based on the idea of Pan-Hellenism. This was the idea that Greek owed some decency to Greek, a limited conception but still a much higher one than the hostile particularism of city-states. Pan-Hellenism, like federation, never achieved important practical results; but, again like federation, it deserves the most careful study as a recurrent motive for historical events. Its great exponent Isocrates, in the fourth century B.C., took over the idea from the 'sophist' (or critical philosopher) Gorgias, of the fifth century. But Pan-Hellenism had much earlier roots lurking perhaps in the religious unions based on Delphi and other religious centres (p. 114). Yet, owing to the interest of historians in competition rather than in co-operation (p. 182), this fundamental question of the origin of Pan-Hellenism has never received the full treatment that it deserves.

Pan-Hellenism strove to harness nationalist instincts in a wider concept than that of the city-state. It also rose above racialist hostilities engendered by the alleged differences between Ionians, Dorians, etc. (p. 196). A few far-sighted men carried the concept further still. Thus Isocrates described the name of Greece as 'denoting no longer a race but a kind of intellect'; and the truth of this judgment is well borne out by the Lycians, who although only partly Greek used their Greek culture to carry out a federalistic achievement unique in the ancient world (p. 172). But flashes of understanding like that of Isocrates were rare; and indeed Pan-Hellenism by its very nature actually augmented *Greek* racialism while diminishing that based on lesser groups. That is to say, Pan-Hellenism could not rise above the racialist feeling which, ever since the Persian wars, had caused Greeks to regard non-Greeks, however civilised, as 'barbarians'. On the contrary, Pan-Hellenism was frequently directed against the Persians; and this was true of Gorgias and Isocrates themselves.

So Pan-Hellenism was not, by itself, a match for the evils of Greek racialism. Something has been said already concerning the strength of ancient racialism (p. 193). But it may be added here that this is a subject in which our expositions of ancient history have, on the whole, most strikingly failed to keep abreast of modern research. We say that we deplore the Nazi doctrine of the master-race (as a *doctrine* and not merely because we dislike the Nazis); and we say so for what appear to be sound genetical reasons (p. 38). But it is amazing to note how often text-books still in use imply, or even actually assert, their acceptance of precisely similar claims by the Greeks and Romans. It is erroneous to accept their view that they were racially 'superior' to other peoples. Yet we very rarely see, in discussions of the ancient world, the warning—against this myth—which it would be salutary for the student to receive.

Indeed, warnings were offered by the Greeks themselves; and as antidotes to war-mongering and

tribalism these attempts to transcend racialist errors
must be welcomed and studied by the historians. The
first steps had been taken by others. One great step
forward had been the replacement of henotheism
—the idea that each political unit had its own special
god (p. 191)—by monotheism, the conception that
there is one God for all the world, and that all men
are his children. An approach to this view—belief
in the common fatherhood or providence of God—
seems to appear in the Egyptian Hymn to Amen, in
the days of Thothmes III (c. 1479-1447 B.C.). It
gained force under that most startling and original
minded of all the Pharaohs, the religious reformer
and 'heretic' Akhenaton (fourteenth century), who
stressed that Aton, the sun, shone equally on Egyptians and their Syrian and Nubian subjects. His
'heresy' died with him. But monotheism later
returned in the most vivid and brilliant form under
the great Jewish prophets of the eighth and seventh
centuries, starting from Amos and Hosea and culmi-
nating in that almost unequalled writer who has left
us the second part of the Book of Isaiah ('Deutero-
Isaiah'). Monotheistic, too, are the noble doctrines
of the Persian religious leader Zoroaster, who created
the mighty religion bearing his name, which may
perhaps have been adopted by Darius and was
greatly to influence Christianity. But the question
whether Zoroaster preceded or followed the Hebrew
prophets is one of the questions most disputed by
scholars today.

These religious thinkers had established the
universal Fatherhood of God. But the logical deduction from the Fatherhood of God is a hypothesis
which profoundly opposes the passions of aggressive

nationalism, namely, the universal Brotherhood of Man. The Jewish prophets had shown signs of making this deduction, but they had not explicitly done so. This outstanding conception, however, reached three widely separated civilisations in about the sixth century B.C.—the most remarkable instance that could be discovered of the parallel developments of great ideas and simultaneous emergence of outstanding men to propagate them. For—only a few years after the writings of 'Deutero-Isaiah' and conceivably of Zoroaster also—Buddha (d. 483 (?)), Mahavira (the founder of Jainism), Confucius (d. 479 (?)), Laotse, and the Ionian natural philosophers such as Heraclitus of Ephesus, are believed to have been contemporary.

All of them laid great and, as far as we are aware, new stress on the brotherhood of mankind. This is implicit in the Buddhist notion of *dharma*, in which toleration is insisted on; and it later became explicit under the Buddhist rule of Asoka (p. 47). The whole teaching of Confucius was based on the theory that human society depends on the sympathy of men for each other. It is summed up by the word *jen*, which has been variously translated as fellow-feeling or humanity, and bears a close resemblance to the Christian doctrine of Love. In the fifth century B.C. the relevance of this teaching to social and political affairs, and to nationalism, was elaborated and developed by the Confucian Mo Ti (Motse), the 'prophet of China', who based his ideal society on the love of mankind: 'mutual love without discrimination is needed in the whole Great Society . . . one should regard other States exactly as one regards one's own State'.

At the same time as Buddha, Confucius, and Laotse are believed to have been paving the way for the eastern versions of the doctrine of the Brotherhood of Man, the pre-Socratic physical philosopher Heraclitus of Ephesus, in Ionia, made a similar assertion which likewise struck at the evils of particularism. 'Those who speak with understanding', he said 'must hold fast to what is *common to all* (*koinon*) as a city holds fast to its law, *and even more strongly*.' For all human laws are fed by the one divine law. Heraclitus is proverbially obscure, but it may be that further research will increasingly show the decisive part that he played in the history of thought. At present, interpretations are contradictory; and this is not surprising since, among other provocative utterances, he apparently expressed belief in the inevitability of war (p. 181). But, here, he is deducing from the universality of divine providence the brotherhood of man.

Near the end of the fifth century B.C., or a little later, the idea was given explicit political shape by certain of the 'sophists'. The 'sophists' were travelling lecturers, some inferior but others exceedingly brilliant, who sought to provide various forms of higher education. The emphasis of their instruction came to be laid on ruthless argumentation. This was to have its bad side—the mere indulgence in mental acrobatics—but it also had a very good side, namely, the application of cold rationality to some of the beliefs that had prevented the Greek world from finding peace. Thus one of these 'sophists', Antiphon, rendered explicit the suggestion of Heraclitus: all men, he said, are alike in essential respects, including not only Greeks but barbarians. At this same period the ethical implications of this doctrine were given expression by the philosopher Democritus, of Abdera in Thrace. Democritus is chiefly famous for his development of the atomic theory in its ancient form (originated by his master Leucippus of Miletus, often considered the last of the pre-Socratic physical philosophers). But Democritus, true to the spirit of his time, had even more to say. He recognised the value of States, but remarked—in what sounds a familiar aphorism today, but was striking enough in his own society—'to the wise man, the whole world is open, and the native land of a good soul is the whole universe'.

But the full elaboration of the doctrine of the Brotherhood of Man was reserved for a later philosophical school, that of the Stoics. In our educational programmes and general books it is almost invariably the case that Stoicism is totally neglected in favour of the writings of Plato and Aristotle. Plato and Aristotle, it is true, were its predecessors and in part its masters; but—partly owing to their preoccupation with the city-state—the direct influence of their teaching on ancient history was incomparably less than that of Stoic teaching, with its belief in the universality handed down from Heraclitus and Democritus. Soon after the death of Aristotle (322 B.C.), the Stoic school was founded at Athens by Zeno of Citium in Cyprus (335–263 B.C.). Cyprus and Citium were under strong Phoenician and Syrian influences; and there is little doubt that this applies to Zeno too—his mother-tongue may well have been a Semitic language. The Stoics taught the universal Brotherhood of Man. But such ideas were in the air, and—though the immediate source is disputed—inspired the liberality of Alexander's concept of empire, which was the first attempt to put the idea into practice on a large scale.

But the concept of the Brotherhood of Man did not bring the world a Greek peace. Like other ideas which have political implications, universalism, true cosmopolitanism, became smirched and distorted in the course of time. But its birth was one of the great moments of history, because it rose above suicidal sovereignties and the aggressive nationalisms that fed them. Nor is its importance in the ancient world by any means limited to its origins. The Greeks failed to curb aggressive nationalism through the only peaceful means available, namely, federation (p. 173). So the choice next lay between the continuation of international anarchy and its elimination by forcible means. Rome achieved the latter. Such a solution would be ruinous today; and even in the ancient world, when weapons had achieved less destructiveness, it was a second-best solution (p. 174). None the less, the paradox was fully worked out. However forcible the means, the aggressive nationalisms that had always racked the world were eliminated.

And in the Roman Empire which emerged there was much talk and serious thought of the Brotherhood of Man. Stoicism had been introduced to the governing class of Rome in the second century B.C., when the Stoic Panaetius of Rhodes became an intimate of Scipio Aemilianus. From then onwards it achieved vast influence far exceeding that of any other philosophical school; it became an integral part of the Roman statesman's conscious and unconscious education. Its doctrines were given a wide circulation by Cicero; and recent research has shown that it played a very large part in the lofty conception of their duty to the empire as a whole which characterised the best Roman emperors.

They acted as though they believed in the Brotherhood of Man, and the same idea occurs abundantly in the writings of the mature *Pax Romana*—Latin writers like the Spaniard Seneca the Younger and the north Italian Pliny the Younger, and perhaps with even greater emphasis those who did not even write in Latin—Greeks like the travelling lecturer Aristides. The same Stoic idea is likewise ever-present in the minds of the great Roman lawyers, Salvius Julianus, Papinian, and Ulpian—the first from Tunisia, the second perhaps African or Syrian, and the third from Tyre in Phoenicia. Their whole work was inspired by the ethical concepts which follow from this doctrine.

Finally, by means of this diffusion of Greek Stoicism throughout the Roman world, this idea of the universality of the empire passed directly into the universality of the Christian Church. This was the final answer of the ancient world to the aggressive nationalism which had disfigured the whole of its history; and it was to be an answer based, not on force as had been the Roman Empire, but on free co-operation. So far it has not curbed aggressive nationalism; so far, in all history, the only curb that has been successful over a very wide area has been the forceful one of the Roman Empire. This is a situation which is of peculiar relevance to ourselves. For today it is imperative that we should repeat the achievement of the Roman Empire, but repeat it with a difference—for today the elimination of particularism must somehow be achieved by peaceful and not by forcible means.

CHAPTER VII

THE SOCIAL STRUCTURE

IT was suggested that the aggressive nationalism to which so much ancient warfare must be ascribed owes a great deal to irrational emotions of a racialist character. Similar feelings also contributed greatly to a second important cause of war: the division of society into a steep gradation of hereditary social, political, and economic classes—much steeper and more rigorous than exists in most parts of Europe today. This is a subject which needs to be approached with caution, since it has provided the springboard for many famous leaps into theory. On the other hand, it is a subject of undeniable importance, and is still greatly neglected by many ancient historians; slavery, for example, is a subject which though fundamental is often unaccountably ignored. Marxists have made some interesting points, which the student will disregard at his cost; but they persuade some people to disregard them, by assigning to them an absolute priority of importance that they do not possess. It remains true, however, that what may briefly be described as the 'class-struggle' is one of the most significant themes of antiquity, and this is particularly true in relation to our present discussion of the causes of ancient war.

But first let us give a brief account of certain features of these class-distinctions. A striking example is provided by the hereditary caste-system of India. This was originally caused by the desire of the Indo-European-speaking immigrants and invaders to put an end to the prevalent racial intermingling with the earlier Dravidian-speaking population. Here, despite the powerful protests of Buddha and his contemporary Mahavira, the founder of Jainism, the caste-system remained rigid. Similarly, Chinese society was firmly based on the hereditary division between the mass of peasant proprietors and a small oligarchy. This situation is reflected in the words of Confucius and his most distinguished followers. Mencius, for example—who has been described as the 'Saint Paul of Confucius'—though he concedes that 'without the peasant the gentleman has nothing to eat', balances this by the reminder that 'without the gentleman the peasant cannot be governed'; and the point is, indeed, a commonplace of the Chinese classics.

Generally speaking, these sharp gradations are found all over the civilised world throughout ancient history. Classical Greece is no exception. As usual too, Greek literature provides clear formulation. The clearly marked, hereditary, social hierarchy is strongly and explicitly defended by the poets Theognis, of Megara in the Corinthian isthmus (sixth century B.C.), and Pindar the Boeotian (518–438 B.C.). By the time of the Stoics, and even before, doubts had begun to arise regarding the justice of slavery. But it is taken for granted by Plato and Aristotle.

They are not, it is true, wholly representative of their age in one respect, for they did not favour the government by large gatherings which was the chief feature of Greek 'democracy' (p. 200). But their verdict as regards slavery was one that would have been shared by democrats. For slaves had no part in these 'democracies'; they did not possess the franchise any more than women did (p. 233). The franchise was also withheld from large groups of resident aliens (Metics, e.g. at Athens) and of other subordinate populations, the 'dwellers round about' (Perioeci, e.g. in Thessaly and at Sparta). These often attained a large proportion of the population; but they were not members of Assemblies and so had no part in the 'democracy' at all.

H. P. Hall remarks: 'that the Athenian democracy kept slaves does not make it any the less a democracy as far as the freemen were concerned'. That is true, if we exclude also Metics and Perioeci, and if we interpret 'democracy' in the strict Greek sense of control by the *demos*, the citizenry. But it is no less true that the 'democracies' do not provide any real exception to the rule that rigorous hereditary class-distinctions were universal in the ancient world. 'To the Greek, "democracy" meant, not the overthrow of privilege, but merely the extension of its area' (E. M. Walker). That is to say, the respect in which the 'democracies' chiefly differed from the oligarchies—other than the vesting of sovereignty in the community—lay in the larger size of their hereditary privileged group. But even so this privilege did not extend to nearly the whole of the adult male community; in Athens, for example, it extended to less than half of it.

This point is curiously illustrated by Sparta. Sparta came to be regarded as the enemy of 'democracy'. Yet, within the charmed circle of privilege, the small proportion of the population that possessed the hereditary franchise enjoyed an extraordinary degree of equality *one with another*, and all participated in the election of the chief officials. This was

really a *reductio ad absurdum* of 'democracy', and yet
by the Greek definition it ought to be described as
'democratic' (Wade-Gery). For the enormous numbers of Helots and Dwellers Around (Perioeci) were
irrelevant to that term, which was only concerned
with citizens. So, according to Greek terminology,
this ruthless totalitarian government was wholly in
accordance with 'democratic' principles. What is
more, it was one of the earliest governments to
possess this character. Toynbee mentions it as the
first of all; but there are certain reasons for attri-
buting a somewhat earlier date to similar régimes in
cities of Crete ((?) *c.* 675 B.C.: van Effenterre). However, Sparta vies with Chios as providing the earliest
known use of the word *demos* to mean the citizen-
body.

By a further irony, it was the equality, one with
another, of the Spartan citizen-minority—and particularly their equality in land-ownership—which, in
the following century, inspired 'democratic' Athenian
demands for a redistribution of land. At Athens
reforms gradually took place, though the conception
of citizenship narrowed again under Pericles (fifth
cent. B.C.). But the memory of Sparta's democratic
primacy remained; and this was later stressed by
would-be social and communistic reformers at Sparta
in the third century B.C. (p. 228). The character of
Spartan 'democracy' provides one of the reasons why
even 'democracies' in ancient Greece do not constitute
any real exception to the rigorous hereditary class-
distinction which is so much more striking a feature
of the ancient world than it is in present-day Europe.

These political and social gradations were closely
accompanied by even more sharply defined economic

gradations; and this is only to be expected in a
society in which economic conditions were closely
dependent on political power. So economic conditions, too, in almost every ancient society and at
almost every epoch achieved a degree of harshness
that is not found in very many European countries
today. This, too, is a factor which the historian is
unable to ignore, especially today when economic
freedom, 'freedom from want', is duly recognised as
an aim of mankind alongside of political freedom. It
is true that in Greece, at least, there was not great
wealth; but for the vast mass of the populations of
Greece and all other parts of the ancient world at all
its epochs—even including many citizens—life was
exceedingly miserable. 'Ever since the dawn of civilisation, most people in civilised communities have
led lives full of misery' (Russell); and that truth is
even more emphatically applicable to the ancient
world than it is to the present day. 'Of many, perhaps most, cultures it is true that only a small
oligarchic minority reaped any benefit from such
progress as was made' (John Baillie).

Thus at the dawn of our historical record we find
the Sumerian monarch Urukagina telling of his
endeavours to relieve the misery of the very poor;
and this theme of crushing poverty recurs throughout
ancient history, whenever we are able to see behind
royal propaganda or aristocratic literary traditions.
The providers of the grim forced labour of the Egyptian pyramid builders, whether slaves or serfs, must
have lived appallingly hard lives, and the mighty
megalithic stones of the Andean city of Tiahuanaco
seem to tell a similar story. An echo of such conditions comes down to us in the record of Solomon's

agreement with his Phoenician ally Hiram of Tyre: 'And King Solomon raised a levy out of all Israel; and the levy was thirty thousand men. And he sent them to Lebanon . . . and Solomon had threescore and ten thousand that bare burdens, and fourscore thousand hewers in the mountains; beside the chief of Solomon's officers which were over the work, three thousand and three hundred. . . .' (I Kings, vi, 13–16). Many of these were, presumably, at other times, 'free' men. And so was the Chinese poet, earlier than Confucius, who wrote: 'bitter my poverty and want, for no man cares of my distress. Can these things be? . . . you do not know the people starve? You have known early enough, but you do not act' (*Book of Odes*). No doubt the economic condition of free men was not always much better than that of slaves, notably at Sparta, where the aristocracy ruthlessly controlled a Helot population at least seven times as large as their own (p. 116).

As Zimmern points out, Greek thought gives us no help with the labour problem—'how to secure that a good life for the customer shall be compatible with a good life for the producer'. However, Greek thinkers did at least appreciate that the economic troubles were closely connected with political conditions. This was understood by Thucydides, and also by his Athenian contemporary, the orator Antiphon, who saw in such inequalities the principal cause of the political disturbances and class-struggles that ruined Greek city-life (p. 221). In the following century Aristotle accepted this conclusion and elaborated further on the close interaction between inadequate economic policies and political stability. Two of his contemporaries knew where these failures were leading Greek civilisation. For a certain Heraclides, a philosopher from Heraclea in N.W. Asia Minor, remarked that it was easy enough to be good when you had enough to eat; and Isocrates even concluded that 'the needy may well be pardoned if they have no care *for the State*'. And from the fourth century B.C. matters became worse still; the greater part of the Greek population, citizens and all, sank into proletarianism, unemployment, and semi-starvation. This time, governments did not regard the emigrations of the eighth and seventh centuries (p. 113) as worth repeating.

These economic inequalities are always with us in the ancient world; and so is the rigid hereditary hierarchy of privilege which accompanied and in part caused them. But both these subjects attain particular importance in connection with the primary topic of this study, the prevalence of wars in ancient history. This particularly applies to the climactic Greek and Roman periods to which we are devoting special attention. For in these, the smouldering ill-effects of excessive class-differentiation erupted into wars of three different kinds. These comprise:

(1) interventions by Greek city-states in each other's class-wars;

(2) the encouragement of Greek and Roman aggressiveness by the hope of acquiring cheap slaves;

(3) revolts by slaves and proletariats against Rome.

Let us consider these three sorts of war briefly. As regards the first of them, class-wars broke out in Greece when the barriers of class began to be lowered just sufficiently for discontent to become articulate. Revolutionary economic changes such as the introduction and extension of coinage had not solved the inherent contradictions of a poor country rent by particularism (p. 162). So there were, in many cities, long periods of ferocious civil war between the privileged 'oligarchs' and the now vociferous 'democrats', who were citizens, but badly off. The Greek word for this sort of war is *stasis*. It has been made famous by Thucydides, who gives a general description of this phenomenon in connection with one of its earliest appearances at Corcyra (Corfu) in 427 B.C. In the course of a brilliant and terrible account of the atrocious characteristics of this strife, Thucydides points out that Corcyra provided one of the first of many instances of reprisals by the badly governed; of the attempt to end poverty by the seizure of the property of others; and of the massacre of creditors by their debtors. Extremism and revengefulness prevailed on all sides: 'advocates of extreme measures always seemed trustworthy . . . in this contest the blunter wits were most successful . . . they at once boldly had recourse to action'. He sums up as follows: 'Death raged in every shape . . . so bloody was the march of the revolution . . . later on practically the whole Greek world was convulsed in the same way.' Plato, in a vivid phrase, speaks of cities divided as if between two armies watching each other. 'It was accepted as a common doctrine that it might be justifiable to spill citizen blood in order to snatch a party advantage' (Cary and Haarhoff).

Thus class-war in Greek city-states caused much internal bloodshed. But it was also a serious cause of external war. For the parties to these struggles formed the habit of seeking assistance from outside. In these cases class-warfare had reached such ferocity that it took precedence even over so strong a force

as nationalism (p. 20); political parties took on an
international character. This had already happened
long before the classic outbreak of *stasis* at Corcyra.
It is particularly conspicuous as an accompaniment
of the movement which set up dictators ('tyrants') in
the seventh and sixth centuries B.C., usually as
champions of the newly rising mercantile middle
class. The disaffected nobilities frequently sought
help from other cities, and such help was readily
given. Sparta was particularly ready for such interventions. Spartan troops helped the noblemen of
Sicyon to put down its anti-Dorian tyrant; Spartan
troops had to be bought off by the tyrant Polycrates
of Samos, with a bribe of specially struck false coins
(P. N. Ure). It was the Spartans, again (under
Cleomenes I), who were called in by the noble
Alcmaeonid family of Athens to drive out the son
of its tyrant Pisistratus. This constant, if involun-
tary, fomentation of external wars by the tyrannies
is one of the reasons why Plato regards this as the
very worst form of government.

Tyrannies had disappeared from the mainland of
Greece by about 500 B.C. But Sicily, where revolutions were particularly frequent since the inequalities
of wealth and status were particularly grave (Plato),
now showed that they could be caused as well as
terminated by these interventions from outside. For
at Syracuse the aristocratic government of landlords
(*Gamoroi*), faced with a revolt of the serf-population,
themselves called in a tyrant (Gelon) from Gela next
door (485 B.C.). Indeed, in such causes the Sicilian
factions were constantly ready to call in even the
Carthaginians. On the mainland, the oligarchic systems which by now had mostly taken the place of

the tyrannies retained this fatal propensity to encourage, intentionally or unintentionally, the outbreak of wars through outside intervention. This
became one of the most prominent and dangerous
features of Greek class-warfare. In this *stasis*, ironi-
cally enough, both sides constantly stressed their
attachment to the ancestral constitution with its
implications of autonomy and autarky (p. 161); yet
both sides were continually prepared to call in other
cities to support their cause by forcible means.

This was clearly appreciated by Thucydides. In
the days of the Peloponnesian War, 'efforts were
everywhere made by the popular leaders to bring in
the Athenians, and by the oligarchs to bring in the
Spartans. In peace there would have been neither
the excuse nor the desire to issue such invitations;
but in war-time . . . the two sides in the revolutions
never lacked the opportunity to secure the aid of
foreign intervention.' Plato, too, sees clearly this
weakness in the oligarchic system: 'just as a sick
body . . . is sometimes at strife with itself . . . so is
this sick city. It falls ill and makes war on itself on
the smallest pretext, *whenever the one party or the
other manages to obtain help from outside*.' Later this
same sacrifice of patriotism to party played a great
part in the extension of Roman rule. Roman intervention was often invited; and the inviters included
not only Greek cities but even the oligarchs of
Carthage, who, finding Hannibal too progressive for
their liking, invoked the conquerors against him
(196 B.C.).

So these solicitations of forcible help from outside,
due in the last resort to the rigidity of internal
structure, contributed formidably to the everlasting

recurrence of ancient wars. But such invocations of outside help for purposes of *stasis* were only one side of a wider phenomenon which was greatly conducive to international anarchy, namely, the Greek propensity to 'collaboration' and treachery. 'Greek history furnishes not only shining examples of patriotism, but equally conspicuous instances of treason, and some of the traitors are among the most eminent of Greek statesmen' (F. R. Earp).

Among the best-known cases are those of the Athenian Themistocles, the hero of Salamis, who ended his days as a satellite of Artaxerxes I of Persia; and his compatriot Alcibiades who fled to the Spartans and told them the best ways to win the Peloponnesian War. Among the Spartans, too, King Cleomenes I, the ejector of the Athenian tyrants, later tried to break up the Peloponnesian League; and King Pausanias, the victor of Plataea, was accused first of treasonable negotiations with Persia and then of conspiring with the serf-population of Helots. Such cases of treachery all played a prominent part in fomenting hostility between cities.

'So many instances of treason in great men are hard to find elsewhere,' says F. R. Earp. In an acute analysis of this phenomenon and of its apparent contradiction to the intense nationalism of the Greeks (p. 198), he concludes that this too is a product of the combative instinct (p. 180). A Greek firmly believed that 'a man should hate and injure his enemy' even when the enemy was within the same city; and in these small States political life reached such a pitch of intensity that such enmities were bound to exist despite all the claims of nationalism. Moreover, as Earp points out, the patriotism of a

Greek was to some extent of a practical, debit-and-credit character, 'something external and self-regarding'. That he regarded his relations with his city (as with his gods) in this light is shown by his tendency to recount his services to the State in a more direct and boastful fashion than would create a good impression today.

In the case of less distinguished people than the most famous of the traitors (and in some of their cases too), a frequent cause of treachery was the obvious one, poverty. The temptation to secure a new source of income was often very great, and resistance to it was often unsuccessful. Herodotus, from Halicarnassus in S.W. Asia Minor remarked that no Spartan could resist a bribe; and in the second century B.C. Polybius, himself a Greek (from Megalopolis in Arcadia), commented on the extreme dishonesty of Greeks handling public funds. At all events, whatever the causes, 'collaboration' was a frequent phenomenon in Greek life. The availability of collaborators exacerbated the emotional and acquisitive tendencies of city-states, and tempted them to interfere forcibly in each other's affairs. This, then, is an important respect in which the unfortunate relations between groups and classes inside cities provided incentives to external wars.

A second respect in which this was so lies in the institution of slavery—the existence of people with no political rights or very few. Slavery was universal in the ancient world. No civilised community could sustain itself without it. It was less prominent in India and China than in other great civilisations; but even there it existed. At certain centres and certain periods, it attained especially formidable dimensions; and these were usually times when the lot of the 'free' poor, too, was particularly grim, owing to the easy alternative of slave labour.

In the great empires of the second and first millennia B.C., the numbers of slaves reached new heights, notably under Assyrian rule. Slavery again greatly increased after c. 500 B.c. in Greece, where a great market was established on the island of Chios, off Asia Minor—always a source of manpower, and eventually through the descendants of its slaves the motherland of many people of all sorts and regions throughout the Mediterranean (p. 238). It is con-jecturally estimated that in c. 430 B.c. a total popula-tion of 155,000 in Athens and the Piraeus included 70,000 slaves, and a total population of 315,000 in Attica included 115,000 slaves (A. W. Gomme). A further terrible boom occurred during the Roman Republic, and especially in the days of the great eastern wars of the second and first centuries B.C. Between one-fifth and one-third of the population of Rome itself consisted of slaves. In this period the chief market was another Aegean island within easy reach of Asia Minor, Delos. During these two periods the conditions of slaves, at their worst, were un-speakable. It would be difficult to exceed the miseries of slave-labour at the silver-mines of Laurion from which Athens drew her wealth, or on the great Italian ranches of the second century B.C., of which Cato the Elder—exemplar of antique Roman virtue—remarked that it was cheaper to work slaves to death and replace them than to treat them well.

The abundance of slaves during these two periods was caused by war. That is to say, cheap slave-labour was obtainable by means of war. Naturally enough, this provided ruling classes and governments with a strong incentive to further wars. We may mention here, as prototypes, the wars fought by the Spartans (the First and Second Messenian Wars, traditionally assigned to the eighth and seventh centuries B.C.), to overcome the Helots—in quantities vastly outnumbering their conquerors and requiring the latter to maintain perpetual mobilisation. The Helots were not slaves, but serfs; but here again wars were fought to secure forced labour. 'Love of power . . . will cause the governors to desire conquest. This motive is very much reinforced when the vanquished are made into slaves instead of being exterminated' (Russell). 'War in the ancient world was not merely a political enterprise: it was commercial as well . . . a considerable part of the spoils of war, legally or illegally, stuck to the fingers of the generals, officers and soldiers, in the shape of gold and silver, cattle and slaves' (Rostovtzeff).

As in earlier times, Asia Minor was a great source of slaves for Rome. Many prisoners of the wars against Mithridates of Pontus swelled the slave-market (and the Roman taxpayers added to the stream by the enslavement of debtors and their children). A rougher type of slave was forthcoming in enormous numbers from Caesar's brutally con-ducted Gallic campaigns. These are but two of many instances of aggressive war being welcomed by the ruling group as a source of profit. It is also significant that the Roman senate was for a long time, in the second century B.C., very reluctant to suppress the pirates who infested the Mediterranean—because these too greatly enriched the slave-markets by kid-napping innumerable people and selling them as

slaves (H. A. Ormerod). It was not until, at the end
of the century, the pirates had become a major sea-
power threatening the Roman administration itself
that those in power at Rome were reluctantly obliged
to risk foregoing this supply of slaves by gradually
undertaking the essential defensive task.

Simultaneously, in the eastern part of the Mediterranean, the economic situation of the 'free' population was continuing to deteriorate; and there was a
vast impoverished proletariat as well as huge numbers of ill-used slaves. In Egypt, for example, we
learn from the Rosetta Stone of full prisons, bank-
ruptcies, bandits, and confiscations. It is not surprising that the flash-point was reached more than once,
and that there were times when the ruling groups
of the area were in real danger of a catastrophe.
Movements of reform from above were few and
shortlived, though their effects remained. One can
cite the remarkable but ill-fated 'communistic' attempts of Agis IV (244–241 B.C.) and Cleomenes III
(235–219) of Sparta (now much changed from its
former self), and of the only two truly democratic
reformers in Rome's history, the brothers Tiberius
and Gaius Gracchus (d. 133, 122 B.c). These attempts,
though not immediately successful, exacerbated the
feelings that prevailed over a vast area.

It is not surprising that in these circumstances
there were many serious outbreaks of violence against
the Romans and the Greek oligarchs whom they
placed or maintained in power. These can only be
described as class-wars; and these class-struggles
against the empire represent the third category of
warfare which was directly caused by the structure
of society. In the first years of the second century

B.C., soon after the exacting Second Punic War, Rome felt the need to use force against slaves and other depressed groups in several parts of Italy. But the first dangerous risings occurred in the same decade as witnessed the failure of Ti. Gracchus. These occurred far apart from each other, in Sicily and Asia Minor. The movement in Sicily was a rebellion of slaves (under leaders named Eunus and Salvius), and the outbreak in Asia Minor (under an Attalid bastard Aristonicus) a revolt against Roman annexation which combined nationalism with an appeal to slaves and impoverished people generally.

Nor was that all, for in Sicily there was a further slave-revolt in 103–99 B.C., accompanied (as was usual in these struggles) by appalling cruelties on both sides. We must also reckon as a class-war the great revolt of Italians (Marsian War, 90–89) fought in order to obtain citizenship. Spartacus led huge armies of slaves to control large areas of S. Italy. All the revolts were finally crushed with terrible ruthlessness, the credit for the defeat of Spartacus being assumed by Pompey. But thirty years later Pompey's son Sextus himself mobilised large numbers of slaves in an attempt to wrest the control of the Mediterranean from Octavian (the young Augustus).

The latter was the victor, and his establishment of the imperial régime marks the definitive defeat of revolutionary movements, though certain attempts were made by emperors to break down the impassable barriers between classes (p. 238). The new era also marked the termination of slave-wars, though huge numbers of Jews were sold as slaves by Titus and Hadrian. But on the whole slaves now greatly decreased in number, and those that remained were treated with deepening humanitarianism. Their place as the poorest members of society was increasingly taken by the urban proletariat (already a great problem under the Republic), and also by the new class of peasant-farmers (*coloni*). When in the third century A.D. the western part of the empire began to disintegrate in anarchy,[1] bankruptcy and class-warfare and brigandage begin anew. Sicily, again, was the centre of a peasant-revolt under Gallienus (A.D. 260–8). Large numbers of Gallic peasants, too, called the Bagaudae, took to the *maquis*; they were dealt with by an imperial army in 285, but were still heard of in the fifth century. Aided by catastrophic inflation and other disasters, due in part to technological and industrial stagnation (F. W. Walbank), the differences between classes now became again as fantastically great as they had ever been in the great empires of the Middle East. There was a vast and ever-widening gulf between an enormously expensive hereditary bureaucracy and an utterly impoverished and wretched proletariat and peasantry. This contrast, because of the consequent total lack of unity or cohesion against outside threats, has been widely recognised to be among the chief causes of the disintegration of the Roman Empire.

In China, similar events had already played a leading part in the downfall of the Han Empire. The rebellion which started it on the downward path bore the name of T'aip'ing, a name which was consequently given to a nineteenth-century movement of reform. The original revolt had occurred towards the end of the second century, when 'misgovernment,

[1] See also below, p. 241.

together with an agrarian crisis in Szechuan, brought on a peasant revolt in A.D. 184 which marked the beginning of the end for the Han dynasty' (L. C. Goodrich).

All these wars, in China, Greece, Rome, and elsewhere, were directly caused by extreme hereditary differentiation of political and economic classes, which was so persistent a feature of ancient history. This differentiation must be ranked with international anarchy and aggressive nationalism as one of the principal causes of ancient wars.

CHAPTER VIII

THE CHOICE OF RULERS

THE steep class-differentiations of the ancient world very probably contributed to wars in another and less direct way also. We have mentioned Broad's observation that one of the evil features of political life today lies in the fact that the pace is so largely set by backward and evilly disposed people (p. 179). But there is every reason to suppose that the people in charge of politics and administration (which were combined in a way that does not exist now) in the ancient world were less satisfactory than they are here today. For, throughout much the greater part of ancient history, far less rational care was taken in their selection than is generally taken now. This was because of the sharp differentiation of classes that has been discussed. At least until the beginning of our era, birth and wealth played a much larger role in the selection of officials than would be accorded to them in any highly-developed country today (p. 214). This greatly limited both the number of available candidates and the chance of the emergence of merit. It therefore greatly decreased the probability of efficiency; so the odds were naturally weighted in favour of the breakdown in efficiency represented by a lapse into war.

Moreover, ancient aristocracies were often naturally warlike, and saw little distinction between the peaceful occupation of hunting and the warlike occupation of fighting battles; compare, today, the designation of regiments as Chasseurs, Jäger, etc. In

India the elevated Kshatriya caste was proverbially militaristic. In Egypt, even in the last days of its independence, we find a pugnacious warrior class; the Homeric 'chivalry' has similar characteristics. Later, the Spartans lived in arms; and the Athenians too spent much of their time thinking and training for wars (Zimmern)—not necessarily defensive ones. The ruling class of the Roman Republic sought above all else *gloria*—military renown; this caused Caesar and many before him to plunge vast regions into unprovoked war. Augustus wanted to avoid war whenever he could (p. 123); but, owing to the widespread taste for *gloria*, he was obliged—for propaganda purposes—to dress up his diplomatic successes (notably with the Arsacid Parthians) in the guise of military triumphs.

It is conceivable that the invariable exclusion of women from the franchise and from political posts (apart from a few very exceptional queens) increased this pugnacity. At any rate the Athenian comic dramatist Aristophanes thought so, and believed that women are more likely than men to resent aggressive wars. The subject of his play the *Lysistrata*, produced in the black days of the Peloponnesian War, is an imaginary *coup d'état* of women with the expressive purpose of stopping the slaughter.[1]

It was not wholly unappreciated in Greece and Rome that the hereditary differentiation between the classes would not, in itself, necessarily produce leaders of merit. The Athenians *elected* to such of their posts as required technical skill; but, in spite of the

---

[1] Much more could be said about the role of women in antiquity. This role was far smaller among the Greeks than among the Romans.

marked equality between citizens, birth and wealth still seem, even in the most 'democratic' days, to have played quite a part in the selection (Sundwall). However, as regards the appointment of other officials, the Greek democracies succeeded in making a thoroughgoing departure from such considerations. For they appointed them by *lot*.

This was a determined step away from the age-long hierarchic principles; but it unfortunately represented no step at all in the direction of appointment by merit. It merely substituted one faulty criterion for another, that of egalitarianism. That is to say, it assumed not only that all citizens should possess equal rights before the law—a doctrine which is fundamental to civilised society—but also something quite different as well: namely, that all citizens should be regarded as equally fit for political and administrative office. This latter interpretation is a purely sentimental and irrational one. It was revived by the theoreticians (though not the practical men) of the French and American Revolutions (D. Thomson). It still draws much lip-service; and 'from misunderstandings of it (equality) have sprung half the errors which democratic practice has committed' (Bryce).

But there is also wide recognition now that the only fair and practicable form of equality is equality *of opportunity*. This is not provided by methods such as the lot; for talents and qualities are unevenly divided among people (J. B. S. Haldane), and the lot does not give talents a proper opportunity to emerge. 'The respect in which democracy attempts to treat its citizens as equals . . . is precisely the respect which alone makes possible the rise of true eminence to the top' (Spitz). 'It is just to treat men as equal until some reason other than preference, such as need, capacity or desert, has been shown to the contrary' (Carritt). *La carrière ouverte aux talents*, 'the aristocracy of noble minds' (Santayana), is—if and when it is put into force, and granting an adequate (even if imperfect) process of selection (p. 236)—a valuable corrective to thoroughgoing egalitarianism. The latter served some purpose as an emotional reaction from racialism; but it did not provide any basis at all for the selection of an *élite*.

This was clearly appreciated by Plato, and probably no less clearly by his master Socrates, that extraordinarily acute and realistic observer of the institutions of his day. Plato commented that the Athenian version of 'democracy' was illogical, since it dispensed 'a sort of equality to equals and unequals alike'. Socrates and Plato—despite his preoccupation with racialist conceptions—and another pupil of Socrates, named Antisthenes, devoted enormous attention to the question of merit in rulers. They anticipated Burnham's assertion that the existence of a minority of rulers is 'a universal feature of all organised societies of which we have any record'. The great contribution of Socrates was to stress the importance, in that group, of intellectual honesty— the necessity of a mutual check by morals and brain.

Nor was it only in Greece that such investigations were proceeding. Confucius had already given much consideration to the problem. Indeed, his chief aim —which failed in his lifetime but bore much fruit later on—was to train a loyal and efficient body of men who could combine what are regarded today as the 'political' and administrative functions (p. 232). How was this to be done? Owing to the absence, in the ancient world, of our distinction between these two functions, it is clear that one basic principle had to be applied to the whole field; that is to say, the criterion of merit was inevitably the best.

This is, it is true, a highly abstract assertion; for it does not answer the questions as to how merit is to be defined, and what processes of selection can best assure it, and who is going to do the selecting. 'There is no infallible selection of the wise or good . . . we are reduced to trial and error' (Carritt). This is not the place to attempt a closer definition. All that needs to be said here is that even a relatively imperfect system of allotting political and administrative control on grounds of merit is far preferable to any system which uses criteria wholly or largely unconnected with merit. The former category, whatever its imperfections, is much less likely to produce aggressive wars than the latter. It is a counsel of despair to say that the selection of leaders 'goes beyond what can be reasonably demanded from a mere institution' (Popper); or that, when selected, their hierarchy may be as vicious as the worst aristocracy or plutocracy (D. Thomson). The attempt has to be made.

Unfortunately, despite all the discussions of philosophers, it cannot be said that at most times the controllers of policy in Greek city-states were selected on grounds of real merit. Indeed, there are only two fields in ancient history in which a determined attempt was made to tackle this vital question of the selection of the *élite*; neither system was entirely satisfactory by modern standards, but both represented a step away from aggressiveness, inefficiency, and anarchy. The first of these attempts was made

in China, when it became customary, in the early years
of the Han régime, for the admission to public careers
to be made dependent on a written examination. We
hear of this from 165 B.C., and especially after 125 B.C.
This was a big step forward; but it does not represent
unmixed gain. For subjects were limited to theology
and classical literature; candidates were only selected
from lists provided by the provincial authorities; and
a candidate had to possess private means, if only to
enable him to secure the requisite tutoring to ensure
success in the examination.

The second attempt to select rulers according to
merit was made by the Roman emperors of the
period 30 B.C.–A.D. 180. The Romans were scarcely
ever 'democratic' in an egalitarian sense; for example,
the fundamental concept of Roman law was not
equality but *suum cuique*—each man his own.
Augustus felt the same. Yet he was by no means
satisfied with the gross inefficiency and dishonesty
which had characterised the oligarchic and aristocratic governments of the Roman Republic. These
qualities had not been felt incompatible with the
traditional Roman virtues, which stressed fierce concepts like *gloria* (p. 233). Augustus was second to none
in his ostensible professions of Roman traditionalism,
but in reality he wanted a change. He wanted peace,
and he wanted the efficiency which alone could produce it, and which had been so rare in the governments of the ancient world. So it was essential that
the selection of really important posts should be
governed by merit; and his successors, too—while
allowing the nobility enough posts (especially decora-
tive ones) to prevent discontent—followed this same
practice.

One of the greatest problems facing these emperors was the control of many huge provinces; and the governors of the most important of these were now chosen directly, from among men who had strong qualifications of experience, by the emperors and their immediate advisers. In most cases these made determined attempts to choose the most experienced, capable, and honest men—a total change from the practice of the Republic. Many of the men thus chosen had attained the necessary qualifications despite humble birth and poverty. During the civil wars 'new men' had risen to the top, and this particular feature of an otherwise grim period was retained by successive imperial governments.

The field from which these new men were derived was widened by a further factor. The practice of freeing slaves, hardly heard of in Greece before Hellenistic times, had reached enormous proportions in Rome. Augustus regulated it, but with a view not to stopping the flow but to ensuring that it produced useful freedmen. Very many of these came from Asia Minor, the great home of manpower and slaves. In due course they, along with other people promoted for merit, reached the highest offices. The Roman Empire of this period, unlike the earlier Greek world, was to a large extent governed by people chosen on grounds of merit. Thus the results were a great deal better than those produced by the erroneous or haphazard earlier methods or lack of methods.

Naturally, however, any process of personal selection is bound to be to some extent arbitrary; and in this case its success largely hinged on the personalities of emperors. In general, it was never long before a line of emperors appointed on a hereditary basis produced a bad one. This was only to be expected, for the odds were long—the Mendelian 'laws' of inheritance provide incalculables enough; and to these must be added the environmental factors and the intervention of maternal strains. Such long odds are dangerous when on them depends the autocratic political and administrative control of millions. Thus within a hundred years the dynasty of Caesar and Augustus had produced emperors who were pathological cases, or at least wholly irresponsible, such as Caligula and Nero; and then, in the next dynasty, the brother of the most popular of emperors, Titus, was the most unpopular, Domitian (p. 125).

On the murder of Domitian (A.D. 96), the lesson was learnt. The elderly lawyer who succeeded him, Nerva, instituted what became for a time a regular procedure when he had recourse to the method of *adoption*—the designation of a successor, chosen on grounds of merit, from outside his own family; and indeed the two brilliant emperors who were the first to be thus adopted, Trajan and Hadrian, were neither of them even Italian (they were Spanish).[1]

This spectacular breakaway from haphazard methods of selection had a no less spectacular result. For its direct effect was a series of long reigns of four of the finest emperors Rome ever had; and their maintenance of the *Pax Romana* throughout the vast empire was the only long period of peace that the ancient world ever saw—and a longer one than the modern world has ever seen. It is true that the first of these four emperors, Trajan, was warlike, but his wars did not incommode most of the many million

[1] Adoption outside the emperor's house had previously been tried, unsuccessfully, by Galba in A.D. 69.

inhabitants of the empire; and his three successors, all of them emperors by adoption, were all of them peaceful—Hadrian (117–138), Antoninus Pius (138–161) and Marcus Aurelius (161–180). Adoption, it is true, is again a selective method which is not perfect and has an element of risk; but its results were strikingly more successful than the hereditary principle or the lot. The measure of its success is shown by the unprecedented (and still unequalled) maintenance of the Roman Peace. Two of the main causes of war were removed—international anarchy was replaced (at a price) by a vast empire; aggressive nationalism, with no enemy to excite it, was less interesting than the Brotherhood of Man. Even class-differentiation was giving less trouble than usual; slaves were fewer and more humanely treated, prosperity and paternalism reached many. Such was the situation under a succession of emperors chosen on grounds of merit.

But 'when Marcus Aurelius, by promoting his son Commodus . . . to the throne, reverted to the dynastic principle of succession in place of the "choice of the best", it was an ill day for the empire' (H. H. Scullard, A.D. 166). Commodus was inevitably murdered, and a civil war broke out (A.D. 193–196) no less terrible than that which had terminated the Augustan dynasty. And many such civil wars soon followed. The happy secret was lost. Adoption was only rarely attempted again (p. 126). Fresh efforts to establish dynasties all ended in bloodshed; and force replaced merit as the requirement.

This collapse of the selection of emperors on grounds of merit is one of the chief causes of the disintegration of the empire. For, rather as had happened in the days of Greek *stasis* (p. 221), the internal strife to which it gave rise both encouraged external intervention (which, by a grim coincidence, first began to be really dangerous under Marcus Aurelius), and grievously weakened the resources by which it could be met.[1] When, a hundred years after the fatal decision of Marcus Aurelius, the terrible emergency forced a fresh series of able emperors to the top (p. 126), it was too late. *The empire could not support indefinitely the burden of constant civil, dynastic wars as well as constant foreign wars; no empire could.* It is true the geographical unity of the Roman dominions was temporarily re-asserted (A.D. 268–324). But this could now only be done at a cost of further terrible hardship and impoverishment. The western territories, especially, were still ravaged by external aggressions, and by the dynastic up-heavals and exaggerated class inequalities (p. 230) which invited such aggressions; and these provinces could not be retained indefinitely. By the fifth century A.D. they were crude and warlike indepen-dent kingdoms: international anarchy and aggressive nationalism, the normal features of earlier millennia, were dominant again—as they still are.

But, more than a century before these ominous developments, the centre of the empire had shifted. Asia Minor, which was relatively invulnerable to northern incursions and was now unchallenged as a reservoir of men and money (p. 71), resumed the leading position which it had held over Shubbilu-liuma, 1700 years previously. But Constantine, with

[1] The economic collapse and appalling impoverishment, caused by this dual strain, are discussed in my book *Roman Imperial Money*, now in the press.

his Mediterranean inheritance and Illyrian origin, situated his capital not in the highlands but across the straits at Byzantium (*c.* 330), where he combined the advantages of the land-mass Anatolia with those of the sea. The Byzantine dominion survived for over a thousand years, but it was never within reach of establishing world-peace or anything like it. For the breach in the impoverished Roman Empire, made possible by internal dissensions due to the unsound social structure and (in particular) to the failure to maintain merit as the criterion for its leadership, had let loose again those age-long causes of war, international anarchy and aggressive nationalism. The chance had been lost, and so far it has never come again.

LIST OF DATES

A. FAR EAST

(a) *India.* 4000–3000 B.C. Rise of Indus Civilisation; 2300 in touch with Akkad; 6/5 c.[1] Buddha (d. 483?), Mahavira; 322–298 Chandragupta Maurya; 273–232 Asoka; A.D. 48 Kushans in India; A.D. 120–162 Kanishka; 320–647 Gupta empire.

(b) *China.* From 22/20 c. Hsia (?); 14/12 c. Shang (= Anyang); 11/10–8 c. Chou; 6/5 c. Confucius (d. 479 ?), Laotse; 220 B.C. 'First Universal Emperor' (Ch'in); 202 B.C.–A.D. 220 Han Empire.

B. NEAR AND MIDDLE EAST

(a) 2500–1150 B.C. *Important States:* Sumer 25, 21 c.;[2] Akkad-Babylon 24/33, 18/17 c.; Egypt 20/18, 15/13 c; Assyria 18 c.; Elam 18, 12 c.; Manda 18 c.; Mitanni 15/14 c.; Hittites 14/13 c.

(b) 13/11 c. Wanderings of Peoples. Collapse of kingdoms.

(c) 12/8 c. *Lesser States.* Sidon 12/10 c.; Tyre 10/8 c.; Carchemish 12/9 c.; Assyria 11 c.; Jews 10 c.; Urartu 10/8 c.; Phrygia 10/8 c.

(d) 9/4 c. *Great Empires.* Assyria 883–681 (fell 612); Media 7 c.; Babylon-Chaldaea 6 c.; Persia 550–327— conquered by Alexander.

(e) 250 B.C.–A.D. 230 Arsacid Parthians; A.D. 224–636 Sassanid Persians.

C. GREECE AND ITALY

(a) *Early Period.* From 2000 B.C. 'Achaean' invasions of Greece; 'Terramaricoli' in Italy; rise of Crete. 16/15 c., great age of Cnossus. 12 c., great age of

---

[1] c. = century B.C. (unless explicitly stated to be A.D.). E.g. 6/5 c. = 6th and 5th centuries B.C.

[2] The dates represent roughly the zeniths of states. Earlier dates are very uncertain.

Mycenae; 'Villanovans' reach Alban hills. 11 c., 'Dorian' invasions of Greece; migrations to Ionia.

(b) *City-states.* 10/9 c., their formation in Greece. 8/c., Greek colonisation; Rome united; Etruscan domination in central Italy. 7/6 c., lawgivers; 'tyrants'; Ionian philosophers; Carthaginian sea-power. 5 c., Greeks repel Persians, Carthaginians, Etruscans; climax of thought and art; Athenian 'democracy' and empire (checked by Peloponnesian War); zenith of slavery; early federations. 4 c., Plato and Aristotle.

(c) *Hellenistic Age, Rise of Rome.* 359–323 B.C., conquests of Philip and Alexander. 4/early 3 c., Hellenistic kingdoms; Rome suppresses Latins and Samnites; Aetolian and Achaean Leagues. 3 c., first two Punic Wars; economic deterioration starts in E. Mediterranean; communist experiments at Sparta. 2/1 c., Greek states and Carthage absorbed by Rome; boom in slave-trade (risings) and piracy; breakdown of Republican government, completed by Caesar.

(d) *The Roman Principate.* 30 B.C.–A.D. 14, Augustus; A.D. 69–166, climax of Pax Romana. 3 c. A.D., totalitarian monarchy; military and economic collapse; oriental monarchy; 4 c. A.D., Constantine—move to Christianity and Byzantium; 5 c. A.D., West breaks away.

INDEX

(see also List of Contents *at beginning)*

Revised December, 1967

hARPER ⚜ TORChBOOKS

HUMANITIES AND SOCIAL SCIENCES

American Studies: General

LOUIS D. BRANDEIS: Other People's Money, *and How the Bankers Use It*. ‡ Ed. with an Intro. by Richard M. Abrams TB/3081

THOMAS C. COCHRAN: The Inner Revolution. *Essays on the Social Sciences in History* TB/1140

HENRY STEELE COMMAGER, Ed.: The Struggle for Racial Equality TB/1300

EDWARD S. CORWIN: American Constitutional History. *Essays edited by Alpheus T. Mason and Gerald Garvey* △ TB/1136

CARL N. DEGLER, Ed.: Pivotal Interpretations of American History Vol. I TB/1240; Vol. II TB/1241

A. HUNTER DUPREE: Science in the Federal Government: *A History of Policies and Activities to 1940* TB/573

A. S. EISENSTADT, Ed.: The Craft of American History: *Recent Essays in American Historical Writing* Vol. I TB/1255; Vol. II TB/1256

CHARLOTTE P. GILMAN: Women and Economics: *A Study of the Economic Relation between Men and Women as a Factor in Social Evolution*. ‡ Ed. with an Introduction by Carl N. Degler TB/3073

OSCAR HANDLIN, Ed.: This Was America: *As Recorded by European Travelers in the Eighteenth, Nineteenth and Twentieth Centuries. Illus.* TB/1119

MARCUS LEE HANSEN: The Atlantic Migration: 1607-1860. *Edited by Arthur M. Schlesinger* TB/1052

MARCUS LEE HANSEN: The Immigrant in American History. TB/1120

JOHN HIGHAM, Ed.: The Reconstruction of American History △ TB/1068

ROBERT H. JACKSON: The Supreme Court in the American System of Government TB/1106

JOHN F. KENNEDY: A Nation of Immigrants. △ *Illus.* TB/1118

LEONARD W. LEVY, Ed.: American Constitutional Law: *Historical Essays* TB/1285

LEONARD W. LEVY, Ed.: Judicial Review and the Supreme Court TB/1296

LEONARD W. LEVY: The Law of the Commonwealth and Chief Justice Shaw TB/1309

HENRY F. MAY: Protestant Churches and Industrial America. *New Intro. by the Author* TB/1334

RALPH BARTON PERRY: Puritanism and Democracy TB/1138

ARNOLD ROSE: The Negro in America TB/3048

MAURICE R. STEIN: The Eclipse of Community. *An Interpretation of American Studies* TB/1128

W. LLOYD WARNER and Associates: Democracy in Jonesville: *A Study in Quality and Inequality* ¶ TB/1129

W. LLOYD WARNER: Social Class in America: *The Evaluation of Status* TB/1013

American Studies: Colonial

BERNARD BAILYN, Ed.: Apologia of Robert Keayne: *Self-Portrait of a Puritan Merchant* TB/1201

BERNARD BAILYN: The New England Merchants in the Seventeenth Century TB/1149

JOSEPH CHARLES: The Origins of the American Party System TB/1049

HENRY STEELE COMMAGER & ELMO GIORDANETTI, Eds.: Was America a Mistake? *An Eighteenth Century Controversy* TB/1329

CHARLES GIBSON: Spain in America † TB/3077

LAWRENCE HENRY GIPSON: The Coming of the Revolution: 1763-1775. † *Illus.* TB/3007

LEONARD W. LEVY: Freedom of Speech and Press in Early American History: *Legacy of Suppression* TB/1109

PERRY MILLER: Errand Into the Wilderness TB/1139

PERRY MILLER & T. H. JOHNSON, Eds.: The Puritans: *A Sourcebook of Their Writings* Vol. I TB/1093; Vol. II TB/1094

EDMUND S. MORGAN, Ed.: The Diary of Michael Wigglesworth, 1653-1657: *The Conscience of a Puritan* TB/1228

EDMUND S. MORGAN: The Puritan Family: *Religion and Domestic Relations in Seventeenth-Century New England* TB/1227

RICHARD B. MORRIS: Government and Labor in Early America TB/1244

KENNETH B. MURDOCK: Literature and Theology in Colonial New England TB/99

WALLACE NOTESTEIN: The English People on the Eve of Colonization: 1603-1630. † *Illus.* TB/3006

JOHN P. ROCHE: Origins of American Political Thought: *Selected Readings* TB/1301

JOHN SMITH: Captain John Smith's America: *Selections from His Writings. Ed. with Intro. by John Lankford* TB/3078

LOUIS B. WRIGHT: The Cultural Life of the American Colonies: 1607-1763. † *Illus.* TB/3005

American Studies: From the Revolution to 1860

JOHN R. ALDEN: The American Revolution: 1775-1783. † *Illus.* TB/3011

MAX BELOFF, Ed.: The Debate on the American Revolution, 1761-1783: *A Sourcebook* △ TB/1225

RAY A. BILLINGTON: The Far Western Frontier: 1830-1860. † *Illus.* TB/3012

EDMUND BURKE: On the American Revolution: *Selected Speeches and Letters*. ‡ *Edited by Elliott Robert Barkan* TB/3068

WHITNEY R. CROSS: The Burned-Over District: *The Social and Intellectual History of Enthusiastic Religion in Western New York, 1800-1850* △ TB/1242

GEORGE DANGERFIELD: The Awakening of American Nationalism: 1815-1828. † *Illus.* TB/3061

---

† The New American Nation Series, edited by Henry Steele Commager and Richard B. Morris.

‡ American Perspectives series, edited by Bernard Wishy and William E. Leuchtenburg.

* The Rise of Modern Europe series, edited by William L. Langer.

** History of Europe series, edited by J. H. Plumb.

¶ Researches in the Social, Cultural and Behavioral Sciences, edited by Benjamin Nelson.

§ The Library of Religion and Culture, edited by Benjamin Nelson.

Σ Harper Modern Science Series, edited by James R. Newman.

º Not for sale in Canada.

△ Not for sale in the U. K.

CLEMENT EATON: The Freedom-of-Thought Struggle in the Old South. *Revised and Enlarged. Illus.* TB/1150
CLEMENT EATON: The Growth of Southern Civilization: 1790-1860. † *Illus.* TB/3040
LOUIS FILLER: The Crusade Against Slavery: 1830-1860. † *Illus.* TB/3029
DIXON RYAN FOX: The Decline of Aristocracy in the Politics of New York: 1801-1840. ‡ *Edited by Robert V. Remini* TB/3064
WILLIAM W. FREEHLING, Ed.: The Nullification Era: *A Documentary Record* ‡ TB/3079
FELIX GILBERT: The Beginnings of American Foreign Policy: *To the Farewell Address* TB/1200
FRANCIS GRIERSON: The Valley of Shadows: *The Coming of the Civil War in Lincoln's Midwest: A Contemporary Account* TB/1246
FRANCIS J. GRUND: Aristocracy in America: *Social Class in the Formative Years of the New Nation* TB/1001
ALEXANDER HAMILTON: The Reports of Alexander Hamilton. ‡ *Edited by Jacob E. Cooke* TB/3060
THOMAS JEFFERSON: Notes on the State of Virginia. ‡ *Edited by Thomas P. Abernethy* TB/3052
JAMES MADISON: The Forging of American Federalism: *Selected Writings of James Madison. Edited by Saul K. Padover* TB/1226
BERNARD MAYO: Myths and Men: *Patrick Henry, George Washington, Thomas Jefferson* TB/1108
JOHN C. MILLER: Alexander Hamilton and the Growth of the New Nation TB/3057
RICHARD B. MORRIS, Ed.: The Era of the American Revolution TB/1180
R. B. NYE: The Cultural Life of the New Nation: 1776-1801. † *Illus.* TB/3026
JAMES PARTON: The Presidency of Andrew Jackson. *From Vol. III of the Life of Andrew Jackson. ‡ Ed. with an Intro. by Robert V. Remini* TB/3080
FRANCIS S. PHILBRICK: The Rise of the West, 1754-1830. † *Illus.* TB/3067
TIMOTHY L. SMITH: Revivalism and Social Reform: *American Protestantism on the Eve of the Civil War* TB/1229
ALBION W. TOURGÉE: A Fool's Errand. ‡ *Ed. by George Fredrickson* TB/3074
A. F. TYLER: Freedom's Ferment: *Phases of American Social History from the Revolution to the Outbreak of the Civil War. 31 illus.* TB/1074
GLYNDON G. VAN DEUSEN: The Jacksonian Era: 1828-1848. † *Illus.* TB/3028
LOUIS B. WRIGHT: Culture on the Moving Frontier TB/1053

American Studies: The Civil War to 1900

W. R. BROCK: An American Crisis: Congress and Reconstruction, 1865-67 ° △ TB/1283
THOMAS C. COCHRAN & WILLIAM MILLER: The Age of Enterprise: *A Social History of Industrial America* TB/1054
W. A. DUNNING: Essays on the Civil War and Reconstruction. *Introduction by David Donald* TB/1181
W. A. DUNNING: Reconstruction, Political and Economic: 1865-1877 TB/1073
HAROLD U. FAULKNER: Politics, Reform and Expansion: 1890-1900. † *Illus.* TB/3020
HELEN HUNT JACKSON: A Century of Dishonor: *The Early Crusade for Indian Reform. ‡ Edited by Andrew F. Rolle* TB/3063
ALBERT D. KIRWAN: Revolt of the Rednecks: *Mississippi Politics, 1876-1925* TB/1199
ROBERT GREEN MC CLOSKEY: American Conservatism in the Age of Enterprise: 1865-1910 TB/1137
ARTHUR MANN: Yankee Reformers in the Urban Age: *Social Reform in Boston, 1880-1900* TB/1247
WHITELAW REID: After the War: *A Tour of the Southern States, 1865-1866. ‡ Edited by C. Vann Woodward* TB/3066

CHARLES H. SHINN: Mining Camps: *A Study in American Frontier Government. ‡ Edited by Rodman W. Paul* TB/3062
VERNON LANE WHARTON: The Negro in Mississippi: 1865-1890 TB/1178

American Studies: 1900 to the Present

RAY STANNARD BAKER: Following the Color Line: *American Negro Citizenship in Progressive Era. ‡ Illus. Edited by Dewey W. Grantham, Jr.* TB/3053
RANDOLPH S. BOURNE: War and the Intellectuals: *Collected Essays, 1915-1919. ‡ Edited by Carl Resek* TB/3043
A. RUSSELL BUCHANAN: The United States and World War II. † *Illus.* Vol. I TB/3044; Vol. II TB/3045
ABRAHAM CAHAN: The Rise of David Levinsky: *a documentary novel of social mobility in early twentieth century America. Intro. by John Higham* TB/1028
THOMAS C. COCHRAN: The American Business System: *A Historical Perspective, 1900-1955* TB/1080
FOSTER RHEA DULLES: America's Rise to World Power: 1898-1954. † *Illus.* TB/3021
JOHN D. HICKS: Republican Ascendancy: 1921-1933. † *Illus.* TB/3041
SIDNEY HOOK: Reason, Social Myths, and Democracy TB/1237
ROBERT HUNTER: Poverty: *Social Conscience in the Progressive Era. ‡ Edited by Peter d'A. Jones* TB/3065
WILLIAM L. LANGER & S. EVERETT GLEASON: The Challenge to Isolation: *The World Crisis of 1937-1940 and American Foreign Policy* Vol. I TB/3054; Vol. II TB/3055
WILLIAM E. LEUCHTENBURG: Franklin D. Roosevelt and the New Deal: 1932-1940. † *Illus.* TB/3025
ARTHUR S. LINK: Woodrow Wilson and the Progressive Era: 1910-1917. † *Illus.* TB/3023
GEORGE E. MOWRY: The Era of Theodore Roosevelt and the Birth of Modern America: 1900-1912. † *Illus.* TB/3022
RUSSEL B. NYE: Midwestern Progressive Politics: *A Historical Study of Its Origins and Development, 1870-1958* TB/1202
WILLIAM PRESTON: Aliens and Dissenters: *Federal Suppression of Radicals, 1903-1933* TB/1287
WALTER RAUSCHENBUSCH: Christianity and the Social Crisis. ‡ *Edited by Robert D. Cross* TB/3059
JACOB RIIS: The Making of an American. ‡ *Edited by Roy Lubove* TB/3070
PHILIP SELZNICK: TVA and the Grass Roots: *A Study in the Sociology of Formal Organization* TB/1230
IDA M. TARBELL: The History of the Standard Oil Company: *Briefer Version. ‡ Edited by David M. Chalmers* TB/3071
GEORGE B. TINDALL, Ed.: A Populist Reader ‡ TB/3069
TWELVE SOUTHERNERS: I'll Take My Stand: *The South and the Agrarian Tradition. Intro. by Louis D. Rubin, Jr., Biographical Essays by Virginia Rock* TB/1072

Anthropology

JACQUES BARZUN: Race: *A Study in Superstition. Revised Edition* TB/1172
JOSEPH B. CASAGRANDE, Ed.: In the Company of Man: *Twenty Portraits of Anthropological Informants. Illus.* TB/3047
W. E. LE GROS CLARK: The Antecedents of Man: *Intro. to Evolution of the Primates.* ° △ *Illus.* TB/559
CORA DU BOIS: The People of Alor. *New Preface by the author. Illus.* Vol. I TB/1042; Vol. II TB/1043
RAYMOND FIRTH, Ed.: Man and Culture: *An Evaluation of the Work of Bronislaw Malinowski* ¶ ° △ TB/1133
DAVID LANDY: Tropical Childhood: *Cultural Transmission and Learning in a Puerto Rican Village* ¶ TB/1235

2

L. S. B. LEAKEY: Adam's Ancestors: *The Evolution of Man and His Culture.* △ *Illus.*　　TB/1019
EDWARD BURNETT TYLOR: Religion in Primitive Culture. *Part II of "Primitive Culture."* § *Intro. by Paul Radin*　　TB/34
W. LLOYD WARNER: A Black Civilization: *A Study of an Australian Tribe.* ¶ *Illus.*　　TB/3056

Art and Art History

WALTER LOWRIE: Art in the Early Church. *Revised Edition. 452 illus.*　　TB/124
EMILE MÂLE: The Gothic Image: *Religious Art in France of the Thirteenth Century.* § △ *190 illus.*　　TB/44
MILLARD MEISS: Painting in Florence and Siena after the Black Death: *The Arts, Religion and Society in the Mid-Fourteenth Century. 169 illus.*　　TB/1148
ERICH NEUMANN: The Archetypal World of Henry Moore. △ *107 illus.*　　TB/2020
DORA & ERWIN PANOFSKY : Pandora's Box: *The Changing Aspects of a Mythical Symbol. Revised Edition. Illus.*　　TB/2021
ERWIN PANOFSKY: Studies in Iconology: *Humanistic Themes in the Art of the Renaissance.* △ *180 illustrations*　　TB/1077
ALEXANDRE PIANKOFF: The Shrines of Tut-Ankh-Amon. *Edited by N. Rambova. 117 illus.*　　TB/2011
JEAN SEZNEC: The Survival of the Pagan Gods: *The Mythological Tradition and Its Place in Renaissance Humanism and Art. 108 illustrations*　　TB/2004
OTTO VON SIMSON: The Gothic Cathedral: *Origins of Gothic Architecture and the Medieval Concept of Order.* △ *58 illus.*　　TB/2018
HEINRICH ZIMMER: Myth and Symbols in Indian Art and Civilization. *70 illustrations*　　TB/2005

Business, Economics & Economic History

REINHARD BENDIX: Work and Authority in Industry: *Ideologies of Management in the Course of Industrialization*　　TB/3035
GILBERT BURCK & EDITORS OF FORTUNE: The Computer Age: *And Its Potential for Management*　　TB/1179
THOMAS C. COCHRAN: The American Business System: *A Historical Perspective, 1900-1955*　　TB/1080
THOMAS C. COCHRAN: The Inner Revolution: *Essays on the Social Sciences in History* △　　TB/1140
THOMAS C. COCHRAN & WILLIAM MILLER: The Age of Enterprise: *A Social History of Industrial America* TB/1054
ROBERT DAHL & CHARLES E. LINDBLOM: Politics, Economics, and Welfare: *Planning and Politico-Economic Systems Resolved into Basic Social Processes*　　TB/3037
PETER F. DRUCKER: The New Society: *The Anatomy of Industrial Order* △　　TB/1082
EDITORS OF FORTUNE: America in the Sixties: *The Economy and the Society*　　TB/1015
ROBERT L. HEILBRONER: The Great Ascent: *The Struggle for Economic Development in Our Time*　　TB/3030
ROBERT L. HEILBRONER: The Limits of American Capitalism　　TB/1305
FRANK H. KNIGHT: The Economic Organization TB/1214
FRANK H. KNIGHT: Risk, Uncertainty and Profit TB/1215
ABBA P. LERNER: Everybody's Business: *Current Assumptions in Economics and Public Policy*　　TB/3051
ROBERT GREEN MC CLOSKEY: American Conservatism in the Age of Enterprise, 1865-1910 △　　TB/1137
PAUL MANTOUX: The Industrial Revolution in the Eighteenth Century: *The Beginnings of the Modern Factory System in England* ○ △　　TB/1079
WILLIAM MILLER, Ed.: Men in Business: *Essays on the Historical Role of the Entrepreneur*　　TB/1081
RICHARD B. MORRIS: Government and Labor in Early America △　　TB/1244

HERBERT SIMON: The Shape of Automation: *For Men and Management*　　TB/1245
PERRIN STRYKER: The Character of the Executive: *Eleven Studies in Managerial Qualities*　　TB/1041

Education

JACQUES BARZUN: The House of Intellect △　　TB/1051
RICHARD M. JONES, Ed.: Contemporary Educational Psychology: *Selected Readings*　　TB/1292
CLARK KERR: The Uses of the University　　TB/1264
JOHN U. NEF: Cultural Foundations of Industrial Civilization △　　TB/1024

Historiography & Philosophy of History

JACOB BURCKHARDT: On History and Historians. △ *Introduction by H. R. Trevor-Roper*　　TB/1216
WILHELM DILTHEY: Pattern and Meaning in History: *Thoughts on History and Society.* ○ △ *Edited with an Introduction by H. P. Rickman*　　TB/1075
J. H. HEXTER: Reappraisals in History: *New Views on History & Society in Early Modern Europe* △ TB/1100
H. STUART HUGHES: History as Art and as Science: *Twin Vistas on the Past*　　TB/1207
RAYMOND KLIBANSKY & H. J. PATON, Eds.: Philosophy and History: *The Ernst Cassirer Festschrift. Illus.*　　TB/1115
ARNALDO MOMIGLIANO: Studies in Historiography ○ △　　TB/1283
GEORGE H. NADEL, Ed.: Studies in the Philosophy of History: *Selected Essays from* History and Theory　　TB/1208
JOSE ORTEGA Y GASSET: The Modern Theme. *Introduction by Jose Ferrater Mora*　　TB/1038
KARL R. POPPER: The Open Society and Its Enemies △
　　Vol. I: *The Spell of Plato*　　TB/1101
　　Vol. II: *The High Tide of Prophecy: Hegel, Marx and the Aftermath*　　TB/1102
KARL R. POPPER: The Poverty of Historicism ○ △　　TB/1126
G. J. RENIER: History: *Its Purpose and Method* △ TB/1209
W. H. WALSH: Philosophy of History: *An Introduction* △　　TB/1020

History: General

WOLFGANG FRANKE: China and the West. *Trans by R. A. Wilson*　　TB/1326
L. CARRINGTON GOODRICH: A Short History of the Chinese People. △ *Illus.*　　TB/3015
DAN N. JACOBS & HANS H. BAERWALD: Chinese Communism: *Selected Documents*　　TB/3031
BERNARD LEWIS: The Arabs in History △　　TB/1029
BERNARD LEWIS: The Middle East and the West ○ △　　TB/1274

History: Ancient

A. ANDREWES: The Greek Tyrants △　　TB/1103
ADOLF ERMAN, Ed. The Ancient Egyptians: *A Sourcebook of Their Writings. New material and Introduction by William Kelly Simpson*　　TB/1233
MICHAEL GRANT: Ancient History ○ △　　TB/1190
SAMUEL NOAH KRAMER: Sumerian Mythology △　　TB/1055
NAPHTALI LEWIS & MEYER REINHOLD, Eds.: Roman Civilization. *Sourcebook I: The Republic*　　TB/1231
NAPHTALI LEWIS & MEYER REINHOLD, Eds.: Roman Civilization. *Sourcebook II: The Empire*　　TB/1232

History: Medieval

P. BOISSONNADE: Life and Work in Medieval Europe: *The Evolution of the Medieval Economy, the 5th to the 15th Century.* ○ △ *Preface by Lynn White, Jr.* TB/1141
HELEN CAM: England before Elizabeth △　　TB/1026
NORMAN COHN: The Pursuit of the Millennium: *Revolutionary Messianism in Medieval and Reformation Europe* △　　TB/1037

3

History: Renaissance & Reformation

History: Modern European

C. G. JUNG & C. KERÉNYI: Essays on a Science of Mythology: *The Myths of the Divine Child and the Divine Maiden* TB/2014
DORA & ERWIN PANOFSKY : Pandora's Box: *The Changing Aspects of a Mythical Symbol.* △ *Revised edition. Illus.* TB/2021
ERWIN PANOFSKY: Studies in Iconology: *Humanistic Themes in the Art of the Renaissance.* △ 180 *illustrations* TB/1077
JEAN SEZNEC: The Survival of the Pagan Gods: *The Mythological Tradition and its Place in Renaissance Humanism and Art.* △ 108 *illustrations* TB/2004
HELLMUT WILHELM: Change: *Eight Lectures on the I Ching* △ TB/2019
HEINRICH ZIMMER: Myths and Symbols in Indian Art and Civilization. △ 70 *illustrations* TB/2005

Philosophy

G. E. M. ANSCOMBE: An Introduction to Wittgenstein's Tractatus. o △ *Second Edition, Revised* TB/1210
HENRI BERGSON: Time and Free Will: *An Essay on the Immediate Data of Consciousness* o △ TB/1021
H. J. BLACKHAM: Six Existentialist Thinkers: *Kierkegaard, Nietzsche, Jaspers, Marcel, Heidegger, Sartre* o △ TB/1002
CRANE BRINTON: Nietzsche. *New Preface, Bibliography and Epilogue by the Author* TB/1197
MARTIN BUBER: The Knowledge of Man. △ *Ed. with an Intro. by Maurice Friedman. Trans. by Maurice Friedman and Ronald Gregor Smith* TB/135
ERNST CASSIRER: The Individual and the Cosmos in Renaissance Philosophy. △ *Translated with an Introduction by Mario Domandi* TB/1097
ERNST CASSIRER: Rousseau, Kant and Goethe. *Introduction by Peter Gay* TB/1092
FREDERICK COPLESTON: Medieval Philosophy o △ TB/376
F. M. CORNFORD: Principium Sapientiae: *A Study of the Origins of Greek Philosophical Thought. Edited by W. K. C. Guthrie* TB/1213
F. M. CORNFORD: From Religion to Philosophy: *A Study in the Origins of Western Speculation* § TB/20
WILFRID DESAN: The Tragic Finale: *An Essay on the Philosophy of Jean-Paul Sartre* TB/1030
A. P. D'ENTRÈVES: Natural Law: *An Historical Survey* △ TB/1223
MARVIN FARBER: The Aims of Phenomenology: *The Motives, Methods, and Impact of Husserl's Thought* TB/1291
MARVIN FARBER: Phenomenology and Existence: *Towards a Philosophy within Nature* TB/1295
HERBERT FINGARETTE: The Self in Transformation: *Psychoanalysis, Philosophy and the Life of the Spirit* ¶ TB/1177
PAUL FRIEDLÄNDER: Plato: *An Introduction* △ TB/2017
J. GLENN GRAY: The Warriors: *Reflections on Men in Battle. Intro. by Hannah Arendt* TB/1294
WILLIAM CHASE GREENE: Moira: *Fate, Good, and Evil in Greek Thought* TB/1104
W. K. C. GUTHRIE: The Greek Philosophers: *From Thales to Aristotle* o △ TB/1008
G. W. F. HEGEL: The Phenomenology of Mind o △ TB/1303
F. H. HEINEMANN: Existentialism and the Modern Predicament △ TB/28
ISAAC HUSIK: A History of Medieval Jewish Philosophy JP/3
EDMUND HUSSERL: Phenomenology and the Crisis of Philosophy. *Translated with an Introduction by Quentin Lauer* TB/1170
IMMANUEL KANT: The Doctrine of Virtue, *being Part II of the Metaphysic of Morals. Trans. with Notes & Intro. by Mary J. Gregor. Foreword by H. J. Paton* TB/110

IMMANUEL KANT: Groundwork of the Metaphysic of Morals. *Trans. & analyzed by H. J. Paton* TB/1159
IMMANUEL KANT: Lectures on Ethics. § △ *Introduction by Lewis W. Beck* TB/105
IMMANUEL KANT: Religion Within the Limits of Reason Alone. § *Intro. by T. M. Greene & J. Silber* TB/67
QUENTIN LAUER: Phenomenology: *Its Genesis and Prospect* TB/1169
MAURICE MANDELBAUM: The Problem of Historical Knowledge: *An Answer to Relativism. New Preface by the Author* TB/1338
GABRIEL MARCEL: Being and Having: *An Existential Diary.* △ *Intro. by James Collins* TB/310
GEORGE A. MORGAN: What Nietzsche Means TB/1198
H. J. PATON: The Categorical Imperative: *A Study in Kant's Moral Philosophy* △ TB/1325
PHILO, SAADYA GAON, & JEHUDA HALEVI: Three Jewish Philosophers. *Ed. by Hans Lewy, Alexander Altmann, & Isaak Heinemann* TB/813
MICHAEL POLANYI: Personal Knowledge: *Towards a Post-Critical Philosophy* △ TB/1158
WILLARD VAN ORMAN QUINE: Elementary Logic: *Revised Edition* TB/577
WILLARD VAN ORMAN QUINE: From a Logical Point of View: *Logico-Philosophical Essays* TB/566
BERTRAND RUSSELL et al.: The Philosophy of Bertrand Russell. *Edited by Paul Arthur Schilpp* Vol. I TB/1095; Vol. II TB/1096
L. S. STEBBING: A Modern Introduction to Logic △ TB/538
ALFRED NORTH WHITEHEAD: Process and Reality: *An Essay in Cosmology* △ TB/1033
PHILIP P. WIENER: Evolution and the Founders of Pragmatism. *Foreword by John Dewey* TB/1212
WILHELM WINDELBAND: A History of Philosophy
Vol. I: *Greek, Roman, Medieval* TB/38
Vol. II: *Renaissance, Enlightenment, Modern* TB/39
LUDWIG WITTGENSTEIN: The Blue and Brown Books o TB/1211

Political Science & Government

JEREMY BENTHAM: The Handbook of Political Fallacies: *Introduction by Crane Brinton* TB/1069
C. E. BLACK: The Dynamics of Modernization: *A Study in Comparative History* TB/1321
KENNETH E. BOULDING: Conflict and Defense: *A General Theory* TB/3024
CRANE BRINTON: English Political Thought in the Nineteenth Century TB/1071
ROBERT CONQUEST: Power and Policy in the USSR: *The Study of Soviet Dynastics* △ TB/1307
EDWARD S. CORWIN: American Constitutional History: *Essays edited by Alpheus T. Mason and Gerald Garvey* TB/1136
ROBERT DAHL & CHARLES E. LINDBLOM: Politics, Economics, and Welfare: *Planning and Politico-Economic Systems Resolved into Basic Social Processes* TB/3037
JOHN NEVILLE FIGGIS: The Divine Right of Kings. *Introduction by G. R. Elton* TB/1191
JOHN NEVILLE FIGGIS: Political Thought from Gerson to Grotius: 1414-1625: *Seven Studies. Introduction by Garrett Mattingly* TB/1032
F. L. GANSHOF: Feudalism △ TB/1058
G. P. GOOCH: English Democratic Ideas in the Seventeenth Century TB/1006
J. H. HEXTER: More's Utopia: *The Biography of an Idea. New Epilogue by the Author* TB/1195
SIDNEY HOOK: Reason, Social Myths and Democracy △ TB/1237
ROBERT H. JACKSON: The Supreme Court in the American System of Government △ TB/1106
DAN N. JACOBS, Ed.: The New Communist Manifesto *and Related Documents. Third Edition, Revised* TB/1078
DAN N. JACOBS & HANS BAERWALD, Eds.: Chinese Communism: *Selected Documents* TB/3031

7

Psychology

Sociology

GERHART B. LADNER: The Idea of Reform: *Its Impact on Christian Thought and Action in the Age of the Fathers*   TB/149
ARTHUR DARBY NOCK: Early Gentile Christianity and Its Hellenistic Background   TB/111
ARTHUR DARBY NOCK: St. Paul º △   TB/104
ORIGEN: On First Principles. △ *Edited by G. W. Butterworth. Introduction by Henri de Lubac*   TB/311
JAMES PARKES: The Conflict of the Church and the Synagogue: *The Jews and Early Christianity*   TB/821
SULPICIUS SEVERUS et al.: The Western Fathers: *Being the Lives of Martin of Tours, Ambrose, Augustine of Hippo, Honoratus of Arles and Germanus of Auxerre.* △ *Edited and translated by F. R. Hoare*   TB/309
JOHANNES WEISS: Earliest Christianity: *A History of the Period A.D. 30-150. Introduction and Bibliography by Frederick C. Grant*   Volume I   TB/53
                                               Volume II TB/54

Christianity: The Middle Ages and The Reformation

ANSELM OF CANTERBURY: Truth, Freedom and Evil: *Three Philosophical Dialogues. Ed., trans., and Intro. by Jasper Hopkins & Herbert Richardson*   TB/317
JOHN CALVIN & JACOPO SADOLETO: A Reformation Debate. *Edited by John C. Olin*   TB/1239
G. CONSTANT: The Reformation in England: *The English Schism, Henry VIII, 1509-1547* △   TB/314
CHRISTOPHER DAWSON, Ed.: Mission to Asia: *Narratives and Letters of the Franciscan Missionaries in Mongolia and China in the 13th and 14th Centuries* △
                                                        TB/315
JOHANNES ECKHART: Meister Eckhart: *A Modern Translation by R. B. Blakney*   TB/8
DESIDERIUS ERASMUS: Christian Humanism and the Reformation: *Selected Writings. Edited and translated by John C. Olin*   TB/1166
ÉTIENNE GILSON: Dante and Philosophy △   TB/1089
WILLIAM HALLER: The Rise of Puritanism △   TB/22
HAJO HOLBORN: Ulrich von Hutten and the German Reformation   TB/1238
JOHAN HUIZINGA: Erasmus and the Age of Reformation. △ *Illus.*   TB/19
A. C. MC GIFFERT: Protestant Thought Before Kant △ *Preface by Jaroslav Pelikan*   TB/93
JOHN T. MC NEILL: Makers of the Christian Tradition: *From Alfred the Great to Schleiermacher* △   TB/121
G. MOLLAT: The Popes at Avignon, 1305-1378 △   TB/308
GORDON RUPP: Luther's Progress to the Diet of Worms º △   TB/120

Christianity: The Protestant Tradition

KARL BARTH: Church Dogmatics: *A Selection* △   TB/95
KARL BARTH: Dogmatics in Outline △   TB/56
KARL BARTH: The Word of God and the Word of Man
                                                     TB/13
RUDOLF BULTMANN et al: Translating Theology into the Modern Age: *Historical, Systematic and Pastoral Reflections on Theology and the Church in the Contemporary Situation. Volume 2 of Journal for Theology and the Church, edited by Robert W. Funk in association with Gerhard Ebeling*   TB/252
WHITNEY R. CROSS: The Burned-Over District: *The Social and Intellectual History of Enthusiastic Religion in Western New York, 1800-1850* △   TB/1242
NELS F. S. FERRÉ: Swedish Contributions to Modern Theology. *New Preface by the Author. Additional chapter by William A. Johnson*   TB/147
ERNST KÄSEMANN, et al.: Distinctive Protestant and Catholic Themes Reconsidered. *Volume 3 of Journal for Theology and the Church, edited by Robert W. Funk in association with Gerhard Ebeling*   TB/253

SOREN KIERKEGAARD: On Authority and Revelation: *The Book on Adler. Translated by Walter Lowrie. Intro. by Frederick Sontag*   TB/139
SOREN KIERKEGAARD: Crisis in the Life of an Actress *and Other Essays on Drama.* △ *Trans. with Intro. by Stephen D. Crites*   TB/145
SOREN KIERKEGAARD: Edifying Discourses. *Edited with an Introduction by Paul Holmer*   TB/32
SOREN KIERKEGAARD: The Journals of Kierkegaard. º △ *Ed. with Intro. by Alexander Dru*   TB/52
SOREN KIERKEGAARD : The Point of View for My Work as an Author: *A Report to History.* § *Preface by Benjamin Nelson*   TB/88
SOREN KIERKEGAARD: The Present Age. § △ *Translated and edited by Alexander Dru. Introduction by Walter Kaufmann*   TB/94
SOREN KIERKEGAARD: Purity of Heart △   TB/4
SOREN KIERKEGAARD: Repetition: *An Essay in Experimental Psychology.* △ *Translated with Introduction & Notes by Walter Lowrie*   TB/117
SOREN KIERKEGAARD: Works of Love: *Some Christian Reflections in the Form of Discourses* △   TB/122
WALTER LOWRIE: Kierkegaard: *A Life*   Vol. I   TB/89
                                       Vol. II TB/90
JOHN MACQUARRIE: The Scope of Demythologizing: *Bultmann and His Critics* △   TB/134
PERRY MILLER & T. H. JOHNSON, Editors: The Puritans: *A Sourcebook of Their Writings*   Vol. I   TB/1093
                                       Vol. II TB/1094
WOLFHART PANNENBERG, et al.: History and Hermeneutic. *Volume 4 of Journal for Theology and the Church, edited by Robert W. Funk in association with Gerhard Ebeling*   TB/254
JAMES M. ROBINSON et al.: The Bultmann School of Biblical Interpretation: New Directions? *Volume 1 of Journal for Theology and the Church, edited by Robert W. Funk in association with Gerhard Ebeling*
                                                     TB/251
F. SCHLEIERMACHER: The Christian Faith. △ *Introduction by Richard R. Niebuhr*   Vol. I   TB/108
                                       Vol. II TB/109
F. SCHLEIERMACHER: On Religion: *Speeches to Its Cultured Despisers. Intro. by Rudolf Otto*   TB/36
TIMOTHY L. SMITH: Revivalism and Social Reform: *American Protestantism on the Eve of the Civil War*
                                                     TB/1229
PAUL TILLICH: Dynamics of Faith △   TB/42
PAUL TILLICH: Morality and Beyond △   TB/142
EVELYN UNDERHILL: Worship △   TB/10

Christianity: The Roman and Eastern Traditions

DOM CUTHBERT BUTLER: Western Mysticism: *The Teaching of Augustine, Gregory and Bernard on Contemplation and the Contemplative Life* § º △   TB/312
A. ROBERT CAPONIGRI, Ed.: Modern Catholic Thinkers I: *God and Man* △   TB/306
A. ROBERT CAPONIGRI, Ed.: Modern Catholic Thinkers II: *The Church and the Political Order*△   TB/307
THOMAS CORBISHLEY, S.J.: Roman Catholicism △   TB/112
CHRISTOPHER DAWSON: The Historic Reality of Christian Culture   TB/305
G. P. FEDOTOV: The Russian Religious Mind: *Kievan Christianity, the 10th to the 13th centuries*   TB/370
ÉTIENNE GILSON: The Spirit of Thomism   TB/313
GABRIEL MARCEL: Being and Having: *An Existential Diary.* △ *Introduction by James Collins*   TB/310
GABRIEL MARCEL: Homo Viator: *Introduction to a Metaphysic of Hope*   TB/397
FRANCIS DE SALES: Introduction to the Devout Life. *Trans. by John K. Ryan*   TB/316
GUSTAVE WEIGEL, S. J.: Catholic Theology in Dialogue
                                                     TB/301

Oriental Religions: Far Eastern, Near Eastern

TOR ANDRAE: Mohammed: *The Man and His Faith* △
TB/62
EDWARD CONZE: Buddhism: *Its Essence and Development*. º △ *Foreword by Arthur Waley*　TB/58
EDWARD CONZE et al., Editors: Buddhist Texts Through the Ages △
TB/113
ANANDA COOMARASWAMY: Buddha and the Gospel of Buddhism. △ *Illus.*
TB/119
H. G. CREEL: Confucius and the Chinese Way　TB/63
FRANKLIN EDGERTON, Trans. & Ed.: The Bhagavad Gita
TB/115
SWAMI NIKHILANANDA, Trans. & Ed.: The Upanishads: *A One-Volume Abridgment* △
TB/114
HELLMUT WILHELM: Change: *Eight Lectures on the* I *Ching* △
TB/2019

Philosophy of Religion

NICOLAS BERDYAEV: The Beginning and the End § △ TB/14
NICOLAS BERDYAEV: Christian Existentialism: *A Berdyaev Synthesis*. △ *Ed. by Donald A. Lowrie*　TB/130
NICOLAS BERDYAEV: The Destiny of Man △
TB/61
RUDOLF BULTMANN: History and Eschatology: *The Presence of Eternity* º
TB/91
RUDOLF BULTMANN AND FIVE CRITICS: Kerygma and Myth: *A Theological Debate* △
TB/80
RUDOLF BULTMANN and KARL KUNDSIN: Form Criticism: *Two Essays on New Testament Research*. △ *Translated by Frederick C. Grant*
TB/96
MIRCEA ELIADE: Myths, Dreams, and Mysteries: *The Encounter between Contemporary Faiths and Archaic Realities* § △ º
TB/1320
MIRCEA ELIADE: The Sacred and the Profane △
TB/81
LUDWIG FEUERBACH: The Essence of Christianity. § *Introduction by Karl Barth. Foreword by H. Richard Niebuhr*
TB/11
ÉTIENNE GILSON: The Spirit of Thomism
TB/313
ADOLF HARNACK: What is Christianity? § △ *Introduction by Rudolf Bultmann*
TB/17
FRIEDRICH HEGEL: On Christianity: *Early Theological Writings*. Ed. by R. Kroner and T. M. Knox　TB/79
KARL HEIM: Christian Faith and Natural Science △ TB/16
IMMANUEL KANT: Religion Within the Limits of Reason Alone. § *Intro. by T. M. Greene & J. Silber*　TB/67
K. E. KIRK: The Vision of God: *The Christian Doctrine of the Summum Bonum* § △
TB/137
JOHN MACQUARRIE: An Existentialist Theology: *A Comparison of Heidegger and Bultmann*. º △ *Preface by Rudolf Bultmann*
TB/125
PAUL RAMSEY, Ed.: Faith and Ethics: *The Theology of H. Richard Niebuhr*
TB/129
EUGEN ROSENSTOCK-HUESSY: The Christian Future *or the Modern Mind Outrun. Intro. by Harold Stahmer*
TB/143
PIERRE TEILHARD DE CHARDIN: The Divine Milieu º △
TB/384
PIERRE TEILHARD DE CHARDIN: The Phenomenon of Man º △
TB/383

Religion, Culture & Society

JOSEPH L. BLAU, Ed.: Cornerstones of Religious Freedom in America: *Selected Basic Documents, Court Decisions and Public Statements. Revised and Enlarged Edition*
TB/118
WILLIAM A. CLEBSCH & CHARLES R. JAEKLE: Pastoral Care in Historical Perspective: *An Essay with Exhibits. New Preface by the Authors*
TB/148
C. C. GILLISPIE: Genesis and Geology: *The Decades before Darwin* §
TB/51
KYLE HASELDEN: The Racial Problem in Christian Perspective
TB/116

WALTER KAUFMANN, Ed.: Religion from Tolstoy to Camus: *Basic Writings on Religious Truth and Morals. Enlarged Edition*
TB/123
KENNETH B. MURDOCK: Literature and Theology in Colonial New England
TB/99
H. RICHARD NIEBUHR: Christ and Culture △
TB/3
H. RICHARD NIEBUHR: The Kingdom of God in America
TB/49
R. B. PERRY: Puritanism and Democracy　TB/1138
PAUL PFUETZE: Self, Society, Existence: *Human Nature and Dialogue in the Thought of George Herbert Mead and Martin Buber*
TB/1059
WALTER RAUSCHENBUSCH: Christianity and the Social Crisis. ‡ *Edited by Robert D. Cross*　TB/3059
KURT SAMUELSSON: Religion and Economic Action: *A Critique of Max Weber's The Protestant Ethic and the Spirit of Capitalism* ¶ º △ *Trans. by E. G. French. Ed. with Intro. by D. C. Coleman*
TB/1131
TIMOTHY L. SMITH: Revivalism and Social Reform: *American Protestantism on the Eve of the Civil War* △
TB/1229

NATURAL SCIENCES
AND MATHEMATICS

Biological Sciences

CHARLOTTE AUERBACH: The Science of Genetics Σ △
TB/568
JOHN TYLER BONNER: The Ideas of Biology. Σ △ *Illus.*
TB/570
A. J. CAIN: Animal Species and their Evolution. △ *Illus.*
TB/519
W. E. LE GROS CLARK: The Antecedents of Man: *An Introduction to Evolution of the Primates*. º △ *Illus.* TB/559
W. H. DOWDESWELL: Animal Ecology. △ *Illus.*　TB/543
W. H. DOWDESWELL: The Mechanism of Evolution. △ *Illus.*
TB/527
R. W. GERARD: Unresting Cells. *Illus.*　TB/541
J. E. MORTON: Molluscs: *An Introduction to Their Form and Functions. Illus.*
TB/529
P. M. SHEPPARD: Natural Selection and Heredity. △ *Illus.*
TB/528
EDMUND W. SINNOTT: Cell and Psyche: *The Biology of Purpose*
TB/546
C. H. WADDINGTON: The Nature of Life: *The Main Problems and Trends in Modern Biology* △
TB/580

Chemistry

J. R. PARTINGTON: A Short History of Chemistry. △ *Illus.*
TB/522

Communication Theory

J. R. PIERCE: Symbols, Signals and Noise: *The Nature and Process of Communication* △
TB/574

Geography

R. E. COKER: This Great and Wide Sea: *An Introduction to Oceanography and Marine Biology. Illus.*　TB/551
F. K. HARE: The Restless Atmosphere △
TB/560

History of Science

MARIE BOAS: The Scientific Renaissance, 1450-1630 º △
TB/583
W. DAMPIER, Ed.: Readings in the Literature of Science. *Illus.*
TB/512
A. HUNTER DUPREE: Science in the Federal Government: *A History of Policies and Activities to 1940* △ TB/573
ALEXANDRE KOYRÉ: From the Closed World to the Infinite Universe: *Copernicus, Kepler, Galileo, Newton, etc.* △
TB/31